dBASE III® Plus
Tips, Tricks, and Traps

George Tsu-der Chou

Que™ Corporation
Carmel, Indiana

Library of Congress Catalog No.: 86-063980
ISBN 0-88022-286-7

90 89   9 8 7 6 5

Interpretation of the printing code: the rightmost double-digit number
is the year of the book's printing; the rightmost single-digit number, the
number of the book's printing. For example, a printing code of 87-3
shows that the third printing of the book occurred in 1987.

dBASE III PLUS Tips, Tricks, and Traps is based on dBASE III Plus
Version 1.0 and 1.1.

Dedicated to

my wife, Jane-Wen
and our children
Doris, Tina, and Tom

Product Director
David Paul Ewing, M.A.

Editorial Director
David F. Noble, Ph.D.

Acquisitions Editor
Terrie Lynn Solomon

Editors
Betty White
Gail S. Burlakoff

Technical Editor
John Cameron

Production
Dan Armstrong
Dennis Sheehan
Carrie L. Torres
Jennifer Matthews
Joe Ramon

Composed in Wiedeman, Megaron, and Que Digital
by Que Corporation

Screen reproductions in this book were created by means of the Inset program from The American Programmers Guild, Ltd., Danbury, Connecticut.

About the Author

George Tsu-der Chou, of Vancouver, Washington, is a consultant in the field of database design and development. He has developed database management systems for a large number of clients, such as Gregory Government Securities, Morley Capital Management, Hi-Tech Electronics, West Coast Lumber Inspection Bureau, NERCO, Inc., and others. These systems include analytical managerial database systems and administrative database management programs that deal with inventory and accounting functions.

The author earned his Ph.D. in Quantitative Methods, with supporting studies in Computer Science, Economics, and Econometrics, from the University of Washington. He is currently a full professor at the University of Portland in Oregon, where he teaches courses in business data processing and data management, quantitative methods, operations research, business forecasting, and other subjects. He has taught computer programming in FORTRAN, COBOL, BASIC, and IBM Assembler.

Dr. Chou wrote the popular *dBASE III Handbook*, *dBASE III Plus Handbook*, and *Using Paradox*, all published by Que Corporation. He is also the author of *Microcomputer Programming in BASIC* and *Computer Programming in BASIC*, both published by Harper & Row. The former has been translated into Spanish and published in Mexico; reprints of that book have also been distributed in the Philippines.

Dr. Chou has also written a financial analytical modeling program, COMPASS (Computer Assisted Portfolio Planning Management System). Combining database and analytical tools, this software represents the first major effort in the computerization of portfolio management. COMPASS, marketed by Morley & Associates, has been adopted by many major banks and financial institutions in the United States and Canada. The COMPASS program also has been licensed to Federate Investors Services as the Asset Allocation software currently used by more than 600 of its bank clients.

Table of Contents

2   Configuring dBASE III Plus 39

3   Creating and Modifying Databases   79

8   Generating Reports and Mailing Lists 237

Trademark Acknowledgments

Que Corporation has made every attempt to supply trademark information about company names, products, and services mentioned in this book. Trademarks indicated below were derived from various sources. Que Corporation cannot attest to the accuracy of this information.

1-2-3, DIF, Lotus, and VisiCalc are registered trademarks of Lotus Development Corporation.

Ashton-Tate, dBASE II, dBASE III, dBASE III Plus, and Framework are registered trademarks of Ashton-Tate Corporation.

Bernoulli and Iomega are registered trademarks of Iomega Corporation.

Clipper and Nantucket are trademarks of Nantucket, Inc.

COMPAQ is a registered trademark of COMPAQ Computer Corporation.

dPROBE is a trademark of Analytical Software, Inc., of Seattle, Washington.

GW-BASIC, Microsoft, Microsoft QuickBasic, Microsoft Word, and Multiplan are registered trademarks of Microsoft Corporation.

Hayes is a registered trademark and Smartmodem 1200 is a trademark of Hayes Microcomputer Products, Inc.

Hercules is a registered trademark of Hercules Computer Technology.

IBM is a registered trademark of International Business Machines Corporation.

MultiMate is a registered trademark of Multimate International Corp., an Ashton-Tate company.

Multiplan is a registered trademark of Microsoft Corporation.

Paradox is a trademark of Ansa Corporation.

PFS is a registered trademark of Software Publishing Corporation.

SideKick, SuperKey, and Turbo Pascal are registered trademarks of Borland International, Inc.

WordPerfect is a registered trademark of WordPerfect Corporation.

WordStar is a registered trademark of MicroPro International Corporation.

Wordtech DB Compiler is a trademark of WordTech Systems, Inc.

Zenith is a registered trademark of Zenith Radio Corporation.

Conventions Used in This Book

For ease of reading, different typefaces are used to distinguish elements of the text. Entries made from the keyboard, messages displayed by dBASE III Plus, and dBASE III Plus menu options are set apart from the text in the following manner:

Keyboard entries that appear in running text are in set in *italics.*

Messages that appear on your screen are set in `digital`.

Menu options, such as **Setup** and **Create** are also set in a contrasting typeface.

In illustrations of the dot-prompt commands and dBASE III Plus functions, angle brackets (< >) are used to indicate variable command elements:

.SET FILTER TO <the filter condition>

Because of space limitations, many command lines are shown as two lines. Normally, they would be entered on a single line at the dot prompt. For example,

.SORT TO ROSTER ON ANNUAL_PAY/D,lAST_NAME
FOR MALE

should be entered on a single line at the dot prompt or in a program file.

Commands are spelled out completely in the text:

. SELECT 1
. DISPLAY FOR STOCK_NO="ANS–DB110"

Figures often show abbreviated forms of the commands

. SELE 1
. DISP FOR STOCK_NO="ANS–DB110"

to demonstrate that commands can be shortened to save time and keystrokes.

Introduction

Ashton-Tate®'s dBASE III® Plus is unquestionably the leading computer program for data-management applications. With its earlier versions—dBASE II® and dBASE III®—dBASE III Plus has revolutionized the way data is managed and manipulated in a microcomputer system.

Beginning users appreciate the "friendly" dBASE III Plus Assistant menu. Those with more experience use dBASE III Plus's powerful programming language to develop programs for efficiently managing large, complex databases. Small wonder that dBASE III Plus is the most popular database-management program on the market.

Scope of the Book

To fully enjoy the program's power and flexibility, you must be familiar with all the dBASE III Plus commands and programming tools. Used intelligently, these commands and tools provide efficient shortcuts for many data-management operations.

One of this book's major objectives is to share with you some *tips*—ideas or simple techniques, "better ways" to use the program—for managing your database. The tips presented here are the accumulation of years of experience working with dBASE III Plus and its earlier versions.

Here also you will find *tricks*—sophisticated techniques you can use to enhance the basic functions of many dBASE III Plus commands and programming tools. Some of the tricks in this book are the result of extensive experimentation with the program. Others were discovered accidentally as I worked on database applications.

All the tips and tricks in this book are meant to help you manage data more effectively. Many will reduce the number of steps required for a given task.

You will also find traps. A *trap* is a potential hazard. Some traps cause annoying results but do not present serious problems. Others, however, may result in a costly loss of valuable information. This book warns you about some of these serious traps, explains how to avoid them, and tells you what to do when you find one. Many traps are followed by tricks that offer solutions to the problem.

Who Should Read This Book

This book is targeted primarily at dBASE III Plus users, but most subjects covered here are relevant also to dBASE III. Many of the tips and tricks have to do with the dot prompt commands and procedures. And users of the Assistant menu can see how to achieve greater power and flexibility with these commands and procedures. If you want to go beyond using the Assistant menu to manage a large, complex database, this book will serve as an excellent guide.

Because this book covers the program's intermediate and advanced features, readers need to understand the commonly used dBASE III Plus commands. To better understand the proper use of these commands, please refer to the *dBASE III Plus Handbook*, 2nd Edition, published by Que Corporation.

Organization of the Book

The first chapter, "System Configuration and General Operations," shows you how to use directories for effective file management. Because more database-management applications are demanding the processing speed and storage capacity of a hard disk, organizing files in a directory has become a necessity. Knowing how to create and maintain a directory is vital to ensuring the integrity of data stored in your files.

This chapter also deals with the procedure for allocating (via the CONFIG.SYS file) sufficient file buffers to dBASE III Plus. Effective ways of issuing commands at the dot prompt are discussed.

Chapter 2, "Configuring dBASE III Plus," focuses on the powerful commands you can include in the CONFIG.DB configuration file. By using these commands, you can set the environment and parameters for the program before it is executed. Once you have set up the CONFIG.DB file properly, you can eliminate many tedious steps in the data-manipulation process. Most important, you can learn how to allocate sufficient memory space to dBASE III Plus and other external programs executed by way of the configuration file. These techniques will help you to avoid losing valuable data.

Chapter 3, "Creating and Modifying Databases," deals with the tips, tricks, and traps related to creating a new database. Shortcuts include borrowing the file structure or records from an existing database to create a new database file. You also will find tips and warnings for modifying the field attributes in an existing file structure. And, because errors frequently result from poorly organized data, the layout of a database file is explained in detail.

Chapter 4, "Entering and Editing Data," discusses the features and proper use of commands related to data entry and modification. You can use this chapter's shortcuts and tricks to take advantage of the dBASE III Plus screen painter, a powerful tool for designing custom data-entry forms.

Chapter 5, "Organizing Data," shows you how to organize files so that you can access them quickly. This chapter also focuses on the program's powerful catalog feature, which allows you to group data files into a catalog. You'll find many tips for creating and using a catalog file to organize your data.

Chapter 6, "Sorting and Indexing Data," deals with using the SORT and INDEX commands to rearrange records in a database file. The chapter explores the strengths and weaknesses of sorting and indexing so that you know when and how to choose the correct operation. You also will learn tricks for overcoming some of these weaknesses.

Chapter 7, "Display Data," introduces special features that enhance the basic functions of commonly used commands for displaying data. (Many of these special features are mentioned briefly but not explained in the dBASE III Plus reference manual.) The tips and tricks for using these special features are the result of experience working with the commands.

Chapter 8, "Generating Reports," focuses on generating mailing lists and producing custom reports. Reporting is one of the most important functions of database management, but the dBASE III Plus report generator has some limitations. To produce moderately complex reports, you need to learn some of this chapter's tips and tricks.

Chapter 9, "Programming in dBASE III Plus Command Language: Program Editing, Memory Variables, and Screen Design," discusses the power of command-language programming. Although you can perform many database-management operations by choosing appropriate options from the Assistant menu, you need the power of program and procedure files for complex data manipulation and sophisticated reports. This chapter shows you how to write many different types of program modules.

Chapter 10, "Programming in dBASE III Plus Command Language: Branching, Looping, Subprograms, and Debugging," continues the discussion of how to write programs. Graphics, statistical, and utility programs are included in this chapter.

Chapter 11, "Advanced Topics," teaches you how to exchange data between dBASE III Plus and other programs. You can use these external programs to enhance the power of dBASE III Plus. This chapter discusses also the dBASE compiler, which can be used to speed up program execution and protect your program code.

Finally, you will find several useful appendixes. Appendix A presents the standard ASCII character codes. Appendix B summarizes the dBASE III Plus function and control keys, and Appendix C contains a summary of the dBASE III commands. The program's built-in functions are summarized in Appendix D. Appendix E lists the file structures for all the database files in this book.

1

Organizing Disk Files and System Configuration

A microcomputer system's most important permanent storage medium is the disk unit, and for a long time the floppy disk was adequate for most database application programs. But with recent advances in database-management programs, storage requirements have changed drastically. The floppy disk is no longer adequate for the power of these new programs.

With more storage space available to you and more files to manage, you need to develop an efficient way to access and manipulate data. Sophisticated organization of your files is the answer. This chapter explores the important use of subdirectories for organizing your disk files.

You can manipulate data even more effectively if you supplement dBASE III Plus with DOS commands. This chapter discusses some of the tips and tricks for using DOS commands within dBASE III Plus.

Finally, this chapter presents shortcuts for executing dBASE III Plus commands as well as procedures for allocating memory for disk files and memory buffers.

Structuring Your Files Efficiently in Directories

Tip:

Save time and trouble by grouping files in separate directories.

Files organized in directories and subdirectories are easily identified and maintained. If you can't remember the exact name of a particular file, for instance, you can display the contents of that file's directory to locate the file.

When you turn on your computer, you start from the *root* directory, which was created automatically when you formatted your disk. The root directory stores the names of other file directories. In turn, these directories can store any number of *subdirectories* at any number of levels.

The structure of all the disk files stored on a given disk can be organized in multiple levels of directories, as you can see in figure 1.1.

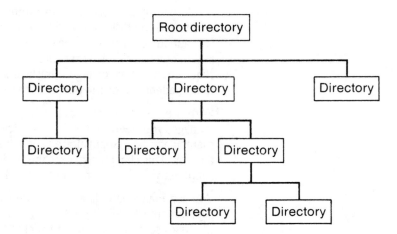

Fig. 1.1. The structure of disk file directories.

You may want to put all the files related to DOS operations in a directory named DOSFILES and all the dBASE III Plus system files in another directory named DBASE.

You can create subdirectories in the DBASE directory for storing groups of files. Also, if you need to access a word-processing program such as WordStar, you can save all your WordStar files in another directory (named WORDPROC) directly below the root directory (see fig. 1.2).

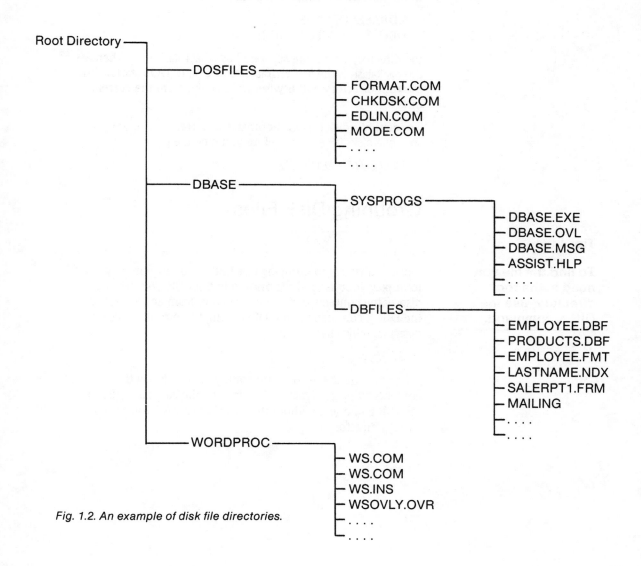

Fig. 1.2. An example of disk file directories.

The Directory Path

Use the directory PATH to access your files easily.

To access your files quickly and easily, you need to know about paths. A directory *path* is a chain of directory names that tell DOS how to move through this chain to find a specific directory or disk file.

In the following examples of paths:

    \DBASE\DBFILES
    DBFILES\EMPLOYEE.DBF

the directory names are separated by a backslash (\). When the backslash is the first character of the path, DOS starts with the root directory. Otherwise, DOS begins from the current directory.

To identify a disk drive other than the current drive, you specify a disk drive name before you type the path:

    D:\LOTUS\DATAFILE

Grouping Disk Files

To find the file you need in the root directory, use the DIR \ command.

Once you've begun grouping files in directories, you may want to display your list of directories to find the file you need. To display the contents of the root directory from any level, use the DIR \ command at the DOS prompt (the root directory is designated by a backslash):

    C>*DIR* \

When you are at the root directory, you can display the contents by simply typing *DIR*, omitting the backslash. (Issuing the DIR command without the backslash always displays the current directory.)

Creating a New Directory

Tip:

Create a directory for your dBASE files.

To create a directory, at the DOS prompt (>), type the DOS command *MD* or *MKDIR* (Make Directory) followed by the name of the directory (*DBASE*, for example):

C>*MD DBASE*

In response to the command, a new directory with the specified name is created under the current directory. If you issue the MD command when you are in the root directory, the new directory becomes a subdirectory of the root directory.

Tip:

To create a subdirectory under a particular directory, specify the parent directory in the MD command.

If you need to create a subdirectory in a directory different from the one you're working in, be sure to include the parent directory in the directory path. If you don't specify the parent directory when you use the MD command to create a subdirectory, you will create a subdirectory in the current directory.

For example, to create a subdirectory named DBFILES under the DBASE directory in the current disk drive, issue the following command at the DOS prompt:

C>*MD \DBASE\DBFILES*

To create the subdirectory DBFILES from the DBASE directory, use the following command without specifying a parent directory:

C>*MD DBFILES*

Monitoring the Current Directory

Trap:

You can lose track of your files if you create a subdirectory from the wrong directory.

Know where you are in the directory structure before you create a subdirectory. Otherwise, you may create the subdirectory under the wrong directory and have trouble finding it later. Be sure to specify the correct directory path in the MD or MKDIR (Make Directory) command unless you want to create a subdirectory under the current directory.

Identifying the Current Directory

Trick:

Use the CD command to identify the current directory.

You can identify the current directory in a number of ways, but the simplest is to issue the CD or CHDIR (Change Directory) command at the DOS prompt:

C>*CD*

Even though the CD command may be used to change from the current directory to a new directory, you can use it to show where you are in the directory structure. For example:

C>*CD*

shows you

C:\DBASE\DBFILES

which means that you are working in DBFILES, a subdirectory of the parent DBASE directory.

Trick:

To always know the current directory path, include the PROMPT pg command in the AUTOEXEC.BAT file.

An excellent way to always know the current directory path is to include in the AUTOEXEC.BAT file the following command:

PROMPT pg

This command yields a DOS prompt made up of the current directory path, followed by a greater-than symbol. The DOS prompt changes as you change directories with the CD command.

For example, if you are in the DBFILES subdirectory of the DBASE directory on the C: drive, the DOS prompt is

C:\DBASE\DBFILES>

Moving between Directories

Use the CD command to switch from one directory to another.

To switch from the current active directory to another directory, issue the DOS command CD or CHDIR (Change Directory) at the DOS prompt, followed by the path and name of the directory you want to switch to.

Moving up in the Directory Structure

To return directly to the root directory from any level of directory, use the CD \ command.

The CD \ command will return you to the root directory from anywhere in the directory structure.

For example, executing the CD \ command from the C:\DBASE\DBFILES subdirectory will return you to the root directory.

```
C>CD
C:\DBASE\DBFILES

C>CD \
C>CD
C:\
```

Use the CD .. command to move to the parent directory.

To move "up" one level from the current directory to its parent directory, use the CD .. (double dot) command.

For example, you can switch from the DBFILES subdirectory of the DBASE directory to the parent directory by issuing the CD .. command at the DOS prompt.

```
C>CD
C:\DBASE\DBFILES

C>CD ..

C>CD
C:\DBASE

C>
```

As you can see, after the CD .. command is executed, the current directory changes from C:\DBASE\DBFILES to C:\DBASE.

Tip:

To move above a parent directory, specify the root directory at the beginning of the directory path.

To move from a given directory to a directory that is higher than its parent directory, specify (in the CD command) a directory path that begins from the root directory.

For example, to move up to the DBASE directory from the SALES directory, which is three levels below the root directory (C:\DBASE\DBFILES\SALES), you must specify a directory path that begins with a backslash (which designates the root directory):

C>*CD \DBASE*

As you can see from the following code

```
C>CD
C:\DBASE\DBFILES\SALES

C>CD DBASE
Invalid directory

C>CD \DBASE

C>CD
C:\DBASE

C>
```

you can't begin the path from a directory below the root directory. Issuing the CD DBASE command from the C:\DBASE\DBFILES\SALES directory results in an **Invalid directory** error message. You must begin the directory path from the root directory (CD \DBASE) in the CD command.

Similarly, if you want to move from the fourth-level REGION1 directory (C:\DBASE\DBFILES\SALES\REGION1) to the DBFILES directory, you must begin the path from the root directory:

```
C>CD
C:\DBASE\DBFILES\SALES\REGION1
```

```
C>CD \DBASE\DBFILES

C>CD
C:\DBASE\DBFILES

C>
```

As you can see from the preceding code, the path must begin with \DBASE.

If you specify the path in the CD command as \DBFILES or DBFILES, you will get an `Invalid directory` error message.

```
C>CD
C:\DBASE\DBFILES\SALES\REGION1

C>CD \DBFILES
Invalid directory

C>CD DBFILES
Invalid directory

C>
```

Moving down in the Directory Structure

Tip:

To move to the subdirectory immediately below the current directory, specify the name of the subdirectory in the CD command.

To switch from a directory to one of its subdirectories, specify the name of the subdirectory in the CD command:

```
C>CD
C:\

C>CD DBASE

C>CD
C:\DBASE

C>CD DBFILES

C>CD
C:\DBASE\DBFILES
```

```
C>CD SALES

C>CD
C:\DBASE\DBFILES\SALES

C>
```

As you can see, you use the CD DBASE command to switch from the root directory to the DBASE directory. Similarly, the CD DBFILES command transfers you from the DBASE directory to its DBFILES subdirectory.

Tip:

To move down more than one level below the current directory, specify the path beginning from one level below the current directory.

To move to a directory below the current directory's immediate subdirectory, the path you specify in the CD command should begin from one level below the current directory.

For example, if you want to move from the second level in the directory structure (C:\DBASE\DBFILES) to a directory at the fourth level, you must begin your path from the third level:

```
C>CD SALES\REGION1
```

With a directory structure of

```
C:\DBASE\DBFILES\SALES\REGION1
```

you can move from the DBASE directory to REGION1 (which is three levels below the current directory) by specifying a path that begins with DBFILES (the current directory's immediate subdirectory).

```
C>CD
C:\DBASE

C>CD DBFILES\SALES\REGION1

C>CD
C:\DBASE\DBFILES\SALES\REGION1

C>
```

Displaying a File Directory

Tip:

Use the DIR command to display the contents of the current file directory.

From the DOS prompt, use the DIR command to display a listing of the current directory.

Tip:

To list files that are not in the current directory, specify the directory path in the DIR command.

You can use one of two methods to list files that are not in the current directory.

You can move from the current directory to the directory containing the files and then issue the DIR command. (For instructions on moving from one directory to another, see this chapter's "Moving between Directories" section.)

Or you can display the contents of a specific directory by specifying the appropriate directory path in the DIR command. Whether you begin the path with the root directory or with a subdirectory depends on which directory structure level you are working in.

Tip:

To list disk files in the root directory from any directory, use the DIR \ command.

Without leaving the current directory, you can list the contents of the root directory by using the DIR \ command from any level in the directory structure:

C>*DIR *

Tip:

To display the contents of the parent directory, use the DIR .. command.

From a subdirectory, you can list files in the parent directory by using the DIR .. (double dot) command:

C>*DIR ..*

Listing Selective Files in a Directory

Tip:

Use a wild card to list files by their types.

From a given directory, you can display a selected group of files by using the asterisk (✱) or the question mark (?) as a masking or "wild card" character.

For example, you would use the DIR ✱.DBF command to display all the database files in the directory. Similarly, the DIR ✱.NDX command will cause all the index files to be displayed.

If you want to list all the files whose names begin with DB, enter the DIR DB??????.✱ command at the DOS prompt. The DIR DB???.DBF command will display all database files with names that begin with DB, followed by up to three other characters.

Deleting an Existing Directory

Tip:

Before you can delete a directory, you must empty it.

You must delete all the files in an existing directory before removing it from the directory structure. Use the ERASE ✱.✱ command to delete all the disk files in the current directory.

If the directory you want to delete contains one or more subdirectories, you must first delete the subdirectories. Erase all the files in the subdirectories before deleting them.

To remove an empty directory, use the RD or RMDIR (Remove Directory) command:

C>*RD* <name of the empty directory to be deleted>

Trap:

The ERASE ✱.✱ command is extremely powerful and potentially destructive.

When the ERASE ✱.✱ command is issued, DOS returns the prompt:

Are you sure (Y/N)?

At this point, you can say whether you really want to erase *all* the files in the current directory. Before you proceed, take a moment to make sure you are in the correct directory. Otherwise, you may have to test your backup procedures or reenter valuable data.

Renaming a Directory

Trap:

DOS does not allow you to change the name of a directory.

For some strange reason, DOS does not allow you to change the name of an existing directory.

Trick:

Create a new directory to rename an existing directory.

To use DOS commands for renaming a directory, create a new directory with the name you want. Copy the contents of the existing directory to the new directory. Then remove the original directory.

Note: Utility programs for renaming directories are available through various Bulletin Board Systems, PC User Groups, and Software Interest Groups.

Displaying Directories within dBASE III Plus

Tip:

Use the DIR or LIST FILES command to display a list of database files.

From within dBASE III Plus, you can display a list of all the database files in the current directory by issuing either the DIR command or LIST FILES command at the dot prompt.

Tip:

To list the names of all the disk files in the current directory, use asterisks as global characters.

Issuing the DIR command at the dot prompt from within dBASE III Plus displays only database files (with the file extension .DBF) in the current directory of the default disk drive.

To list *all* the files in the current directory, you can use asterisks as global characters (or wild cards) in the DIR or LIST FILES command:

    . DIR *.*
    . LIST FILES *.*

When asterisks replace a file name and its extension in a DIR or LIST FILES command, the command tells the program to list files of all names and types.

Tip:

To list disk files of a given type, specify the file extension in the command.

If you want to display files other than database (.DBF) files, use an asterisk (∗) as a global character (or wild card) and specify the file extension in the DIR or LIST FILES command:

. DIR ∗.<file extension>
. LIST FILES ∗.<file extension>

For example:

. DIR ∗.NDX
. LIST FILES ∗.TXT

Tip:

To list disk files with certain file names, use question marks (?) as global characters.

You can list disk files with names that share one or more common characters. To do so, specify the shared characters in the DIR or LIST FILES command and replace the remaining characters in the file name with question marks (?) as global characters.

For example, to display all files with names that begin with *ABC*, issue the following DIR or LIST FILES command at the dot prompt:

. DIR ABC?????.∗

or

. LIST FILES ABC?????.∗

The question marks in the file name allow any character in the name of the files to be matched.

Trick:

Be sure to use the correct number of question marks in the file name.

A file name can be up to eight characters long. Because each question mark replaces a character in the file name, you must be sure to specify exactly as many question marks as there are characters in the file name.

For example, when . DIR ABC?????.* is executed, all file names that are up to eight characters long and begin with ABC are displayed.

If you use two question marks to define a file name that begins with ABC (. DIR ABC??.*), only those files with names that are up to five characters long are displayed.

Tip:

Use the Assistant menu's Tools / Directory options to display files of different types.

To display groups of files by their file types from the Assistant menu, select the **Tools / Directory** options from the menu and, at the prompt, specify a disk drive.

Then you are prompted to specify the type of disk files to be displayed:

> /.DBF Database Files
> /.NDX Index Files
> /.FMT Format Files
> /.LBL Label Files
> /.FRM Report Files
> /.TXT Text Files
> /.VUE View Files
> /.QRY Query Files
> /.SCR Screen Files
> /.* All Files

Trap:

The Assistant menu does not allow use of the ? global character to display files.

You cannot use question marks (?) as global characters to define file names for display. The menu's **Directory** option allows you to display files by file types only, not by file names.

Displaying File Directories
within dBASE III Plus

Tip:

To display files that are not in the current directory, specify the directory path.

Unless you specify a directory path when you issue the DIR or LIST FILES command at the dot prompt, only the files in the current active directory of the default drive are displayed.

To remain in the current active directory and display files in another directory, include the directory path in the DIR or LIST FILES command.

Use the . DIR *.* command to display all the files in the root directory.

All the .SYS files in the DBASE directory are displayed by the command:

   . DIR \DBASE*.SYS

The command

   . LIST FILES \DBASE\DBFILES*.NDX

displays all the index files (.NDX) in the DBFILES directory, which is a subdirectory of the DBASE directory.

Tip:

To display files that are not in the default disk drive, specify the disk drive.

If you do not include the disk drive in the directory path, the default disk drive is assumed. But you can specify a different drive in the path.

For example, if drive C is the default disk drive and you want to display files in drive B or D, you must specify a disk drive in the directory path of the DIR or LIST FILES command, as in:

   . DIR B:*.*

or

   . LIST FILES D:\LOTUS*.PRN

Tip:

Use the SET PATH TO command within dBASE III Plus to access files that are not in the current directory.

From a given directory within dBASE III PLUS, use the SET PATH TO command to gain access to a database file and its associated files in another directory.

To select a database file from the SALEDATA directory, for example, you would specify the directory path:

. SET PATH TO *SALEDATA*

Trap:

If different directories contain files with the same name, only the file in the current directory is used.

If you have more than one database file with the same name (one in the current directory and another in the directory specified in the SET PATH TO command) only the file in the current directory will be selected.

For example, if you are currently working in the DBFILES (C:\DBASE\DBFILES) directory and want to gain access to a database file (SALEITEM.DBF) in the SALEDATA directory (C:\DBASE\SALEDATA), you could issue the following dot commands:

. SET PATH TO \DBASE\SALEDATA
. USE SALEITEM

dBASE III Plus will be able to locate the database file SALEITEM.DBF from the directory C:\DBASE\SALEDATA.

However, if the current directory (C:\DBASE\DBFILES) also contains a database file named SALEITEM.DBF, dBASE III Plus will select that file. The program always searches the current directory first.

If you use a subdirectory structure, different database files can share the same name. But when you select files from these subdirectories, you must be sure to access the correct file.

Trap:

The SET PATH TO command does not change the current directory.

The directory path specified by the SET PATH TO command simply provides a searching path for file retrieval. The command does not change the current directory.

Trap:

You cannot save a new database file to the directory defined by the SET PATH TO command.

The SET PATH TO command instructs dBASE III Plus to search the specified directory path for an existing file.

When you create a database file, the new database created at any point in the processing is saved in the *current* directory, *not* in the directory specified in the SET PATH TO command's path.

For example, if you create a database file named "EMPLOYEE.DBF" in the DBFILES directory (C:\DBASE\DBFILES), the new file is saved in that directory, even though you may have set the path to another directory:

```
. SET PATH TO \DBASE SALEDATA
. CREATE EMPLOYEE
```

Trap:

The path defined by the SET PATH TO command does not affect the DIR command.

When you issue the DIR command, only those files in the current directory are displayed. The DIR command ignores the path defined in the SET PATH TO command (see fig. 1.3).

```
. DIR
Database Files    # Records    Last Update    Size
EMPLOYEE.DBF           10       01/06/87        836

      836 bytes in      1 files.
8216576 bytes remaining on drive.

. SET PATH TO \DBASE\SALEDATA
. USE SALEITEM
. LIST
Record#  STOCK_NO  DSCRIPTION            TYPE                  COST    PRICE
     1   ASH-DB300 dBASE III Plus v1.01  database            395.00   595.00
     2   CLP-DB100 Clipper DB Compiler   database compiler   450.00   595.00
     3   AST-FW200 Framework v2.0        integrated          345.00   349.00
     4   MIC-QB100 Microsoft QuickBasic  language             79.00   109.00
. DIR
Database Files    # Records    Last Update    Size
EMPLOYEE.DBF           10       01/06/87        836

      836 bytes in      1 files.
8216576 bytes remaining on drive.
```

Fig. 1.3. Effects of the SET PATH TO action on the DIR command.

Moving between Directories within dBASE III Plus

From within dBASE III Plus, you can move from the current directory to another directory by using the RUN (or !) command to execute the DOS CD or CHDIR (Change Directory) command.

You can use the RUN command to execute a DOS command at the dot prompt as if you were at the DOS prompt. Because the RUN command puts you in DOS mode temporarily, you can process any CD command at the dot prompt.

For example, from DOS you would switch directly from the current directory to the root directory by issuing the CD \ command at the DOS prompt:

C>*CD* \

Instead of exiting to DOS from dBASE III Plus, you can issue the DOS CD \ command at the dot prompt by adding the word RUN to the command:

. RUN CD \

(For instructions about using the DOS CD command to move between directories, refer to the earlier "Moving between Directories" section in this chapter.)

Accessing the DOS Command Interpreter

You need the COMMAND.COM file to use the RUN command within dBASE III Plus.

Because the COMMAND.COM file contains instructions that translate DOS commands into actions, that file must be present when you execute a DOS command.

If you have a hard disk, put the COMMAND.COM file in the root directory. Then, when you issue the RUN command in dBASE III Plus, the program will be able to locate the file.

If you are using a floppy disk system, you usually start your computer system from drive A, where the COMMAND.COM file is located. After booting the system, you enter the dBASE III Plus program by inserting system disks #1 and #2 in sequence. You must leave system disk #2 in drive A while you work with dBASE III Plus.

Trap:

When the COMMAND.COM file is not in drive A on a floppy disk system, you can't use the RUN command to execute DOS commands.

You could try to solve the problem by copying the COMMAND.COM file to the dBASE III Plus system disk #2, which must be in drive A while you use the program. Unfortunately, the system disk is full of dBASE III Plus programs. There is no room for other disk files.

Trick:

Put the COMMAND.COM file on your data disk in drive B and use the SET COMSPEC command at the DOS prompt to tell the computer where to find the file.

With the COMMAND.COM file on your data disk in drive B, type the following command at the DOS prompt:

A>SET COMSPEC=B:\COMMAND.COM

Be sure to execute the SET COMSPEC command at the DOS prompt *before* you call up the dBASE III Plus program.

Tip:

Use the RUN CD command to monitor the current directory within dBASE III Plus.

From the DOS prompt, you can always determine where you are in the directory structure by using the CD or CHDIR (Change Directory) command without specifying the name of a directory.

You can use the RUN command to execute the DOS CD command from within dBASE III Plus:

```
. RUN CD
```

Changing System Date and Time

Trick:

Change the system date and time by using the RUN command to execute the DOS DATE and TIME commands.

From within dBASE III Plus, you can display the current system date and time on the screen or in your reports by using the built-in functions DATE() and TIME(). For example, you can monitor the current date and time by using the ? operator to display the value of these built-in functions in a dot-prompt command:

```
. ?DATE(),TIME()
01/06/87 22:13:47
```

If you have a built-in clock and calendar that are set automatically to the correct date and time when you start the computer, you probably do not have to change these values.

Otherwise, you may have to set the date and time whenever you start the computer. If you forget to set the date or time or if you want to change their values while you work in dBASE III Plus, the RUN command is handy.

To process the DOS date and time commands within dBASE III Plus, simply issue the RUN command:

```
. ?DATE(),TIME()
01/06/87  22:13:47
. RUN  DATE

Current date is Tue  1-06-1987
Enter new date: 1-05-1987

. RUN  TIME

Current time is 22:23:01.00
Enter new time: 08:00

. ?DATE(),TIME()
01/05/87  08:00:11
```

Deleting Disk Files

To conserve disk space when you're processing data within dBASE III Plus, you sometimes want to delete files you no longer need. For example, whenever you modify the structure of an existing database file, the program includes the changes in a new database (.DBF) file and, at the same time, saves the original data table in a backup (.BAK) file. If you decide to change the data structure back to the original version, you can delete the modified database file and then rename the backup file. Otherwise, it is good practice to clean up your disk space by deleting these backup files.

As you can see from the following examples, you can delete a file by issuing the ERASE command at the dot prompt:

```
. ERASE  EMPLOYEE.BAK
. ERASE  EMPLOYEE.DBF
. ERASE  PRODUCTS.NDX
```

Trap:

You cannot use asterisks (∗) and question marks (?) as global characters in the dBASE III Plus ERASE command to delete a group of files.

Each of the following dot-prompt commands is invalid:

```
. ERASE  ∗.BAK
. ERASE  ABC.∗
. ERASE  ABC????.DBF
```

Trick:

Use the RUN ERASE command to delete selected files from within dBASE III Plus.

You can delete a group of files by using asterisks and question marks as global characters in the RUN ERASE command:

```
. RUN ERASE ∗.BAK
. RUN ERASE ABC.∗
. RUN ERASE ABC????.DBF
```

And, as you can see from the following examples, you can use the RUN command to delete files in other directories:

```
. RUN ERASE B:∗.BAK
. RUN ERASE \DBASE\SALEDATA\∗.NDX
. RUN ERASE D:\LOTUS\SALES\REGION?.WK1
```

Copying Disk Files

Tip:

You can duplicate files by using the COPY FILE command or the RUN COPY command.

You can use the dBASE III Plus COPY FILE command to duplicate the contents of a disk file. (A more flexible method of copying files is using the RUN command to issue the powerful DOS COPY command in dBASE III Plus.)

The COPY FILE command allows you to duplicate a disk file within one directory or from one directory to another. The following examples show how to use the command:

```
. COPY FILE EMPLOYEE.DBF TO B:EMPLOYEE.DBF
. COPY FILE EMPLOYEE.DBF TO D:\BACKUP
  \EMPLOYEE.DBF
```

Trap:

You cannot use asterisks (*) and question marks (?) as global characters (or wild cards) in the COPY FILE command.

Each of the following dot-prompt commands is invalid:

```
. COPY FILE *.DBF TO B:*.DBF
. COPY FILE B:ABC???.DBF TO XYZ???.DBF
```

Trick:

Use the RUN COPY command to copy groups of files within dBASE III Plus.

By using the RUN COPY command at the dot prompt, you can copy groups of disk files from one directory to another. Each of the following commands works:

```
. RUN COPY *.DBF B:*.DBF
. RUN COPY *.BAK D:\BACKUP\*.BAK
. RUN COPY REGION?.DBF B:
```

Renaming Disk Files

Trick:

Use the RUN RENAME command to rename files.

Although you can use the dBASE III Plus RENAME command for renaming a file at the dot prompt, you must comply with certain restrictions when you use this command. A major restriction is that you cannot use asterisks (*) and question marks (?) in the RENAME command.

By using the RUN RENAME command, however, you can rename one or more files with few restrictions. The following commands illustrate ways to use the RUN RENAME command:

```
. RUN RENAME EMPLOYEE.DBF STAFF.DBF
. RUN RENAME *.BAK *.TMP
. RUN RENAME D:\WORDSTAR\*.DOC *.PRG
```

Formatting a Disk within dBASE III Plus

Tip:

Use the RUN FORMAT command to format a blank disk.

Although it is unlikely that you will need to format a disk in dBASE III Plus, you may want to save some of your working files to a floppy disk as backup without leaving the program. To do this, you can format a floppy disk with the RUN command:

```
. RUN FORMAT B:
```

Trap:

The FORMAT.COM file must be accessible while you use the RUN FORMAT command.

One way to gain access to the FORMAT.COM file is to have the file in the current directory when you execute the RUN FORMAT command at the dot prompt.

Trick:

Before entering dBASE III Plus, put the FORMAT.COM file in a separate directory. At the DOS prompt, use a PATH command to tell DOS where to find the file.

Another way to access the FORMAT.COM file from dBASE III Plus is to put the file in a separate directory and then tell DOS where to find it by using a PATH command at the DOS prompt. You will need to do this before you enter dBASE III Plus.

For example, if you put all the DOS command files in a directory named DOSFILES, you can use the following PATH command to tell DOS where to find the command files:

C>PATH C:\DOSFILES

You also can set multiple paths so that DOS will search the directories in these paths for any command or program file that you subsequently request. As you can see from the following example, these paths must be separated by semicolons:

C>PATH C:\DOSFILES;\DBASE;\DBASE\DBFILES

Executing an External Application Program

Tip:

Use the RUN command to execute an external application program.

Executing a non-dBASE III Plus application program from within dBASE III Plus is one of the RUN command's most powerful features.

You can use the command with a commercially developed program (such as WordStar® or Lotus® 1-2-3®) or with a program you've written in a programming language such as BASIC, Pascal, FORTRAN, and so on.

For example, if you want to switch to a word processor such as WordStar in the middle of your dBASE III Plus application, you can issue the following RUN command:

. RUN WS

Tip:

To execute an external application program, be sure that its system files are accessible to dBASE III Plus.

Before you use the RUN command to execute an external application program from within dBASE III Plus, be sure that the working directory contains the system files you need to execute the application.

For example, before you issue the RUN WS command to execute the external WordStar program, you must make sure the current directory contains the WordStar WS.COM program and its associated system files. Otherwise, a **Bad command or file name** error message will be returned.

Because most application programs require more than one file for the different functions provided by the program, be sure that all of these disk files are in the current directory. Otherwise, you may have to change your directory.

While you run an application program at the dot prompt from within dBASE III Plus, whatever you are doing in dBASE III Plus is suspended temporarily. Control of the program is transferred to the application program until you have finished processing in that program. After you exit the external application program, control is returned to dBASE III Plus and processing continues where you left off.

Application programs written in either an interpretive or compiled language also can be executed from the dBASE III Plus dot prompt. For example, you can run a BASIC program (such as MAIN.BAS) that is written in BASICA by using the following command at the dot prompt:

. RUN BASICA MAIN

Again, before you execute the command, be sure that the current directory contains the BASICA.COM system file and the necessary data files for the BASIC program or that these files can be found in the DOS path.

If the BASIC program has been compiled into an executable file such as MAIN.EXE, you can execute the program by using the following command:

. RUN MAIN

Configuring the System
for dBASE III Plus

Tip:

Before entering dBASE III Plus, allocate sufficient files and buffers to the program by configuring the system.

Because dBASE III Plus uses a substantial amount of memory space for data storage and manipulation, you must allocate sufficient RAM (random access memory) to the program before using it.

The dBASE III Plus program consists of a set of commands that instruct the computer to perform the tasks required for managing a database. These commands are coded and stored on the dBASE III Plus system disks.

Before dBASE III Plus is loaded into the computer's memory, the computer must be informed about the environment in which the program is to be operated. For example, the number of disk files that may be used by the program and the amount of memory to be reserved for data storage must be specified before the program is loaded. You provide this type of information in the CONFIG.SYS file in the root directory during the system configuration procedure.

A typical CONFIG.SYS file contains the following two lines for allocating a certain number of files and buffers to application programs such as dBASE III Plus:

```
FILES=20
BUFFERS=15
```

The instructions in the CONFIG.SYS file tell the computer to reserve the disk files and memory buffers for the program.

The CONFIG.SYS file may also contain lines that specify other system devices or parameters. You use a line editor (such as EDLIN.COM that comes with the DOS system) or a text editor to create or modify the contents of the file. (For detailed instructions on using a text editor, refer to its manual.)

By default, DOS ordinarily sets to 8 the number of disk files that can be open at one time. However, because DOS uses 5 of these files, only 3 are available for your application. Because dBASE III Plus can accommodate a total of 15 files, you must set the number of files to 20 in the CONFIG.SYS file to maximize the number of files you can use.

If you do not specify the number of files in the CONFIG.SYS file or if the file is missing, the default setting (FILES=8) is assumed.

Before processing the dBASE III Plus program, DOS must also reserve a certain amount of random access memory (RAM) as temporary working space for the manipulation of data. This temporary working space is reserved in blocks of RAM called *buffers*. The size of this working space influences processing speed when you manipulate data in dBASE III Plus.

If the working space is large, the computer easily finds unused spots in which to store information. As the working space fills with information, DOS takes more time to search for and find the remaining memory available for new information.

In theory, the larger the amount of buffer space you set aside, the faster the processing speed for your data manipulation will be.

Because dBASE III Plus requires a certain minimum of RAM (256K for the most basic applications) and DOS always puts aside memory space for buffers, it is important that you do not use too much memory for buffers. You must be sure that sufficient memory space is available for dBASE III Plus and other application programs.

Allocating Memory Buffers

Tip:

Set more buffers if you have RAM space to spare.

Because each buffer takes up 528 bytes of RAM, you must balance the memory needs of the buffers against those of the application programs.

If your computer has a relatively large amount of RAM (640K, for example), you can experiment with setting the number of buffers to more than 15—to 20, perhaps. In determining your buffer number, be sure to take into account all the memory requirements for your applications, including such RAM-resident programs as SideKick® or a RAM disk.

Trap:

By not reserving sufficient memory in buffers, you run the risk of losing valuable data.

If you do not have enough RAM for reserving a large number of buffers, you run the risk of losing valuable information if you run out of memory space during your dBASE III Plus operations.

On one hand, you want to process your data as quickly as possible by setting a large number of buffers. On the other hand, reserving too much memory space for the buffers and leaving insufficient memory for the application program will result in an **Insufficient memory** error message. Even worse, by exceeding the available memory space you run the risk of losing some or all of your data.

Using Abbreviated Command Words

To reduce typing time and conserve memory space, use the abbreviated forms of the dBASE III Plus commands.

Trick:

Use the abbreviated form of keywords in a command.

When you issue a dBASE III Plus command at the dot prompt or in a program file, the first four characters of each keyword are necessary to identify the command.

For example, you can display the structure of the active database by issuing either the full command:

DISPLAY STRUCTURE

or an abbreviated form of the command:

DISP STRU

You can see that using abbreviated keywords in the commands reduces significantly the amount of typing you have to do.

More important, by using the abbreviated command words when you code a large set of commands in a program file, you reduce the size of the program and conserve the amount of memory needed. As a result, execution time often speeds up.

Refer to table 1.1 for a list of the keywords and abbreviations that can be used in a dBASE III Plus command.

Table 1.1
Abbreviated Command Keywords

Keyword	Abbreviation	Keyword	Abbreviation
ACCEPT	ACCE	IMPORT	IMPO
ALTERNATE	ALTE	INDEX	INDE
APPEND	APPE	INSERT	INSE
ASSIST	ASSI	INTENSITY	INTE
AVERAGE	AVER	LABEL	LABE
BROWSE	BROW	LOCATE	LOCA
CANCEL	CANC	MARGIN	MARG
CARRY	CARR	MEMORY	MEMO
CATALOG	CATA	MEMOWIDTH	MEMO
CENTURY	CENT	MENUS	MENU
CHANGE	CHAN	MESSAGE	MESS
CLEAR	CLEA	ORDER	ORDE
CLOSE	CLOS	OTHERWISE	OTHE
COLOR	COLO	PARAMETERS	PARA
COMMAND	COMM	PRINTER	PRIN
CONFIRM	CONF	PRIVATE	PRIV
CONSOLE	CONS	PROCEDURE	PROC
CONTINUE	CONT	PUBLIC	PUBL
COUNT	COUN	QUERY	QUER
CREATE	CREA	RECALL	RECA
DEBUG	DEBU	RECORD	RECO
DECIMALS	DECI	REINDEX	REIN
DEFAULT	DEFA	RELATION	RELA
DELETE	DELE	RELEASE	RELE
DELIMITERS	DELI	RENAME	RENA
DEVICE	DEVI	REPORT	REPO
DISPLAY	DISP	RESTORE	REST
DOHISTORY	DOHI	RESUME	RESU
EJECT	EJEC	RETURN	RETU
ENDCASE	ENDC	SAFETY	SAFE
ENDDO	ENDD	SCOREBOARD	SCOR
ENDIF	ENDI	SCREEN	SCRE
ERASE	ERAS	SELECT	SELE
ESCAPE	ESCA	STATUS	STAT
EXACT	EXAC	STORE	STOR
FIELDS	FIEL	STRUCTURE	STRU
FILTER	FILT	SUSPEND	SUSP
FIXED	FIXE	TOTAL	TOTA
FORMAT	FORM	TYPEAHEAD	TYPE
FUNCTION	FUNC	UPDATE	UPDA
HEADING	HEAD	WHILE	WHIL
HISTORY	HIST		

Trap:

Use abbreviated command keywords carefully.

When you use the abbreviated command keywords, a few words of caution are in order:

1. You cannot abbreviate the name of a file, a data field, or a memory variable. An abbreviated file name will not allow you to access the file.

2. Although only the first four characters of a keyword are sufficient to execute the command, you can use more than that to identify the keyword.

For example, you can use DISP, DISPL, DISPLA to abbreviate the keyword DISPLAY. However, you may not add any other character to the abbreviated or the original keyword. DISPIT, DISPLAYS, and DISPLAYIT are not valid substitutes for the DISPLAY command. dBASE III Plus will not execute these invalid commands. An `Unrecognized command verb` message will be displayed.

Reissuing an Interactive dBASE III Plus Command

Trick:

Use the ↑ and ↓ keys to reissue a dot command line.

Instead of retyping a dBASE III Plus command you have just typed, you can use the ↑ and ↓ keys at the dot prompt to reissue the command.

In many database-management applications, you can manipulate data by executing a series of interactive dBASE III Plus commands you enter from the keyboard at the dot prompt.

dBASE III Plus saves up to 20 of these commands in a command buffer called a HISTORY buffer. (See Chapter 3 for a detailed discussion of the HISTORY buffer.) When the buffer is full, the new commands you enter replace those entered earlier in a first-in, first-out order.

Redisplaying the contents of the HISTORY buffer is handy when you need to modify a command you've just entered. For example, if you find a typing error when you execute a command at the dot prompt (see fig. 1.4), you can redisplay the command and fix it.

```
. LIST FOR (TYPE="printer" .OR. TYPE="modem") .AND (PRICE-COST)>50

Syntax error.
                                                     ?
LIST FOR (TYPE="printer" .OR. TYPE="modem") .AND (PRICE-COST)>50
Do you want some help? (Y/N) No
```

Fig. 1.4. A command issued at the dot prompt.

Instead of retyping the command, you can recall it by pressing the ↑ key. Each time you press the ↑ key, the most recently entered command is displayed at the dot prompt.

For example, after the error message shown in figure 1.4 appears, press the ↑ key once. The most recently entered command is reissued at the dot prompt (see fig. 1.5).

```
. LIST FOR (TYPE="printer" .OR. TYPE="modem") .AND (PRICE-COST)>50

Syntax error.
                                                     ?
LIST FOR (TYPE="printer" .OR. TYPE="modem") .AND (PRICE-COST)>50
Do you want some help? (Y/N) No
. LIST FOR (TYPE="printer" .OR. TYPE="modem") .AND (PRICE-COST)>50
```

Fig. 1.5. Reissuing a command with the ↑ keystroke.

At this point, you can use the → key to place the cursor at the error (at the end of the word .AND.) and make the necessary correction (insert a period).

After you make the correction, press Enter and execute the command as usual (see fig. 1.6).

```
. LIST FOR (TYPE="printer" .OR. TYPE="modem") .AND (PRICE-COST)>50

Syntax error.
                                                     ?
LIST FOR (TYPE="printer" .OR. TYPE="modem") .AND (PRICE-COST)>50
Do you want some help? (Y/N) No
. LIST FOR (TYPE="printer" .OR. TYPE="modem") .AND. (PRICE-COST)>50
Record# STOCK_NO DIVISION TYPE                     COST   PRICE
      5 NEC-PC660 HW      printer                 560.00 820.00
      6 HAY-M1200 HW      modem                   269.00 309.00
```

Fig. 1.6. Executing the reissued dot command.

If the HISTORY buffer contains more than one command, you can use the ↑ and ↓ keys to scroll up and down the buffer and select the appropriate command. When the command appears at the dot prompt, press Enter to execute it.

Properly Saving dBASE III Plus Data

Trap:

If you switch data disks during data manipulation, you may lose valuable data.

If you store data on a floppy disk in drive B, *do not* switch data disks while you manipulate data.

If dBASE III Plus is configured on a two floppy disk system, drive B usually is designated as the default data-disk drive. Information about the disk files on the default disk drive is saved in a *file allocation table* that tells the computer where data is stored and how it is arranged on the disk.

Whenever you change the contents of the disk files, the file allocation table is updated to reflect the changes and the contents of the file are saved correctly to the disk.

To preserve these updated files, avoid switching data disks during data manipulation. If you change the disks, information in the file allocation table may not agree with your disk files in the current drive. As a result, information in *both* the original and the new disk files can be damaged. Changes made to the original file are saved incorrectly to the new disk.

Trick:

If you must change data disks during your dBASE III Plus session, you need to first issue the CLEAR ALL command to close all the open files and clear all the memory variables.

Then reselect the default disk drive. To do so, either use the SET DEFAULT TO command at the dot prompt or select the Tools/Set drive option from the Assistant menu.

Trap:

Do not turn off the power to quit the program.

Doing so may cause the loss of valuable information or damage the contents of your files.

Trap:

Do not use the Ctrl-Alt-Del key combination to restart the computer before you exit dBASE III Plus.

Doing so may cause data to be lost and may damage your disk file.

Trick:

Always use the QUIT command to exit dBASE III Plus.

The safest way to end a dBASE III Plus session is to exit the program by using the QUIT command. You can execute the command at the dot prompt:

. QUIT

or you can select **Set Up / QUIT dBASE III Plus** from the Assistant menu. Because the QUIT command closes all the open files and saves the contents of all files to disk before terminating the program, no information will be lost.

2

Configuring
dBASE III Plus

dBASE III Plus provides a powerful tool for specifying the commands you need for defining your environment—the configuration file named CONFIG.DB. By predefining the function parameters and commands you need in the CONFIG.DB file, you will be able to do your work more efficiently.

Tip:

**Take advantage of
the CONFIG.DB file
to use dBASE III Plus
more efficiently.**

The CONFIG.DB file can perform many functions for you automatically. At startup, for example, the default data disk drive must be identified to make sure all disk files are saved to the correct disk. The type of display monitor (either a monochrome or color monitor) you are using and its setting (background and foreground colors, for example) must also be supplied. If you are using several memory variables, you may have to reserve sufficient memory space to store the values of the variables properly.

You may want to use an independent word processor or text editor. To save time, you can set the function keys on the keyboard to perform predetermined editing operations. And you can set the size of the keyboard buffers so that a certain number of keys can be stored temporarily as you type ahead.

You can save valuable time by specifying each of these in a configuration file. Because the CONFIG.DB file is the first disk file the computer processes when it enters the program, all the commands stored in the configuration file are executed at startup.

Tip:

Setting up the CONFIG.DB file is easy.

You can set the options and parameters you need in the CONFIG.DB file by using this format:

   <option> = <ON/OFF>

or

   <option> =

Tip:

The CONFIG.DB file is especially useful when you design a turnkey system.

For example, by including the command for executing the first program module (such as the main menu module) in the CONFIG.DB file, control of the program is transferred to the program module as soon as the configuration file is executed.

(If you don't have a CONFIG.DB file, you can set most of these options and parameters at the dot prompt when you enter the program. The format is SET <option> <ON/OFF> or SET <option> to <parameter>.)

Contents of the CONFIG.DB File

Tip:

You need to understand the CONFIG.DB file to use it effectively.

Here is a summary of commands and parameter settings you can use in your CONFIG.DB file:

- Commands for identifying the default disk drive and the type of display monitor

- Keywords for defining the function of a function key

- Keywords for selecting a custom text editor and word processor

- Keywords for reserving memory space for memory variables

- Keywords for allocating memory space

- Keywords for setting the size of the keyboard buffer

- Keywords used by the SET commands for specifying parameter settings

- Other keywords for specifying parameters for controlling data-display operations

Database management operations can be completed efficiently when the settings and commands in the configuration file are chosen appropriately.

Selecting the Default Disk Drive

Tip:

Set the default disk in the configuration file.

Your disk files may be stored in more than one disk drive. In that case, you need to set the default disk drive to the drive that holds your data files. The default data disk drive, which stores all the disk files during your program operations, usually is displayed in the command line at the bottom of the screen. You can use one of several methods to set it.

Assuming that you will be using drive C to store your data, set the data disk drive before you enter the program and add DEFAULT=C to the CONFIG.DB file.

The default disk drive also can be changed while you are in the program. From the Assistant menu, you can set the default by using this option sequence:

Tools/Set drive/<the default drive>

You would type:

Tools/Set drive/C:

At the dot prompt, you can set the default data disk drive by issuing this command:

. SET DEFAULT TO <the default drive>

You would type:

. SET DEFAULT TO C:

Trap:

A directory path specified in the SET DEFAULT TO command has no effect.

If you include a directory path in the command for setting the default disk drive, the path is ignored and no warning message is returned.

The DEFAULT keyword in the CONFIG.DB file identifies the data disk drive. For example, do not include a directory path in the DEFAULT statement, such as

DEFAULT=C:*DBASE\DBFILES*

A directory path specified in the DEFAULT statement will be ignored. And the disk files you create thereafter will not be saved in the specified directory in the DEFAULT drive. To verify the current directory, use the RUN CD command at the dot prompt after you have entered the program.

Defining Function Keys

Tip:

Save time with the default settings of the function keys.

Function keys are set up to perform commonly used program commands. Use these function keys to minimize keystrokes when you issue program commands at the dot prompt.

Each function key can be set to perform a specific function. For example, the first function key (designated F1) is used to invoke the HELP facility. Here are the normal operations assigned to the function keys:

Function Key	Command	Designated Operation
F1	HELP	Access HELP facility
F2	ASSIST	Invoke Assistant menu
F3	LIST	List records in active database file
F4	DIR	Display database files in active directory
F5	DISPLAY STRUCTURE	Display structure of database in use

F6	DISPLAY STATUS	Display current processing status and current setting of function keys
F7	DISPLAY MEMORY	Display values of active memory variables
F8	DISPLAY	Display current records in active database file
F9	APPEND	Append data record to active database file
F10	EDIT	Edit contents of data records in active database file

You can use the F2 through F10 function keys to perform other prespecified operations. (F1 is reserved for the HELP facility.) As a result, you can customize your database operations with these function keys.

Customizing Function Keys

Trick:

For increased power, reassign the function keys to a set of custom operations.

You can create program modules for performing database management functions when you design a turnkey database management system.

For example, your database management system can consist of several program modules, such as INVOICE.PRG, MAILLIST.PRG, and REPORTS.PRG (for preparing invoices, mailing lists, and financial reports, respectively). Rather than writing a menu program in which you select an operation from the main menu, you can designate a function key for each operation. Function keys F2, F3, and F4, for instance, could perform the following operations:

Function Key	Designated Operation
F2	Creating invoices
F3	Producing mailing lists
F4	Generating financial reports

You can define the operation of a function key by specifying the operation in a SET FUNCTION TO command. To define the function key before entering the program, specify the operation as a line in the CONFIG.DB file:

F<function key #> = "<the designated operation>;"

For example, you can designate F2 to execute the INVOICE.PRG program module by including F2="DO INVOICE;" in the CONFIG.DB file. The semicolon (;) at the end of the operation instructs the computer to issue a carriage return (or press Enter). Without the semicolon, you would have to press F2 and then Enter to execute the designated operation.

You also can assign more than one operation to a function key. For example, you can instruct the program to clear the screen before executing the MAILLIST.PRG program by defining F3 as:

F3="CLEAR; DO MAILLIST;"

Trick:

Assign multiple operations to a function key.

The operations assigned to a function key can be entered as a character expression. For example, to clear the screen and execute the MAINMENU.PRG program by pressing F3, include F3="CLEAR; DO MAINMENU;" in the CONFIG.DB file.

Trap:

You can't redefine the operation of the F1 function key.

The F1 function key is confined to the HELP operation by the program. You cannot redefine F1 by using the set function command.

Using an External Text Editor

Tip:

Use an external word processor to edit a text file within dBASE III Plus.

The built-in text editor provided by dBASE III Plus lets you create and modify text files primarily by using one of these file extensions:

.PRG (a program or command file)
.LBL (a label file)
.FMT (a format file)
.TXT (a text file)

Any file that contains a block of text in the ASCII format can be created and edited by such a text editor. To invoke the built-in text editor, enter the following command at the dot prompt:

. MODIFY COMMAND <name of text file to be created or edited>

For example, to create a program called MAINPROG.PRG, you issue this command at the dot prompt:

. MODIFY COMMAND MAINPROG.PRG

The built-in text editor is invoked, and you can enter the text for the program file (see fig. 2.1).

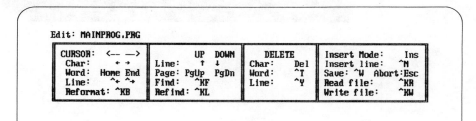

Fig. 2.1. Entering dBASE III Plus text editor.

The top of the screen shows a summary of the keystrokes you can use for editing the contents of the text file. (You can hide or display the summary by toggling the F1 function key.)

The built-in text editor provides many of the basic functions of a text editor. But it lacks some of the powerful features of such stand-alone text editors and word processors as WordStar, Microsoft® Word, WordPerfect®, and MultiMate®. Fortunately, you can use one of these powerful word processors in place of the built-in text editor.

An important fact to remember here is that the text file being edited by an external text editor or word processor must be saved in ASCII format.

To select an external text editor to use within the program, you need to specify the text editor in the CONFIG.DB file. The format of the configuration command in the file is

TEDIT=<name of the text editor>

For example, to choose WordStar as your external text editor, you add TEDIT=WS.COM to the CONFIG.DB file.

After the commands in the CONFIG.DB file are executed and the cursor is at the dot prompt, you can invoke a text editor by issuing MODIFY COMMAND (see fig. 2.2).

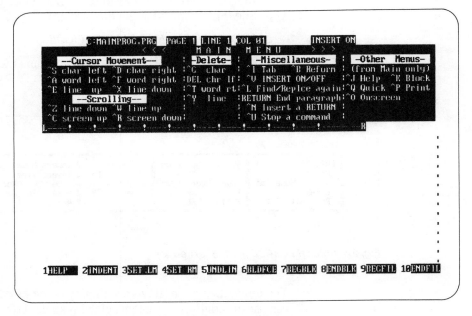

Fig. 2.2. Using WordStar as a word processor for text editing.

Tip:

To use an external text editor, your files must be accessible to DOS.

When you use an external text editor in dBASE III Plus, you must make sure that all the files can be accessed by DOS. The files usually include all the related files that have .COM, .OVR, or .EXE file extensions.

You can save the programs in the current directory so that DOS can find them. For example, if you are in the directory C:\DBASE\DBFILES, all the files required to execute WordStar (such as WS.COM, WSU.COM, WSMSGS.OVR, and WSOVLY1.OVR) can be saved in that directory. If these programs are saved in a separate directory, you must use the

PATH command to tell DOS where to find them. Otherwise, when you attempt to invoke the text editor at the dot prompt, the error message `Bad command or file name` flashes on the screen and the cursor returns to the dot prompt.

Trick:

Use the PATH command to tell DOS where to find the word-processor programs.

If you want to use an external word processor (and the external programs are saved in a separate directory), you must specify—before you enter the program—the path that tells DOS where to find the programs. For example, if all the programs associated with your word processor are saved in the WORDPROC directory, you need to issue the C>PATH \WORDPROC command at the DOS prompt.

Tip:

Use an external word processor to edit the contents of memo fields.

Memo fields in a database table can be used effectively to store large blocks of text. When editing text in the memo field, you can take advantage of some of the powerful editing features offered by external word processors. To do so, you first specify the word processor in the CONFIG.DB file. The format of the configuration command is

WP=<name of the word processor>

For example, to choose WordStar as your external word processor, you add WP=WS.COM to the CONFIG.DB file.

Tip:

Use a DOS PATH command when the external text editor programs are not in the current directory.

Be sure to tell DOS where to find these files by using a DOS PATH command before entering dBASE III Plus. Otherwise, the program won't be able to find and execute the word processor you specified.

After the commands in the CONFIG.DB file are executed and the cursor is at the dot prompt, the external word processor you specified is called up by pressing Ctrl-Home (see fig. 2.3).

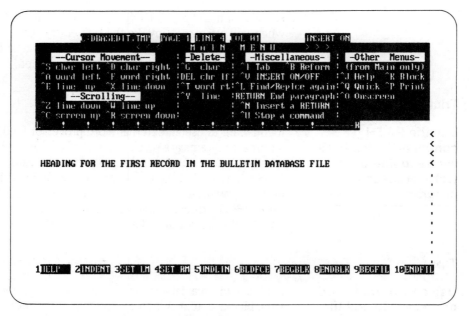

Fig. 2.3. Using WordStar for editing a memo field.

Tip:

The contents of your edited memo fields are held in a temporary file.

When you are using an external word processor such as WordStar to edit text in a memo field, a temporary file is created to hold the contents. (The example in fig. 2.3 is C:DBASEDIT.TMP.) The actual contents of the memo field in the database file are saved in a memo text file (such as BULLETIN.DBT). After you edit the memo field, you can exit from the word processor by using the appropriate command. (In WordStar, you press Ctrl-KD and type *X*.) You then can edit the next data field in the database file.

Tip:

You can edit the contents of memo fields with the built-in text editor.

To invoke the built-in text editor while the cursor is in a memo field, press Ctrl-Home. For example, to add a new record to a database file named BULLETIN.DBF that contains two memo fields named HEADING and TEXT, you issue the USE BULLETIN and APPEND commands at the dot prompt.

In response to the dot-prompt commands, the record to be appended to the database file is displayed. (see fig. 2.4).

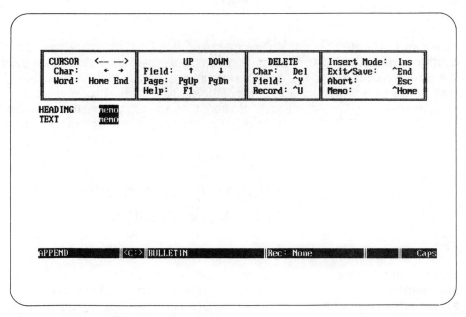

Fig. 2.4. Editing the contents of a memo field.

Then, to edit (or enter) the contents for the first memo field (HEADING), press Ctrl-Home. The built-in text editor is invoked and you can type the text for the memo field (see fig. 2.5).

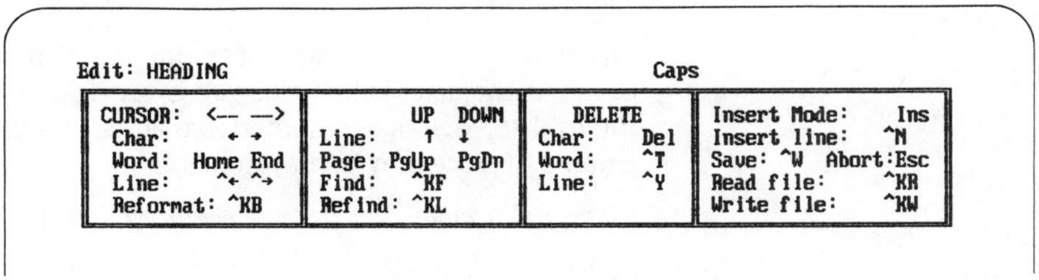

Fig. 2.5. Using the program's text editor for editing a memo field.

The memo field being edited (HEADING) is shown at the top of the screen. After you edit this memo field, press Ctrl-W to save the text in the memo field and continue editing the next data field in the database file.

Trap:

You can't edit the contents of a .DBT file directly with a text editor or a word processor.

A database memo file (.DBT) stores the contents of all the memo fields in the database file, including the control characters for internal organization of the file. If you edit the contents of the database memo file, these control characters could be altered. As a result, information stored in your memo fields might be damaged or lost. You can edit the field contents only by entering the fields themselves while you are editing the database file.

Allocating Memory for Memory Variables

Tip:

Be sure to allocate sufficient memory space when you use several memory variables.

The term *variable* is used in algebra to define a quantity that can assume different values. In dBASE III Plus, a variable is a name assigned to a memory location that can be used to hold a data element. The value stored in a memory variable can be the value in a data field or some other data item. Dates, alphanumeric strings, and numeric values can be stored in memory variables.

During processing, memory variables are stored temporarily in random access memory (RAM). Variables can occupy a varying amount of RAM. For example, an alphanumeric or character variable can contain as many as 254 characters.

The amount of memory an alphanumeric variable occupies equals its character length plus two bytes. The following table shows date, logical, and numeric variables, and the fixed amount of space they occupy in RAM:

Memory Variable Type	Memory Space Used (Bytes)
Alphanumeric or character	Number of characters + 2
Date	9
Logical	2
Numeric	9

The maximum number of memory variables of all types that can be used in the program is 256. Unless otherwise requested, the memory space allocated by the program is limited to 6,000 bytes. This memory limit is sufficient if most of your memory variables are date, logical and numeric variables, or alphanumeric variables that have short character strings.

If you plan to use a number of alphanumeric variables with long character strings, however, you could quickly run short of memory space. Because each alphanumeric variable can hold as many as 254 characters and can occupy as many as 256 bytes, the default amount of memory (6,000 bytes) can accommodate about 23 variables of this size.

When your database management application requires you to use a large amount of memory space for the values of the memory variables, you can exceed the 6,000-byte limit. To allocate the memory you will need in such a case, you can use a configuration line in the CONFIG.DB file. The format of the configuration line is

MVARSIZ=<amount of memory in kilobytes>

For example, if you anticipate using about 10,000 bytes of memory for the memory variables, you can include MVARSIZ=10 in the CONFIG.DB file.

The amount of memory specified in the MVARSIZ is between 1 and 31 kilobytes (between 1,024 and 31,744 bytes). However, when you specify a large amount of memory space for your memory variables, you take memory away from other operations. Therefore, to have enough memory for other data processing operations, you must allocate more memory for the program.

Allocating Memory for dBASE III Plus

If manipulating your database management application requires a large amount of memory, be sure to reserve plenty of RAM space.

When you begin the dBASE III Plus program, DOS allocates a certain amount of RAM for executing the program: a minimum of 256K bytes. This amount of memory is used for (1) holding the program, (2) storing the values of all the memory variables the program needs, and (3) all the working space the program uses during data manipulation.

If your application uses a large amount of memory for the values of the memory variables, you may not have enough memory for other data manipulation. In an extreme case, you will not be able to continue your data manipulation. To prevent this inconvenience—or disaster—you need to calculate your memory needs and reserve them accordingly before you manipulate data.

To reserve memory space for the program, you specify—as a configuration line in the CONFIG.DB file—the maximum amount of memory you anticipate using. The format of the configuration line is

MAXMEM=<amount of memory space in kilobytes>

For example, to reserve 384K for the program, include MAXMEM=384 in your CONFIG.DB file. You can reserve from 256K to 720K of memory for the program.

You might believe that you can safely reserve a lot of memory space for the program with the MAXMEM statement in the CONFIG.DB file. This assumption isn't true, however, if you need to execute other external programs in your application.

Many factors affect the actual amount of RAM you can allocate to your program application. First, RAM is limited by the amount of memory in your hardware (the system board and the extra memory in the other memory boards). RAM resident programs like SideKick or ProKey must be loaded in memory before you can execute dBASE III Plus. In addition, you need to reserve enough memory space to execute external programs, such as an external text editor or word processor. Therefore, if you have a limited amount of memory, be sure to calculate your memory needs in advance and allocate memory accordingly.

Allocating Memory Buffers

Tip:

To use a large number of GET commands with PICTURE and RANGE clauses, allocate space in CONFIG.DB.

If you intend to use several GET commands that include the PICTURE and RANGE clauses, you need to allocate extra memory.

You also need to reserve enough memory space for the @..SAY..GET..PICTURE..RANGE commands when you use them to define the format of a field value in a data entry form. For example, if your database table (PAYDATA.DBF) contains these three fields:

Field Name	Field Type	Width	Dec
ID_NO	Character	11	
EMPLY_DATE	Date	8	
SALARY	Numeric	9	2

you can design a custom data entry form that includes these command lines for defining the data format:

```
USE PAYDATA
APPEND BLANK
@10,5 SAY "Employee's Social Security No. " GET ID_NO;
    PICTURE "999-99-9999"
@12,5 SAY "Employment Date " GET EMPLY_DATE;
    RANGE CTOD("1/1/65"), CTOD("6/30/87")
@14,5 SAY "Annual Salary " GET SALARY PICTURE  "##,###.##";
    RANGE 15000,69000
READ
```

The PICTURE clauses in the GET commands define the type of characters entered in the data fields; the RANGE clauses specify the valid range of the data field values. Each time you include one of these GET commands, the program stores it in a temporary memory location (or buffer).

The default number of GET commands you can use is 128. If your database management application requires you to use more than 128 GET commands in your data formatting instructions, you need to increase the limit accordingly. You can include a GETS configuration instruction in the CONFIG.DB file to specify the maximum number of GET commands you will be using. The format of the configuration instruction is

GETS=<maximum number of GET commands>

The RAM space you have on your computer system limits the number of GET commands you can specify.

Tip:

If you want to use several GET commands, increase the BUCKET size accordingly.

The information specified in the PICTURE and RANGE clauses requires not only a number of GET commands but also a certain amount of memory space. For example, when you specify PICTURE "999-99-9999" for the GET command, 11 bytes of RAM are used to store the 11 characters defined in the PICTURE clause.

Memory space for storing the PICTURE and RANGE clauses is allocated by the BUCKET size, which is measured by the number of kilobytes. Unless otherwise specified, the program allocates two kilobytes (BUCKET=2 or 2×1,024 bytes) for saving all the PICTURE and RANGE options.

This default setting provides sufficient memory space to accommodate formatting operations with PICTURE and RANGE clauses in the GET commands of most applications. However, if your application requires an unusually large amount of memory space for saving the PICTURE and RANGE values, you can increase the BUCKET size by including the following line in the CONFIG.DB file:

BUCKET=<size of bucket in kilobytes>

The maximum size of a BUCKET is 31 kilobytes.

Tip:

To increase the BUCKET size, allocate more memory to dBASE III Plus.

Note that all memory allocated in the configuration files for the GETS and BUCKET commands uses part of the RAM space reserved by the MAXMEM command. Therefore, the more memory you put aside for the GET commands and the PICTURE and RANGE values, the less space is available for other program operations. For example, if you plan to use a large amount of memory to manipulate your database, you won't want to waste your space by setting the number of GET commands and the size of the BUCKET too large.

Setting Monitor Colors

Tip:

To display commands and results on your monitor in color, set colors in the configuration file.

When you use a color monitor connected to an IBM color graphics card (or a compatible card), you can display output in colors.

Before entering the program, you can instruct it to display the commands and the results on a color monitor that has predefined colors. Include a COLOR command in the CONFIG.DB file in this format:

COLOR=<color of standard text/background color>,
     <color of enhanced text/background color>,
     <border color>

For example, to set the standard text to white on a blue background and the enhanced text to red on a blue background with a green border, use COLOR=W/B,R/B,G.

Foreground and background colors for the standard and enhanced texts can be set independently. The color of the screen border also can be chosen separately.

After you are in dBASE III Plus, you can change the screen colors by issuing the SET COLOR TO command at the dot prompt. (See Chapter 7 for a detailed discussion of setting screen colors for displaying output.)

Defining Your Own Prompt

Tip:

Instead of using the dot, define your own prompt symbol in the configuration file.

If you do not want to use the dot (.) as the command prompt symbol in the program, you can select your own command prompt.

In the interactive mode of processing, you can choose either the Assistant menu or the dot prompt to issue your processing commands. Although the Assistant menu provides a user-friendly environment for communicating with the dBASE III Plus processor, the dot prompt is the most powerful and flexible way to issue commands for manipulating your data.

Many users have grown accustomed to the dot as a command prompt and find it quite satisfactory. However, new users of the program often complain about the nondescriptive dot. They dislike the dot because it does not provide any information about the action the processor requests. If you agree, you can replace the prompt with your own symbols or messages. To define your own prompt, include a PROMPT configuration line in the CONFIG.DB file in this format:

PROMPT=<a character string>

Character strings used as command prompts can be from 1 to 20 characters long. Here are some examples:

PROMPT=->
PROMPT=Command>
PROMPT=Enter a command:

For example, if you define your command prompt as

Enter a command:

when you are in dot-prompt mode, this string is displayed in place of a normal dot. You then can issue the command at the prompt, and it will look like these examples:

```
Enter a command:USE EMPLOYEE
Enter a command:LIST
```

In this example, you can see there is no space between the cursor (where you begin typing the command) and the last character of the prompt [:]. If you want to separate the prompt and the command, add a blank space at the end of the character string used as the prompt. Even though a space may not show on the monitor, it is a valid string character. If you add a space, the command prompt will look like these examples:

```
Enter a command: USE EMPLOYEE
Enter a command: LIST
```

Executing a Program Automatically

Configure dBASE III Plus to execute a command automatically after entering the program.

You can instruct a turnkey database management system to execute a command automatically at startup.

When you design a database management system, you can create several program modules that perform specific data manipulation operations. Then, if you want to execute one of these dBASE III Plus programs (a .PRG file extension), you can issue the DO command and include the name of the program to be executed. For example, . DO MAINPROG is the dot prompt command for executing a program named MAINPROG.PRG.

This approach for processing your data requires that you know the name of each program module so that you can specify the name in the DO command. If your system is designed for your own use, you shouldn't have a problem because you probably can remember the program modules involved in your database application.

If you create program modules intended for other people to use, you need to design a turnkey system that doesn't require users to remember the names of all the program modules. Users just select menu items by pressing designated keys to perform specified tasks. (A detailed discussion about this procedure appears in Chapter 9.) A program that automatically specifies all the menu choices as soon as you enter dBASE III Plus is especially useful.

To execute a dot prompt command as soon as you enter the program, include the following command in the CONFIG.DB file:

COMMAND=<the dBASE III Plus command>

Here are two examples:

COMMAND=DO MAINMENU
COMMAND=DO DBFILES\MAINMENU

If you examine the CONFIG.DB file contents originally supplied by the program (by issuing the TYPE CONFIG.DB command at the DOS prompt), you can see COMMAND=ASSIST in the configuration file. When the configuration line is executed, the Assistant menu is displayed automatically. If you delete this line from the configuration file, the cursor moves to the dot prompt when you invoke the program.

On the other hand, when you include another program command in its place (such as DO MAINMENU), that command is executed automatically when the program is invoked. Control of the program then shifts to the program module to be executed. After the program module is executed, unless directed otherwise in the program, the dot prompt regains control.

Therefore, do not attempt to execute more than one program module via the CONFIG.DB file. If you do, the second DO command in the configuration line will not be executed.

The ALTERNATE File

Tip:

Assign a default ALTERNATE file during configuration.

When the program is in interactive mode and is processing a program command via the dot prompt, you can save a list of all commands issued to a text file. This convenient method documents your data processing operations. Such a command list is especially useful in the program development stage, because it documents all the processing steps in your application.

To save program commands issued at the dot prompt, with their related output on the screen, you use the SET ALTERNATE TO and SET ALTERNATE ON commands. An ALTERNATE file example is shown in figure 2.6. (Chapter 3 provides a detailed discussion of the creation of an ALTERNATE file and its functions.)

To assign a name to an ALTERNATE file, use the ALTERNATE command in the CONFIG.DB file:

ALTERNATE=<name of the text file>

The name of the text file may or may not include the directory path or a file extension. If you do not include a file extension, the .TXT extension is assumed automatically. Unless otherwise specified, the directory from which the program is invoked is

```
. SET ALTERNATE TO LISTING.TXT
. SET ALTERNATE ON
. USE EMPLOYEE
. DISPLAY FOR POSITION="Sales Rep"
Record#  ID_NO     FIRST_NAME   LAST_NAME   POSITION   EMPLY_DATE MALE
     4   732-88-4589 Doris Y.    Taylor      Sales Rep  08/14/83   .F.
     7   554-34-7893 Vincent M.  Corso       Sales Rep  07/20/84   .T.

. SET ALTERNATE OFF
. CLOSE ALTERNATE
. TYPE LISTING.TXT

. USE EMPLOYEE
. DISPLAY FOR POSITION="Sales Rep"
Record#  ID_NO     FIRST_NAME   LAST_NAME   POSITION   EMPLY_DATE MALE
     4   732-88-4589 Doris Y.    Taylor      Sales Rep  08/14/83   .F.
     7   554-34-7893 Vincent M.  Corso       Sales Rep  07/20/84   .T.

. SET ALTERNATE OFF
```

Fig. 2.6. Saving screen contents in a text file with the SET ALTERNATE ON command.

assumed. To save the text file in another directory, be sure to specify it accordingly. Here are some examples:

ALTERNATE=*LISTING.TXT*
ALTERNATE=B:*LISTING.DOC*
ALTERNATE=C:*DBASE\\DBFILES\\LISTING.TXT*

Tip:

If you use a large ALTERNATE file, be sure you have enough disk space to hold it.

The text file created by the SET ALTERNATE TO command requires a certain amount of disk space. You need to make sure you have enough space on your disk drive and in the file directory before you create the text file. Otherwise, the error message `ALTERNATE could not be opened` is displayed.

The BELL Command

To turn the beeping sound on or off during a data-entry operation, set the BELL command in configuration.

As a warning or a reminder, the program beeps during certain data-entry operations. For example, when you enter data that fills the specified width of a data field, a beeping sound warns you that the cursor has moved to the next data field. The beeping sound can be turned on by including the BELL command in the CONFIG.DB file; it can be turned off by including the BELL=OFF command.

If you do not specify one of these commands in the CONFIG.DB file, the bell will be set by default to ON.

The CARRY Command

To allow the contents of an existing data record to be carried over to another record, set CARRY to ON during configuration.

When you add new data records to a database file by using the APPEND and INSERT commands, you can carry the contents of a preceding record to the next record. You then can create new data records by replicating the contents of an existing record.

The data replication operation is useful when most of the field values in the new records are the same as the existing record. Instead of entering all the data field values via the keyboard, you can copy the contents of an existing record to a new record and then make modifications. (The replication of data records is discussed in Chapter 3.)

To invoke the replication operation, you issue the SET CARRY ON command at the dot prompt. The SET CARRY OFF command deactivates the replication operation. CARRY=ON and CARRY=OFF are the configuration commands you can include in the CONFIG.DB file for the replicating operation. Normally, the program starts by assuming CARRY is set to OFF.

The CATALOG File

When you are designing a turnkey system, assign a catalog file during configuration.

You can group all the related disk files in a catalog file with a .CAT file extension. Then you can see and use only the files for that application. The name of your catalog file also can be specified in your CONFIG.DB file by including this command line:

CATALOG=<name of catalog file>

Cataloging files is an efficient method for organizing your data. An active catalog file, however, occupies one working area (work area 10). As a result, only nine working areas remain for your other data manipulation operations. (The advantages and disadvantages of using catalog files in database management are discussed in Chapter 5.)

The CENTURY Command

Define the CENTURY command during configuration.

If you use dates from different centuries, be sure to use the CENTURY command to display the century prefix properly.

When the contents of a date variable or a date field are displayed, the century prefix for a date normally does not appear. For example, if you issue the ?DATE() command at the dot prompt, the system date displayed by the command may look like 01/25/87. If you want to show the century prefix, however, you can issue the SET CENTURY ON command at the dot prompt:

```
. SET CENTURY ON
. ?DATE()
01/25/1987
```

The default century setting is OFF. When you use dates that are not in the 20th century, you set CENTURY to ON. jFor example, if you use a date variable from the 19th century and another one from the 20th century in your application, but you don't set CENTURY to ON, you cannot distinguish one century from another (see fig. 2.7).

```
. SET CENTURY OFF
. ADATE=CTOD("07/04/1776")
07/04/76
. BDATE=CTOD("07/04/1976")
07/04/76
. ?ADATE,BDATE
07/04/76 07/04/76
. ?"Number of days in between =",BDATE-ADATE
Number of days in between =      73048
. SET CENTURY ON
. ?ADATE,BDATE
07/04/1776 07/04/1976
```

Fig. 2.7. Displaying the century prefix with the SET CENTURY ON command.

As shown in figure 2.7, variables ADATE and BDATE show the same value when they are displayed with the question mark (?) after SET CENTURY OFF is executed. However, you can see that the two dates are correctly stored internally when you display the number of days between the two dates (73,048 days).

You also can set century ON and OFF by including CENTURY=ON or CENTURY=OFF in the CONFIG.DB file.

The CONFIRM Command

Tip:

Set the CONFIRM operation during configuration.

To ensure that a data value is correctly entered in a data field, use the CONFIRM command to control the cursor movement.

Normally, when you enter data in a data field with the APPEND or EDIT operation, the cursor moves automatically to the next field as soon as the current field is filled. However, you can force the cursor to stay in the same data field. Then you can press Enter to confirm the entered value and make sure the data value is correctly entered in the data field.

To keep the cursor in the data field after data entry, issue the SET CONFIRM ON command at the dot prompt before you begin entering data. (The default setting of the CONFIRM operation is OFF.) To invoke the CONFIRM operation before entering the program, include the CONFIRM=ON configuration line in the CONFIG.DB file.

The CONSOLE Command

**Set CONSOLE to ON
and OFF during
configuration.**

To avoid displaying some of the output elements and prompt
messages produced by the INPUT, ACCEPT, and WAIT
commands, you can use the SET CONSOLE OFF command.

In providing output, you can use one of the ? and ??
commands to display the values of memory variables or data
fields along with the necessary labels:

> ?"Value of variable XYZ = ",XYZ
> ??"Employee's Social Security #:", ID_NO

To assign values to memory variables, you use the following
character strings as prompts in the ACCEPT, INPUT, and
WAIT commands:

> ACCEPT "Enter the account number :" TO ACCTNO
> INPUT "Enter value of the sale :" TO SALE
> WAIT "Are these items correct [Y/N]? " TO ANSWER

When these commands are given, the generated output
normally is displayed on the screen because the program
assumes that the screen or console is on by default. For
example, when the input commands shown in
CONSOLE.PRG are executed (see fig. 2.8), the screen displays
all the prompt messages and the values produced by the ? and
?? commands (see fig. 2.9).

```
. TYPE CONSOLE.PRG
CLEAR
SET CONSOLE ON
ACCEPT "             Enter the account number :" TO ACCTNO
INPUT "             Enter amount of the sale :" TO SALE
?
?
WAIT "             Are the items correct [Y/N]?" TO ANSWER
@10,1 SAY "Values of the memory variables:"
?
?"ACCTNO = "+ACCTNO
?? "     SALE = "+STR(SALE,8,2)
??"     ANSWER ="+ANSWER
RETURN
```

Fig. 2.8. Directing output to the screen with the SET CONSOLE ON command.

```
          Enter the account number :A12345
          Enter amount of the sale :289.95


          Are the items correct [Y/N]?Y



   Values of the memory variables:

   ACCTNO = A12345     SALE =   289.95     ANSWER =Y
```

Fig. 2.9. Effects of the SET CONSOLE ON command.

If you replace SET CONSOLE ON with SET CONSOLE OFF, however, neither the prompt messages in the ACCEPT, INPUT, and WAIT commands nor the output elements generated by the ? and ?? commands are displayed. An exception is that the character string displayed by the @..SAY command still appears on the screen.

You can set CONSOLE to ON or OFF only by using the SET command in a program or by including CONSOLE=ON or CONSOLE=OFF in the CONFIG.DB file. The SET CONSOLE ON and SET CONSOLE OFF commands have no effect when they are issued at the dot prompt.

The DEBUG Command

Tip:

Set DEBUG during configuration.

When you execute a dBASE III Plus program, you can locate all the program errors if you invoke the SET DEBUG ON command at the dot prompt. You also can invoke the DEBUG operation by including the DEBUG=ON configuration line in the CONFIG.DB file. To terminate the DEBUG operation, issue the SET DEBUG OFF command at the dot prompt.

Normally, when DEBUG is set to ON, all the error messages in the program you are executing are displayed on the screen. However, to avoid interference between the program's operations (such as requesting data entry) and the error messages, you can route the error messages to the printer by using the SET ECHO ON command in conjunction with SET DEBUG ON.

Decimals

Tip:

Specify the number of decimal places for displayed values during configuration.

The minimum number of decimal places used by dBASE III Plus for displaying both the results of the numeric functions SQRT(), LOG(), and EXP(), and the arithmetic operation of division is set by default to two:

```
. ?SQRT(10)
   3.16
. ?LOG(10)
   2.30
. ?EXP(10)
      22026.47
. ?10/3
   3.33
```

You have two choices for showing more decimal places in the results of these numeric functions and calculations. First, you can specify the value in the function argument with more decimal places. Then the returning values of the functions will be displayed with the same number of decimals as the argument:

```
. ?SQRT(10.000000)
   3.162278
. ?LOG(10.00000)
   2.30259
. ?EXP(10.0000)
22026.4658
. ?10.0000000000/3
            3.3333333333

.
```

If the argument of these functions is a numeric memory variable, you can express the value in the desired number of decimal places when you assign it to the variable:

```
. A=10
10
. ?LOG(A)
 2.30
. A=10.0000
10.0000
. ?LOG(A)
          2.3026
. B=5.000
5.000
. ?EXP(B)
    148.413
. ?A/B
               2.0000
```

Second, you can define the number of decimal places for these values by issuing the SET DECIMALS TO command at the dot prompt:

. SET DECIMALS TO <number of decimal places to display>

For example, when you set the number to 4 by using the SET DECIMALS TO command, all the values resulting from the SQRT(), LOG(), and EXP() functions and the division operation are displayed in four decimal places. A maximum of 15 decimal places can be set.

```
. SET DECIMALS TO 4
. ?SQRT(10)
 3.1623
. ?LOG(10)
 2.3026
. ?EXP(10)
     22026.4658
. ?10/3
  3.3333
. A=10
10
. B=5
5
. ?LOG(A)
          2.3026
. ?EXP(5)
        148.4132
. ?A/B
               2.0000
```

The number of decimal places also can be set by including this configuration line in the CONFIG.DB file:

DECIMALS=<number of decimal places to display>

Remember that the number of decimals defined by this step and the SET DECIMALS TO command do not affect the accuracy of the numeric values stored in the computer memory. The SET DECIMALS TO and DECIMALS commands affect only the displayed values of the SQRT( ), LOG( ), and EXP( ) functions and the division operation. Results from other numeric functions and arithmetic operations will not be affected by these commands.

The DELETED Command

Tip:

Set DELETED during configuration.

You can filter out the records marked for deletion from the database file by using the SET DELETED command without the PACK operation.

Normally, to remove data records from the active database file, you first mark these records by issuing the DELETE command and then use the PACK command. However, before packing the data records, remember that the records marked for deletion are treated as unmarked records when you apply the LIST and LOCATE operations (see fig. 2.10).

Figure 2.10 shows that the records marked for deletion (records #4 and #7) still appeared when the LIST operation was executed. The record pointer pointed to the "deleted" record when the LOCATE command was performed. If you do not want to use these "deleted" records in the LIST and LOCATE operations, you can issue the SET DELETED ON command before the operations (see fig. 2.11).

Figure 2.11 shows that the records marked for deletion were not displayed by the LIST command. Furthermore, you cannot find these records by using the LOCATE operation.

You should know, however, that the SET DELETED ON command does not hide the "deleted" record from the GOTO, GO TOP, and GO BOTTOM operations.

```
. SET DELETE OFF
. USE EMPLOYEE
. DELETE FOR POSITION="Sales Rep"
     2 records deleted
. LIST
Record#  ID_NO        FIRST_NAME   LAST_NAME      POSITION   EMPLY_DATE MALE
      1  123-45-6789 Thomas T.     Smith          President  03/01/1981 .T.
      2  254-63-5691 Tina Y.       Thompson       VP         09/22/1982 .F.
      3  467-34-6789 Peter F.      Watson         Manager    10/12/1982 .T.
      4 *732-08-4589 Doris Y.      Taylor         Sales Rep  08/14/1983 .F.
      5  563-55-8900 Tyrone T.     Thorsen        Engineer   06/20/1982 .T.
      6  823-46-6213 Cathy J.      Faust          Secretary  04/15/1983 .F.
      7 *554-34-7893 Vincent M.    Corso          Sales Rep  07/20/1984 .T.
      8  321-65-9007 Jane W.       Kaiser         Accountant 11/22/1982 .F.
      9  560-56-9321 Tina K.       Davidson       Trainee    05/16/1986 .F.
     10  435-54-9876 James J.      Smith          Trainee    01/23/1986 .T.

. LOCATE FOR POSITION="Sales Rep"
Record =        4
. DISPLAY
Record#  ID_NO        FIRST_NAME   LAST_NAME      POSITION   EMPLY_DATE MALE
      4 *732-08-4589 Doris Y.      Taylor         Sales Rep  08/14/1983 .F.
```

Fig. 2.10. Listing and locating deleted records.

```
. SET DELETE ON
. LIST
Record#  ID_NO        FIRST_NAME   LAST_NAME      POSITION   EMPLY_DATE MALE
      1  123-45-6789 Thomas T.     Smith          President  03/01/1981 .T.
      2  254-63-5691 Tina Y.       Thompson       VP         09/22/1982 .F.
      3  467-34-6789 Peter F.      Watson         Manager    10/12/1982 .T.
      5  563-55-8900 Tyrone T.     Thorsen        Engineer   06/20/1982 .T.
      6  823-46-6213 Cathy J.      Faust          Secretary  04/15/1983 .F.
      8  321-65-9007 Jane W.       Kaiser         Accountant 11/22/1982 .F.
      9  560-56-9321 Tina K.       Davidson       Trainee    05/16/1986 .F.
     10  435-54-9876 James J.      Smith          Trainee    01/23/1986 .T.

. LOCATE FOR POSITION="Sales Rep"
End of LOCATE scope
. DISPLAY
Record#  ID_NO        FIRST_NAME   LAST_NAME      POSITION   EMPLY_DATE MALE
```

Fig. 2.11. Effects of the SET DELETED ON command.

Trap:

When you use SET DELETED ON, the records marked for deletion still are subject to the INDEX and REINDEX operations.

Contrary to what you might expect, the SET DELETED ON operation does not exclude any records marked for deletion when you apply the INDEX and REINDEX operations (see fig. 2.12).

For example, the EMPLOYEE.DBF database file contains 10 records—two that have been marked for deletion. However, when you index the database file, all the records are indexed.

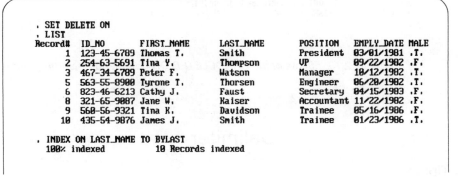

```
. SET DELETE ON
. LIST
Record#   ID_NO        FIRST_NAME     LAST_NAME      POSITION    EMPLY_DATE MALE
      1   123-45-6789 Thomas T.       Smith          President   03/01/1981 .T.
      2   254-63-5691 Tina Y.         Thompson       VP          09/22/1982 .F.
      3   467-34-6789 Peter F.        Watson         Manager     10/12/1982 .T.
      5   563-55-8900 Tyrone T.       Thorsen        Engineer    06/20/1982 .T.
      6   823-46-6213 Cathy J.        Faust          Secretary   04/15/1983 .F.
      8   321-65-9087 Jane W.         Kaiser         Accountant  11/22/1982 .F.
      9   560-56-9321 Tina K.         Davidson       Trainee     05/16/1986 .F.
     10   435-54-9876 James J.        Smith          Trainee     01/23/1986 .T.

. INDEX ON LAST_NAME TO BYLAST
100% indexed          10 Records indexed
```

Fig. 2.12. Pointing to a deleted record.

Trap:

The records marked for deletion when you use SET DELETED ON will not be sorted by the SORT operation; they will be deleted.

When you use SET DELETED ON, the records marked for deletion are excluded from the sorting operation. When you issue the SORT command, these records are removed from the database (see fig. 2.13).

In addition to issuing the SET DELETED ON or SET DELETED OFF commands at the dot prompt, you also can include the DELETED=ON command in the CONFIG.DB file. If you do not set the DELETED command to ON, the program automatically sets the command to OFF.

```
. SET DELETE OFF
. LIST
Record#   ID_NO          FIRST_NAME      LAST_NAME       POSITION   EMPLY_DATE MALE
       7 *554-34-7893 Vincent M.      Corso           Sales Rep  07/20/1984 .T.
       9  560-56-9321 Tina K.         Davidson        Trainee    05/16/1986 .F.
       6  823-46-6213 Cathy J.        Faust           Secretary  04/15/1983 .F.
       8  321-65-9087 Jane W.         Kaiser          Accountant 11/22/1982 .F.
       1  123-45-6789 Thomas T.       Smith           President  03/01/1981 .T.
      10  435-54-9876 James J.        Smith           Trainee    01/23/1986 .T.
       4 *732-08-4589 Doris Y.        Taylor          Sales Rep  08/14/1983 .F.
       2  254-63-5691 Tina Y.         Thompson        VP         09/22/1982 .F.
       5  563-55-8900 Tyrone T.       Thorsen         Engineer   06/20/1982 .T.
       3  467-34-6789 Peter F.        Watson          Manager    10/12/1982 .T.

. SORT ON LAST_NAME TO SORTLAST
100% Sorted          10 Records sorted
. SET DELETE ON
. SORT ON FIRST_NAME TO SRTFIRST
100% Sorted           8 Records sorted
.
```

Fig. 2.13. Effects of the SET DELETED ON command on sorting records.

Delimiter

Tip:

Define DELIMITER symbols during configuration.

Delimiters mark data elements in data fields when you import or export data from or to a non-dBASE file. For example, delimiters can be a pair of symbols for enclosing a data element by marking the beginning and ending characters of the data element. Any valid ASCII character can be used as a delimiter symbol.

The operations for defining and invoking delimiters can be completed in the CONFIG.DB file by including these two lines:

DELIMITER=<the delimiter symbols>
DELIMITER=ON

Here are some examples:

DELIMITER="[]"
DELIMITER=ON

If you do not define your own delimiters, the program uses the colon (:) as the data field delimiter.

The DEVICE Command

Tip:

Define output routing during configuration.

Normally, output generated by @..Say.. commands is displayed on the screen. However, you can instruct the program to route the output to your printer by issuing the SET DEVICE TO PRINT command at the dot prompt or by including the DEVICE=PRINT command in the CONFIG.DB file. The normal setting for the DEVICE command is SCREEN.

The ECHO Command

Tip:

Set the ECHO command during configuration.

The ECHO operation instructs the program to display every command being executed so that you can monitor operations as they are completed by the program. This useful tool traces the execution process step-by-step. To invoke the ECHO operation, you insert the SET ECHO ON command at the beginning of your program or issue the command at the dot prompt. You can save a few keystrokes if you set the echo operation to ON by including the ECHO=ON command in your CONFIG.DB file.

If both the ECHO and DEBUG commands are on when you debug your program, all the commands are echoed automatically to the printer.

Using the Escape Key

Tip:

Define ways to terminate dBASE III Plus operations during configuration.

When you press the Esc key, you stop whatever the program is doing at the time. You can prevent the execution of an incorrect command by pressing Esc. However, if you press Esc in certain operations, you may get undesirable results. For example, if you accidentally press Esc when you enter data in a record, all the data you entered is lost. When you rearrange your data records with one of the SORT, INDEX, or REINDEX operations, the integrity of the data can be damaged if you press Esc. For these and other database applications, you will need to disable the Esc key.

To disable the Esc key, you issue the SET ESCAPE OFF command at the dot prompt or in your program. Or, you can include the ESCAPE=OFF command in your CONFIG.DB file.

The EXACT Command

Tip:

Define data match control during configuration.

When you search data records in a database file by using the LOCATE, FIND, or SEEK commands, the program matches only as many characters as specified in the search key. For example, if you want to find only the employee whose first name is Jo, you normally issue these commands:

    . USE EMPLOYEE
    . LOCATE FOR FIRST_NAME="Jo"

Unless you instruct the program to do otherwise, all the first names that begin with "Jo" (such as Joe, Joseph, John, and Jon) are considered a match. To ensure that the program searches for the employee's exact first name (Jo), you can issue the SET EXACT ON command at the dot prompt. Or, you can specify the EXACT=ON command in the CONFIG.DB file. As a result, the search operation finds only the record that yields an exact match.

The HEADINGS Command

Tip:

Set field HEADINGS ON and OFF during configuration.

When you use the LIST, DISPLAY, SUM, or AVERAGE commands, the output to be displayed also includes the column headings of field names and their related information. These headings can be suppressed either by issuing the SET HEADINGS OFF command at the dot prompt or by using the HEADINGS=OFF command in the CONFIG.DB file.

The HELP Command

Tip:

Deactivate the HELP feature during configuration.

If the message Do you want some help?(Y/N) annoys you every time you improperly enter a command, you can suppress the message by using the HELP command.

If you improperly issue a dBASE III Plus command when the program is in interactive mode, you will be asked whether you need help. This question can be annoying if you have already recognized your mistake. To eliminate this error message, include the HELP=OFF command in your CONFIG.DB file. The HELP command does not activate or disable the F1 help function key, however.

The HISTORY Buffer

Tip:

Size the HISTORY buffer during configuration.

One of the powerful features in dBASE III Plus is the capability to save the commands you have just entered in an area called the HISTORY buffer. Later, the buffer's contents can be replayed like a script. (Chapter 3 discusses how you activate and use the HISTORY buffer in your database management operation.)

Before saving a set of commands in a HISTORY buffer, you need to define the size of the buffer in terms of the maximum number of commands you anticipate storing. To size the HISTORY buffer in the CONFIG.DB file, use this command:

HISTORY=<number of commands>

Although the default limit is 20, the HISTORY buffer can hold 16,000 commands. After setting the buffer size, you start saving commands in the HISTORY file by issuing the SET HISTORY ON command at the dot prompt. Invoke the SET HISTORY OFF command at the dot prompt to terminate the saving operation.

Setting Screen INTENSITY

Tip:

Set INTENSITY OFF during configuration.

If you want to turn off enhanced video mode during full screen editing, issue the SET INTENSITY OFF command at the dot prompt or add an INTENSITY=OFF line to the CONFIG.DB file. Intensity is set ON by default.

Setting the MARGIN

Tip:

Define a report MARGIN during configuration.

When you print reports and screen output, you can set the left margin by issuing this MARGIN command in the CONFIG.DB file:

MARGIN=<number of characters>

Setting MEMOWIDTH

Tip:

Set memo width on the screen display during configuration.

You can use memo fields to store large blocks of textual data. If you try to display memos fields that are wider than your screen, however, your text will be displayed in a disorganized manner. To display such memo fields, you specify the desired memo width in the CONFIG.DB file by using the following line:

MEMOWIDTH=<number of characters>

The width (number of characters) specified in the command determines the width of the text displayed on the screen or the printer. The minimum number of characters specified for the width of a memo field is 8. The default width is 50 characters.

PRINT Status

Tip:

Set printer status during configuration.

If you want to turn on your printer before entering dBASE III Plus, include the PRINT=ON command in the CONFIG.DB file.

SAFETY

Tip:

SAFETY is set ON by default.

The SAFETY=ON default provided by dBASE III Plus warns you before you execute the COPY, ZAP, or SORT commands if you will be overwriting (and therefore destroying) an existing file. It is not advisable to set SAFETY OFF.

TYPEAHEAD

Tip:

Size the keyboard buffer during configuration.

As you enter program commands from the keyboard, your keystrokes are stored temporarily (and in sequence) in a typeahead buffer. If the buffer is filled before you finish typing, you will hear a warning beep.

The typeahead buffer normally holds 20 keystrokes. This small buffer size can be restrictive when you type fast or when you want to enter several commands at one time from the keyboard. If you are concerned about running out of space, you can increase the size of the keyboard buffer by using the TYPEAHEAD command. The size of the typeahead buffer can be increased up to 32,000 keystrokes in the CONFIG.DB file with the following line:

TYPEAHEAD=<number of keystrokes>

Here is an example:

TYPEAHEAD=100

If you set the typeahead buffer size to zero, the INKEY and ON KEY commands are disabled.

Keywords in the CONFIG.DB File

Tip:

Keywords and commands that can be included in the CONFIG.DB file.

In addition to the commands commonly used in the CONFIG.DB file, you can use other keywords to define additional processing environments or operations. However, some of these commands can be better executed at the dot prompt. Table 2.1 shows a summary of all the keywords recognized by CONFIG.DB.

Table 2.1
Keywords and Commands Recognized by CONFIG.DB File

Keyword with possible setting	*Dot prompt command**
ALTERNATE=<name of text file>	SET ALTERNATE TO <file name>
BELL=ON/Off	SET BELL ON/off
BUCKET=<bucket size (2)>	SET BUCKET TO <bucket size>
CARRY=on/OFF	SET CARRY on/OFF
CATALOG=<name of catalog file>	SET CATALOG TO <file name>
CENTURY=on/OFF	SET CENTURY on/OFF
COLOR=<color list>	SET COLOR TO <color list>
COMMAND=<dBASE III Plus command>	The dBASE III Plus command
CONFIRM=on/OFF	SET CONFIRM on/OFF
CONSOLE=ON/off	SET CONSOLE ON/off
DEBUG=on/OFF	SET DEBUG on/OFF
DECIMALS=<number of decimals (2)>	SET DECIMALS TO <decimals>
DEFAULT=<default disk drive>	SET DEFAULT TO <disk drive>
DELETED=on/OFF	SET DELETED on/OFF
DELIMITER=<delimiters (:)>	SET DELIMITERS TO <delimiters>
DELIMITER=on/OFF	SET DELIMITERS on/OFF
DEVICE=SCREEN/PRINT	SET DEVICE TO SCREEN/print
ECHO=on/OFF	SET ECHO on/OFF
ESCAPE=ON/off	SET ESCAPE ON/off
EXACT=on/OFF	SET EXACT on/OFF
GETS=<max number of GETS (128)>	not available
HEADINGS=ON/off	SET HEADING ON/off
HELP=ON/off	SET HELP ON/off
HISTORY=<number of commands (20)>	SET HISTORY TO <number of commands>
INTENSITY ON/off	SET INTENSITY ON/off

Keyword with possible setting	*Dot prompt command* *
MARGIN=<left margin (0)>	SET MARGIN TO <left margin>
MAXMEM=<memory space (256KB)>	not available
MEMOWIDTH=<memo width (50 chars.)>	SET MEMOWIDTH TO <memo width>
MENU=ON/off	SET MENUS ON/off
MVARSIZ=<memory size (6K bytes)>	not available
PATH=<DOS path>	SET PATH TO <DOS path>
PRINT=on/OFF	SET PRINT on/OFF
PROMPT=<character string>	not available
SAFETY=ON/off	SET SAFETY ON/off
SCOREBOARD=ON/off	SET SCOREBOARD ON/off
STATUS=ON/off	SET STATUS ON/off
STEP=on/OFF	SET STEP on/OFF
TALK=ON/off	SET TALK ON/off
TEDIT=<name of text editor>	not available
TYPEAHEAD=<keystrokes (20)>	SET TYPEAHEAD TO <keystrokes>
UNIQUE=on/OFF	SET UNIQUE on/OFF
VIEW=<name of view file>	SET VIEW TO <view file name>
WP=<name of word processor>	not available

* Default settings are described in capital letters and parentheses.

3

Creating and Modifying Databases

Layout of a Database File

Every database management program organizes its data in a unique way, and the dBASE III Plus program is no exception. Because errors can occur if you don't understand the program, this chapter discusses the organization of data in dBASE III Plus.

Tip:

Understanding the layout of a database file will help you to be more efficient.

The information stored in a database file is divided into three components: the file header, the data record section, and the end-of-file (EOF) marker.

The *file header* contains valuable information: the structure of the file and the record count. The *data record* section contains information about all the records saved in an existing file. And the *end-of-file (EOF) marker* tells dBASE III Plus where to stop reading records.

Tip:

Find the record you want quickly by using the information in the file header.

The record count displayed in the header allows the program to find a specified record in the database file without reading every record in the file.

For example, if you issue the GO BOTTOM command at the dot prompt and you know the current record number and the total number of records in the file, the program can position its record pointer at the desired record and not have to search the record section sequentially.

Tip:

To determine the date of your last update of a file, check the information in the file header.

The LIST STRUCTURE or DISPLAY STRUCTURE command displays all the data fields and their attributes, along with the number of records in the file and the date of the last update (see fig. 3.1).

Did you notice something strange about the character count in the field width column? If you add all the field widths (11 + 15 + 15 + 10 + 8 + 1), the sum is 60 instead of 61, as shown after **** Total ****. The extra character is reserved for the deletion marker after you issue the DELETE command.

```
. USE EMPLOYEE
. DISP STRU
Structure for database: C:EMPLOYEE.dbf
Number of data records:      10
Date of last update    : 01/26/1987
Field  Field Name  Type       Width   Dec
    1  ID_NO       Character      11
    2  FIRST_NAME  Character      15
    3  LAST_NAME   Character      15
    4  POSITION    Character      10
    5  EMPLY_DATE  Date            8
    6  MALE        Logical         1
** Total **                      61
```

Fig. 3.1. Displaying the file structure of EMPLOYEE.DBF.

Trap:

The record count in your file will not be updated if you exit the file improperly.

Usually, every time you add new records to the database file (by using one of the APPEND or INSERT commands) or remove records from the database file (by using the ZAP command or the DELETE and PACK commands), the record count is updated accordingly.

If you improperly exit from the data entry operation, however, the record count will not be updated, even though you've added new records to the file. The record count will be smaller than the actual number of records in the file. And as a result, you won't have access to all the records in the file when the database file is selected.

On the other hand, if you improperly exit from the data deletion process (by mistakenly pressing the Esc key during the PACK operation, for example), the record count is not updated after certain records are permanently removed from the file. In this case, the record count shows more records than are actually in the file. As a result, the cursor reaches the end-of-file mark before the program retrieves the correct number of records.

Tip:

Data records are saved sequentially.

As shown in figure 3.2, the contents of the first data record (123-45-6789Thomas T . . .) are stored right after the file header. Information about the other data records is saved sequentially in this section.

```
. USE EMPLOYEE
. LIST
Record#  ID_NO       FIRST_NAME   LAST_NAME   POSITION    EMPLY_DATE MALE
      1  123-45-6789 Thomas T.    Smith       President   03/01/1981 .T.
      2  254-63-5691 Tina Y.      Thompson    VP          09/22/1982 .F.
      3  467-34-6789 Peter F.     Watson      Manager     10/12/1982 .T.
      4  732-08-4589 Doris Y.     Taylor      Sales Rep   08/14/1983 .F.
      5  563-55-8900 Tyrone T.    Thorsen     Engineer    06/20/1982 .T.
      6  823-46-6213 Cathy J.     Faust       Secretary   04/15/1983 .F.
      7  554-34-7893 Vincent M.   Corso       Sales Rep   07/20/1984 .T.
      8  321-65-9087 Jane W.      Kaiser      Accountant  11/22/1982 .F.
      9  560-56-9321 Tina K.      Davidson    Trainee     05/16/1986 .F.
     10  435-54-9876 James J.     Smith       Trainee     01/23/1986 .T.
```

Fig. 3.2. Listing records in the EMPLOYEE.DBF file.

Tip:

---

dBASE III Plus tells the program where to stop reading.

When you issue the LIST command, the program continuously lists the contents of the records until it reaches the end-of-file mark. Similarly, when you search a database for a record with a particular key field (by using the LOCATE, SEEK, or FIND commands, for example) and the end-of-file marker is encountered, you are told that no record matching the key field exists.

Tip:

To examine the information saved in your data records, use the LIST or DISPLAY ALL command.

You can examine records, such as the employment records in figure 3.2, by using either the LIST or DISPLAY ALL command.

Trap:

The layout of a file cannot be displayed by using the dBASE III Plus commands.

The information in a database file is saved in an ASCII format, including various control characters. However, the actual layout of the file components cannot be displayed by using such commands as LIST, DISPLAY, or TYPE. For example, if you issue the TYPE EMPLOYEE.DBF command after the dot prompt, the program displays scrambled text and incomprehensible symbols as shown in figure 3.3.

```
. TYPE EMPLOYEE.DBF
♦W8◄

65-9087Jane W.        Kaiser         Accountant19821122F 560-56-9321Tina K.
    Davidson      Trainee   19860516F 435-54-9876James J.       Smith        T
rainee    19860123T
```

Fig. 3.3. Displaying a database file by using the TYPE command.

Tip:

Use DEBUG.COM to examine the layout of the database file.

You can examine the actual layout of the database file by using DEBUG.COM (a file that comes with the DOS system disk). To display the contents of a file, copy the DEBUG.COM file to the directory that contains that file. Then issue the DEBUG command at the DOS prompt (such as C>*DEBUG EMPLOYEE.DBF*). In response to the command, the DEBUG file displays a dash [–] prompt to ask for the next command (see fig. 3.4).

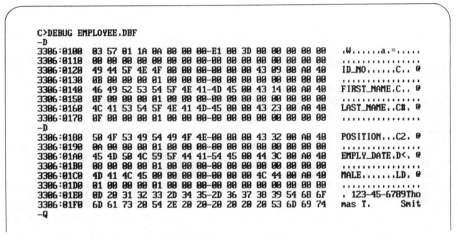

Fig. 3.4. Using the DOS DEBUG command to display contents of a database file.

You then can enter the letter *D* to display (or dump) a section of the database file contents. The program displays the first eight lines of the file and then asks you for another command. When you enter *D*, another set of eight lines is displayed. To terminate the display and exit from the DEBUG program, enter *Q* (for quit).

Tip:

The display is divided into three major columns.

The first column (1556:0100, for example) is a set of numbers that represent the memory locations where the file contents are stored. The numbers may appear differently on your screen, depending on your computer system and the RAM resident programs (SideKick and RAM disk, for example) you loaded in memory before you invoked the DEBUG program.

The middle column is a section of numeric codes (in hexadecimal format) that correspond to the contents of the file displayed in the third column. If you are not familiar with hexadecimal numbers, you can think of them as machine codes that are relevant only to the computer. They are not significant for examining the file contents.

The third column contains the actual contents of the database file. Except for some control characters, you can see such field names as ID_NO, FIRST_NAME, and LAST_NAME.

Saving Data to Disk

Trick:

To avoid losing data, close your file frequently when entering new records.

If you experience system errors that cause you to shut off your computer and restart it before you close the file, you may lose some or all of the new records you have entered. A power failure during your data entry process also has a disastrous effect on the integrity of your data records.

When you add data records to an existing database file by issuing the APPEND or INSERT command, the information is not saved immediately in the disk file. Instead, the information is held temporarily in the RAM working area. Similarly, at this point, only the record count in RAM is updated; the record count of the database file on the disk is not revised.

The data records and updated record count held in the RAM working area are copied back to the disk file only when you close the file.

When you modify the contents of your database, exit to the dot prompt by pressing Ctrl-End—*not the Esc key*—to close a file.

Closing Database Files

Trick:

To close an active file without opening another one, issue the USE command.

You can close an active database file with the USE command:

. USE XYZ
. . . . .
. USE

You also can close an active file by replacing it with another database file in the current active work area. Issue the USE command and type the name of the file that will replace the active one. Here is an example:

. USE XYZ
. . . . .
. USE ABC

When you issue the USE ABC command while the XYZ database is active in the work area, the active database closes.

Tip:

You can close multiple files with one command.

CLOSE ALL closes most of the files currently open. These files include all the database (.DBF), format (.FMT), index (.NDX), label (.LBL), memo (.DBT), query (.QRY), text (.TXT), and view (.VUE) files. The only files not affected by the CLOSE ALL command are catalog (.CAT), memory variable (.MEM), and program (.PRG).

CLOSE DATABASES closes only the database, index, and format files that are open in the work areas.

Tip:

Only one work area is active.

Although you can simultaneously open as many as 10 files in 10 separate work areas, only one area can be the active or primary work area. The other areas are inactive or secondary work areas.

Borrowing an Existing Data Structure

Use the COPY STRUCTURE TO command to borrow a data structure from an existing database file.

Often you need to duplicate part or all of the contents of a file in a new file. For example, you can borrow the structures from one set of data files to create a set of new tables for other applications. Or, if the data related to all your products is stored in a database file, you can split the contents into several files.

To borrow structure from an existing database file:

1. Select the database file from which you are borrowing the structure.

2. Use the COPY STRUCTURE TO command to copy the structure to a new database file.

You might, for instance, own a small computer store and want to create a new file to store information about the items you have in stock. To borrow the structure from an existing database file (PRODUCTS.DBF) to create a new database file (HARDWARE.DBF), issue the following commands:

. USE PRODUCTS
. COPY STRUCTURE TO HARDWARE

After these two commands are given, the program sets up a new database file (HARDWARE.DBF) that has the borrowed structure. To examine the data structure, select the database file and issue the DISPLAY STRUCTURE command after the dot prompt (see fig. 3.5).

```
. USE PRODUCTS
. COPY STRUCTURE TO HARDWARE
. USE HARDWARE
. DISPLAY STRUCTURE
Structure for database: C:HARDWARE.dbf
Number of data records:        0
Date of last update    : 01/26/1987
Field  Field Name  Type       Width    Dec
    1  STOCK_NO    Character      9
    2  DIVISION    Character      2
    3  TYPE        Character     20
    4  COST        Numeric        7      2
    5  PRICE       Numeric        7      2
** Total **                     46
```

Fig. 3.5. Copying an existing file structure in a new database file.

Splitting the Contents of an Existing Database File

Trick:

Organize your data in a master file.

In many database management applications, you can organize your data effectively by storing all the data records for a particular item in one master file. You can then store subsets of the records in their own files. For example, you can store—in a master database PRODUCTS.DBF file—all the products your store carries (see fig. 3.6).

```
. LIST
Record#  STOCK_NO  DIVISION TYPE                   COST    PRICE
      1  CPQ-SP256 HW       system             1359.00 1895.00
      2  ZEN-SL101 HW       system             1695.00 2399.00
      3  IBM-AT640 HW       system             3790.00 4490.00
      4  ZEN-MM012 HW       monitor              89.00  159.00
      5  NEC-PC660 HW       printer             560.00  820.00
      6  HAY-M1200 HW       modem               269.00  389.00
      7  SEA-HD020 HW       hard disk           398.00  495.00
      8  IOM-HD040 HW       hard disk          2190.00 2790.00
      9  PAR-GC100 HW       graphic card        279.00  389.00
     10  HER-GC100 HW       graphic card        199.00  239.00
     11  ASH-DB300 SW       database            395.00  595.00
     12  ANS-DB110 SW       database            525.00  695.00
     13  CLP-DB100 SW       database compiler   450.00  595.00
     14  WOR-DB100 SW       database compiler   469.00  595.00
     15  LOT-L0123 SW       spreadsheet         289.00  359.00
     16  MIC-WS330 SW       word processing     229.00  269.00
     17  MIS-WD300 SW       word processing     229.00  289.00
     18  AST-FW200 SW       integrated          345.00  395.00
     19  MIC-QB100 SW       language             79.00  109.00
     20  BOL-PA300 SW       language             39.50   69.50
```

Fig. 3.6. Data records in the PRODUCTS.DBF file.

You can split the master database file into two database files—one that saves the data for the hardware items and another one that stores information about the software products. For example, you can copy the data structure from PRODUCTS.DBF to two new database files named HARDWARE.DBF and SOFTWARE.DBF:

. USE PRODUCTS
. COPY STRUCTURE TO HARDWARE
. COPY STRUCTURE TO SOFTWARE

Once you've created the structures of the HARDWARE.DBF and SOFTWARE.DBF database files, you can copy selected records in the master database file and save them in the new files. To do so, use the following APPEND FROM command and the necessary filtering condition:

. APPEND FROM <name of database file> <the filtering condition>

The filtering condition determines which set of records will be affected by the APPEND FROM operation. Here are some examples:

. APPEND FROM PRODUCTS FOR RECNO( )>=11
. APPEND FROM PRODUCTS FOR DIVISION="HW"
. APPEND FROM PRODUCTS FOR TYPE="printer"
. APPEND FROM PRODUCTS FOR DIVISION="SW" .AND. TYPE="database"
. APPEND FROM PRODUCTS FOR PRICE>=200.00
. APPEND FROM PRODUCTS FOR (PRICE−COST)>100

To copy all the records related to the hardware products from PRODUCTS.DBF to HARDWARE.DBF, use the FOR DIVISION="HW" filtering condition in the APPEND FROM command (see fig. 3.7).

```
. USE HARDWARE
. LIST

. APPEND FROM PRODUCTS FOR DIVISION="HW"
     10 records added
. LIST
Record#  STOCK_NO  DIVISION  TYPE              PRICE     COST
      1  CPQ-SP256 HW        system         1895.00  1359.00
      2  ZEN-SL101 HW        system         2399.00  1695.00
      3  IBM-AT640 HW        system         4490.00  3790.00
      4  ZEN-MM012 HW        monitor         159.00    89.00
      5  NEC-PC660 HW        printer         820.00   560.00
      6  HAY-M1200 HW        modem           389.00   269.00
      7  SEA-HD020 HW        hard disk       495.00   390.00
      8  IOM-HD040 HW        hard disk      2790.00  2190.00
      9  PAR-GC100 HW        graphic card    389.00   279.00
     10  HER-GC100 HW        graphic card    239.00   199.00
```

Fig. 3.7. Appending hardware records from the PRODUCTS.DBF database file.

Similarly, by using the FOR DIVISION="SW" filtering condition in the APPEND FROM command, you can copy all the records related to the software items from the master database file to the SOFTWARE.DBF database file (see fig. 3.8).

```
, USE SOFTWARE
, LIST

, APPEND FROM PRODUCTS FOR DIVISION="SW"
     10 records added
, LIST
Record#  STOCK_NO  DIVISION  TYPE                 COST    PRICE
       1  ASH-DB300 SW        database            395.00   595.00
       2  AMS-DB110 SW        database            525.00   695.00
       3  CLP-DB100 SW        database compiler    450.00   595.00
       4  WOR-DB100 SW        database compiler    469.00   595.00
       5  LOT-LO123 SW        spreadsheet          289.00   359.00
       6  MIC-WS330 SW        word processing      229.00   269.00
       7  MIS-WD300 SW        word processing      229.00   289.00
       8  AST-FW200 SW        integrated           345.00   395.00
       9  MIC-QB100 SW        language              79.00   109.00
      10  BOL-PA300 SW        language              39.50    69.50

,
```

Fig. 3.8. Appending software records from the PRODUCTS.DBF database file.

Creating HISTORY

Tip:

Use the HISTORY buffer to review previously issued commands.

The HISTORY buffer is a handy reference file for reviewing the commands you've issued via the dot prompt. For example, during your data manipulation process, you might have forgotten the name of the database you created or the name of the index file you used for rearranging the records in a certain file. By listing the contents of the HISTORY buffer, you can retrieve the name of the database and index file.

Each time you issue a dot prompt command, the program saves the command in a temporary HISTORY buffer. HISTORY is not a disk file, so you have no need to (and cannot) assign a file name to it.

The default size of the HISTORY buffer is 20 commands. When the buffer is full, new commands replace the ones entered earlier, in a first-in, first-out order. As a result, while the cursor is at the dot prompt, you can use the LIST HISTORY command to display as many as 20 previously entered commands (see fig. 3.9).

```
. SET HISTORY TO 40
. USE EMPLOYEE
. INDEX ON LAST_NAME TO BYNAME
  100% indexed            10 Records indexed
. FIND Smith
. DISP
Record#   ID_NO      FIRST_NAME      LAST_NAME      POSITION    EMPLY_DATE MALE
       1  123-45-6789 Thomas T.      Smith          President   03/01/1981 .T.

. SEEK "Taylor"
. DISP
Record#   ID_NO      FIRST_NAME      LAST_NAME      POSITION    EMPLY_DATE MALE
       4  732-00-4589 Doris Y.       Taylor         Sales Rep   08/14/1983 .F.

. LIST HISTORY
USE EMPLOYEE
INDEX ON LAST_NAME TO BYNAME
FIND Smith
DISP
SEEK "Taylor"
DISP
LIST HISTORY
```

Fig. 3.9. Listing contents of HISTORY.

When you issue the LIST HISTORY command, the commands are displayed in the order they were saved in the HISTORY buffer (see fig. 3.9). The first two commands (SET HISTORY TO 0 and SET HISTORY TO 40) clear the contents of the current buffer and prepare for saving a set of new commands.

Tip:

You can enlarge your HISTORY buffer.

The default size of the HISTORY buffer is 20 commands. However, you can specify the size you want by using the SET HISTORY TO command:

. SET HISTORY TO <number of commands>

You can specify as many as 16,000 commands in SET HISTORY TO.

Trick:

To clear the HISTORY buffer, first set the buffer size to zero.

Whenever you want to flush the buffer and begin saving a new stream of commands, set the HISTORY buffer size to zero and then reset the size to a desired number of commands. For example, if the current size of the HISTORY buffer is 40, you can clear the buffer's contents by issuing these commands:

. SET HISTORY TO 0
. SET HISTORY TO 40

If you set HISTORY to a number less than the number of commands currently in the buffer, the dBASE III Plus program erases all the existing commands.

Allocating Memory to HISTORY

Tip:

Allocate extra memory when you need a large HISTORY file.

Memory used for holding the commands in the HISTORY file competes with other program operations for RAM space. If you intend to store a large number of commands in the HISTORY buffer, you must use the following MAXMEM command (which can be specified only in the CONFIG.DB configuration file) to increase the memory allocated to the program:

MAXMEM=<memory space to be allocated>

For a detailed discussion about allocating memory space in the program, see Chapter 2.

Tip:

Use an ALTERNATE file to save a screen display.

An ALTERNATE file is a .TXT file that is set up for storing a block of text from the screen display. To create an ALTERNATE file, assign a name to the file with the following dot prompt command:

SET ALTERNATE TO <name of text file>

By activating an ALTERNATE file with the SET ALTERNATE ON command, you instruct the program to start saving the contents that subsequently appear on the screen. After you save the desired information from the screen display, you can terminate the saving operation by issuing the SET ALTERNATE OFF command.

Saving HISTORY to an ALTERNATE File

Trick:

Save the HISTORY buffer in an ALTERNATE file.

When you issue the SET HISTORY TO 0 command to empty the buffer or issue the QUIT command to leave a session, the program erases the current contents of the HISTORY buffer. No command provided by the program saves the HISTORY buffer on the disk for later examination. However, you can list the current contents of the HISTORY buffer on the screen and save the screen display in an ALTERNATE file (see fig. 3.10).

```
. SET ALTERNATE TO LISTING.TXT
. SET ALTERNATE ON
. LIST HISTORY
USE EMPLOYEE
INDEX ON LAST_NAME TO BYNAME
FIND Smith
DISP
SEEK "Taylor"
DISP
LIST HISTORY
CLEAR
SET ALTERNATE TO LISTING.TXT
SET ALTERNATE ON
LIST HISTORY

. SET ALTERNATE OFF
```

Fig. 3.10. Saving the screen display in a text file by using the SET ALTERNATE ON command.

The first command in figure 3.10 designates LISTING.TXT as the ALTERNATE file for saving the contents of the HISTORY buffer. The block of text between the SET ALTERNATE ON and SET ALTERNATE OFF commands is saved in the LISTING.TXT file.

The contents of the ALTERNATE file can be displayed by using the TYPE command after the file is closed (see fig. 3.11).

All the commands stored in the LISTING.TXT file are displayed in response to the TYPE command (see fig. 3.11).

```
. CLOSE ALTERNATE
. TYPE LISTING.TXT

. LIST HISTORY
USE EMPLOYEE
INDEX ON LAST_NAME TO BYNAME
FIND Smith
DISP
SEEK "Taylor"
DISP
LIST HISTORY
CLEAR
SET ALTERNATE TO LISTING.TXT
SET ALTERNATE ON
LIST HISTORY

. SET ALTERNATE OFF
.
```

Fig. 3.11. Listing the text in the ALTERNATE file.

Tip:

Before you display the contents of an ALTERNATE file, close the file.

You must close an ALTERNATE file before you use the TYPE command to display the file's contents, because you cannot list the contents of an open text file. To close the ALTERNATE file, issue either

> . CLOSE ALTERNATE

or

> . SET ALTERNATE TO

Modifying Data Structure

Tip:

You can change the structure of a database file.

When you change the attributes or the number of data fields in a database file, you change the structure of the file. The most direct method for changing the structure of a database file is the MODIFY STRUCTURE command. For example, to modify the structure of the HARDWARE.DBF file, you issue these commands:

> . USE HARDWARE
> . MODIFY STRUCTURE

After executing these commands, the program displays the structure of the active database file on the screen (see fig. 3.12). You then can use the editing keys provided by the program to make the necessary changes. When all the changes are made, press Ctrl-End to save the modified structure in the file.

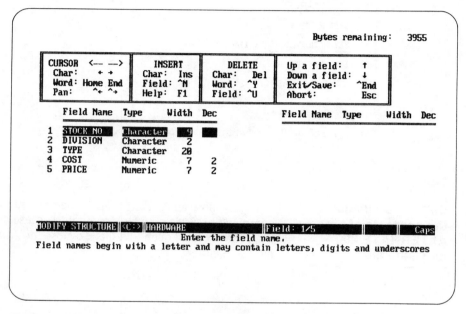

Fig. 3.12. Modifying the file structure of an existing database file.

Converting Character Fields to Numeric Fields

Trap:

You can lose valuable data while converting a character field to a numeric field.

If the file whose structure you want to modify has some data records in it, be cautious. The nonnumeric characters in a character field will be dropped if you convert to a numeric field. For example, if the contents of your character field named ACCT_NO (account number) combine character strings and numeric digits (A1234, 123-45-6789, and so on), some or all of the field contents will be lost if you convert the field to a numeric field.

The amount of information you lose depends on the contents of the character field. In general, if the contents of the character field begin with numeric digits (such as 123-45-6789, as in a Social Security number format), the leading digits (123) are retained. The characters or digits that appear after a nonnumeric character are dropped. (In this case, [-] is treated as a dash.) However, if the character field value begins with a nonnumeric character, such as A1234, all the characters and digits are lost.

If records are in the existing database file, be sure to examine the field contents carefully before you convert a character field to a numeric field.

Trap:

You can lose data during restructuring if you have insufficient memory space.

After you've modified the structure of a database file, data records from the old structure are copied to the new structure. These records are stored temporarily in the working area before they are saved in the disk file. If you haven't allocated sufficient memory space for the working file, some of the information in the database file may be lost.

The default amount of memory allocated to the program is 256K bytes. If you modify the file structure of a large database file, you might not have enough memory space to process the huge number of data records. This is especially true if you have already allocated a fair amount of memory space to the buffers by setting BUFFERS to more than 15 in the CONFIG.SYS file.

If you have more than 256K bytes of RAM, use the MAXMEM command to reserve a larger amount of memory in the CONFIG.DB file for the program.

Changing Field Attributes

Trap:

You can lose the data field if you change a field name and its width at the same time.

A note of caution during file structure modification: you cannot change the name and the width of a data field simultaneously when records are already in the database file. If you try, all the values in that field will be lost.

To change both the name and the width of a data field, you must make the changes in steps. (1) Use the MODIFY STRUCTURE command to edit the field name, (2) save the modified structure in the database file by pressing Ctrl-End, (3) reissue the MODIFY STRUCTURE command to change the field width, and (4) press Ctrl-End to save the modified file.

Repositioning Existing Data Fields

Trick:

You can rearrange your data fields.

In some display operations (such as BROWSE without using BROWSE FIELDS), the screen width limits the number of data fields you can see on the screen. You can move some of the data fields to the beginning of the file structure so that they can be displayed on the same screen by using the BROWSE operation.

For example, if you restructure the HARDWARE.DBF database file, you might switch the PRICE and COST data fields so that PRICE appears before COST on your screen. Such a switching operation can be performed by moving the PRICE field to the front of the COST field.

To move a field from its current position in the structure to a new position, follow these steps:

1. Access the appropriate database and issue the MODIFY STRUCTURE command.

2. Delete the field at the current position.

3. Insert a new field at the new position.

4. Define the new field and the field attributes (field name and width, for example) of the field deleted in Step 2.

For example, to move the PRICE field from the current position (field #5) to the front of the COST field (field #4), follow these steps:

1. Place the cursor anywhere in the PRICE field and press Ctrl-U. The PRICE field is removed temporarily from the structure, and the cursor moves to the beginning of the COST field (see fig. 3.13).

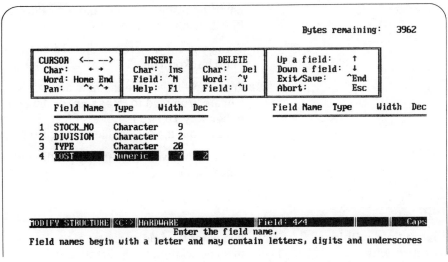

Fig. 3.13. After removing the PRICE data field from the file structure.

2. Press Ctrl-N to insert a blank field in the structure (see fig. 3.14).

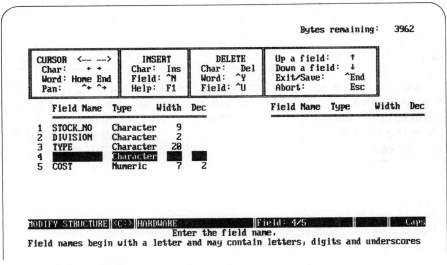

Fig. 3.14. Inserting a blank data field into the file structure.

3. Enter the name, the type, and the field width of the PRICE field in the inserted field.

4. When you see the prompt Should data be COPIED from backup for all fields? (Y/N), type *Y*.

5. Press Ctrl-End to save the new database structure. When you are prompted to Press Enter to confirm, any other key to resume, press Enter. Data then will be copied from the backup file to the current database.

After you have followed these five steps, the PRICE field is repositioned in the structure.

Trap:

Move a field within a structure with caution.

When you enter the field attributes of the inserted field, the field name and width must be identical to the existing field (which has been temporarily deleted).

Before the program creates a new field, it checks to see if the field is one that you deleted earlier. The new field is considered a replacement for the old field only if all the field attributes you enter match those of a deleted field. Otherwise, the program may consider the inserted field as a brand-new field. All the values in the field you were moving are lost.

Trap:

You will lose the field if you leave the restructuring session before the field has been moved.

The deleted field stays in RAM and can be inserted back into the structure as long as you remain in one restructuring session. After you finish a restructuring session by pressing Ctrl-End to save the modified structure, all deleted fields are lost.

Modifying a Memo Field

Trap:

Changing a memo field to a character field and vice versa causes the field contents to be lost.

When you modify the file structure of a database file, do not change a memo field to a character field if the file is not empty. Otherwise, the contents of the memo field will be lost after the file restructuring process. Similarly, do not change a character field to a memo field. If you do, the contents of the character field will be lost as well.

Restoring Damaged Database Files

Trick:

Use the backup .BAK file to restore damaged database files.

If the data in your file has been damaged during the file restructuring process, you can restore the original contents to the file.

Every time the program executes the MODIFY STRUCTURE command, it makes a duplicate copy of the file you are modifying. The duplicate is saved in a disk file with the same name as the active file and a .BAK (for backup) file extension.

If some or all of your file contents are lost or damaged because of unexpected problems in the structure modification process, you can restore the file to its original form from the information saved in the backup file. Restoring the damaged file to its original form involves two steps:

1. Delete the damaged file by using the ERASE command.
2. Rename the backup file (with .BAK file extension) back to its original form (with .DBF file extension).

For example, if the contents of the HARDWARE.DBF file are damaged during restructuring, you can restore the contents to those in the HARDWARE.BAK backup file by entering these commands:

```
. USE
. ERASE HARDWARE.DBF
. RENAME HARDWARE.BAK TO HARDWARE.DBF
```

You must close the database file before you erase and rename it because the program does not let you delete an open file. Remember, you can issue the USE command to close the current active file and not open another database file.

Modifying Database Structure with a Text Editor

Trick:

To change a large file structure, save it in a text file for easy editing.

The usual MODIFY STRUCTURE command procedure for changing a database structure might be sufficient for most applications. But to make substantial changes, you can use a more efficient approach—copying the existing database structure to a text file.

Before copying a database structure to a text file, you must copy the structure to a temporary working file. The contents of the working file then are copied to a text file for editing. To copy a database structure to a working file, use the COPY TO .. STRUCTURE EXTENDED command:

. COPY TO <name of working file> STRUCTURE EXTENDED

The data structure of the working file created by the COPY TO .. STRUCTURE EXTENDED command is set automatically by the program.

Figure 3.15 shows a working file (HWSTRUC.DBF) for the HARDWARE.DBF file. Data records in the working file correspond to field definitions in the original file.

The data structure created automatically by the program for this working file contains four fields: FIELD_NAME, FIELD_TYPE, FIELD_LEN (field length), and FIELD_DEC (decimal places). Each data field definition in the original database structure is saved as a data record in the working database file.

You are now ready to create a text file. Use the COPY TO .. SDF command, which converts the data records in the active database file to lines of ASCII text (in the SDF standard data format). Issue the following command:

. COPY TO <name of text file> SDF

```
. USE HARDWARE
. COPY TO HWSTRUC STRUCTURE EXTENDED
. USE HWSTRUC
. DISP STRUC
Structure for database: C:HWSTRUC.dbf
Number of data records:      5
Date of last update   : 01/26/1987
Field  Field Name  Type       Width   Dec
    1  FIELD_NAME  Character     10
    2  FIELD_TYPE  Character      1
    3  FIELD_LEN   Numeric        3
    4  FIELD_DEC   Numeric        3
** Total **                     18

. LIST
Record#  FIELD_NAME FIELD_TYPE FIELD_LEN FIELD_DEC
      1  STOCK_NO   C                  9         0
      2  DIVISION   C                  2         0
      3  TYPE       C                 20         0
      4  PRICE      N                  7         2
      5  COST       N                  7         2
```

Fig. 3.15. Copying the file structure in a database file by using the COPY STRUCTURE EXTENDED command.

You can convert the contents of your data records when the file is in use by issuing the COPY TO .. SDF command (see fig. 3.16).

```
. USE HWSTRUC
. COPY TO HWASCII SDF
      5 records copied
. TYPE HWASCII.TXT
STOCK_NO C 9 0
DIVISION C 2 0
TYPE     C 20 0
PRICE    N 7 2
COST     N 7 2
```

Fig. 3.16. Converting contents of a database file to a text file.

Tip:

Modify your text file with the text editor.

You can see that the text file contains five lines that represent the contents of a record in the HWSTRUC.DBF file. You are now ready to invoke the text editor to modify the structure in the text file. To use the text editor provided by the program, issue the following command:

. MODIFY COMMAND HWASCII.TXT

The contents of the text file are displayed and you can begin modifying the file (see fig. 3.17).

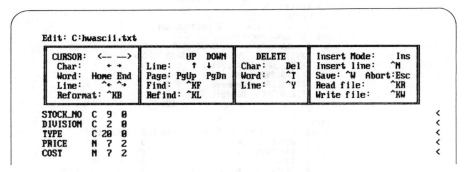

Edit: C:hwascii.txt

CURSOR: <── ──>		UP DOWN	DELETE	Insert Mode: Ins
Char: ← →	Line: ↑ ↓		Char: Del	Insert line: ^N
Word: Home End	Page: PgUp PgDn		Word: ^T	Save: ^W Abort:Esc
Line: ^← ^→	Find: ^KF		Line: ^Y	Read file: ^KR
Reformat: ^KB	Refind: ^KL			Write file: ^KW

```
STOCK_NO  C  9  0                                    <
DIVISION  C  2  0                                    <
TYPE      C 20  0                                    <
PRICE     N  7  2                                    <
COST      N  7  2                                    <
```

Fig. 3.17. Modifying the contents of the HWASCII.TXT file.

You can make changes to the structure by rearranging the fields, adding new data fields, deleting existing fields, or changing the attributes of the fields (see fig. 3.18). However, the field attributes must be entered in the format defined by the program as shown in the HWSTRUC.DBF file. The field name must be defined within the first 10 spaces, followed by field type (1 character width), field length (3 characters), and field decimals (3 characters).

Edit: C:HWASCII.TXT   Ins   Caps

CURSOR: <── ──>		UP DOWN	DELETE	Insert Mode: Ins
Char: ← →	Line: ↑ ↓		Char: Del	Insert line: ^N
Word: Home End	Page: PgUp PgDn		Word: ^T	Save: ^W Abort:Esc
Line: ^← ^→	Find: ^KF		Line: ^Y	Read file: ^KR
Reformat: ^KB	Refind: ^KL			Write file: ^KW

```
STOCK_NO  C  9  0                                    <
DESCRIPTN C 50  0                                    <
TYPE      C 20  0                                    <
PRICE     N  7  2                                    <
COST      N  7  2                                    <
NOTE      M 10  0
```

Fig. 3.18. Changing the text in the HWASCII.TXT file.

Save the edited database structure by pressing Ctrl-W.

Tip:

Convert your text file to a database structure to complete the modification of your file.

Before you convert the text file to a database structure, you must delete the original records in the working file (HWSTRUC.DBF) by issuing the ZAP command. After the working file has been emptied, you can copy the contents of the text file to the working file by using the APPEND FROM .. SDF command (see fig. 3.19).

```
. USE HWSTRUC
. ZAP
Zap C:HWSTRUC.dbf? (Y/N) Yes
. APPEND FROM HWASCII.TXT SDF
      6 records added
. LIST
Record#  FIELD_NAME FIELD_TYPE FIELD_LEN FIELD_DEC
       1  STOCK_NO   C                9         0
       2  DESCRIPTN  C               50
       3  TYPE       C               20         0
       4  PRICE      N                7         2
       5  COST       N                7         2
       6  NOTE       M
```

Fig. 3.19. Saving modified structure back to HWSTRUC.DBF.

Use the contents of the working file to create a new database file (see fig. 3.20) with the CREATE .. FROM command:

. CREATE <name of new database file> FROM <the database file whose records contain the database structure>

```
. CREATE NEWHW FROM HWSTRUC.DBF
. USE NEWHW
. DISPLAY STRUCTURE
Structure for database: C:NEWHW.dbf
Number of data records:       0
Date of last update   : 01/26/87
Field  Field Name  Type       Width    Dec
    1  STOCK_NO    Character       9
    2  DESCRIPTN   Character      50
    3  TYPE        Character      20
    4  PRICE       Numeric         7      2
    5  COST        Numeric         7      2
    6  NOTE        Memo           10
** Total **                      104
```

Fig. 3.20. Creating a new database with file structure in HWSTRUC.DBF.

A new database file with a modified structure has been created. To copy some of the information from the original database file, use the APPEND FROM command (see fig. 3.21).

```
. USE NEWHW
. APPEND FROM HARDWARE
     10 records added
. LIST STOCKNO,TYPE,PRICE,COST
Record#  STOCKNO   TYPE              PRICE     COST
      1  CPQ-SP256 system           1359.00  1895.00
      2  ZEN-SL181 system           1695.00  2399.00
      3  IBM-AT640 system           3790.00  4490.00
      4  ZEN-MM012 monitor            89.00   159.00
      5  NEC-PC660 printer           560.00   820.00
      6  HAY-M1200 modem             269.00   389.00
      7  SEA-HD202 hard disk         398.00   495.00
      8  IOM-HD040 hard disk        2190.00  2790.00
      9  PAR-GC100 graphic card      279.00   389.00
     10  HER-GC100 graphic card      199.00   239.00
.
```

Fig. 3.21. Appending data records from HARDWARE.DBF.

4

Entering and Editing Data

This chapter presents tips, tricks, and traps to help you enter and edit data—and some shortcuts for designing and modifying a custom data-entry form by using the screen painter. First available with dBASE III Plus, the screen painter is a valuable tool for custom designing data-entry forms. You can call up the screen painter from the the Assistant menu or by issuing the CREATE SCREEN and MODIFY SCREEN commands from the dot prompt.

Custom Data-Entry Form

Tip:

Use the screen painter to design a data-entry form.

Instead of writing a program or a format file, you can use the screen painter to design a custom data-entry form on the *blackboard* (dBASE III Plus's name for the monitor). After you save a data-entry form to disk in a *screen* file, you can use the form in the EDIT and APPEND operations.

You create a screen file with the following steps:

1. Select the database file to be used.

2. Create the screen file by invoking the CREATE SCREEN operation.

3. Display the blackboard.

4. Load the data fields you want to display.

5. Modify the field labels and add a title, notes, and boxes.

6. Save the form to a screen file.

You can carry out the first two steps of this operation either by issuing the necessary commands at the dot prompt or by selecting the appropriate options from the Assistant menu.

To create a data-entry form for the EMPLOYEE.DBF database file (in the default disk drive C:), for example, you would type the following commands at the dot prompt:

. USE EMPLOYEE
. CREATE SCREEN EMPLOYEE.SCR

To create the same screen file from the Assistant menu, select the following options:

Set Up/Database file/C:/*EMPLOYEE*/Create/Format/C:/Enter the name of the file:/*EMPLOYEE.SCR*

The file extension (.SCR) is optional. If the extension is left out in the CREATE SCREEN step, the program provides it automatically.

After you execute these commands or menu options, you are ready to design the data-entry form on the screen.

To select the data fields you want to include in the data-entry form, use the **Set Up/Load Fields** options from the menu bar (see fig. 4.1).

After you load the data fields, press F10 to display the blackboard. As you can see in figure 4.2, all the data fields you've loaded are displayed in the upper left corner of the blackboard.

With all the data fields loaded where you want them, you can modify the field names and add more descriptive information to the form by using the editing keystrokes. Figure 4.3 shows a finished data-entry form.

To save the data-entry form, press F10 and then select the **Exit/Save** option from the menu bar.

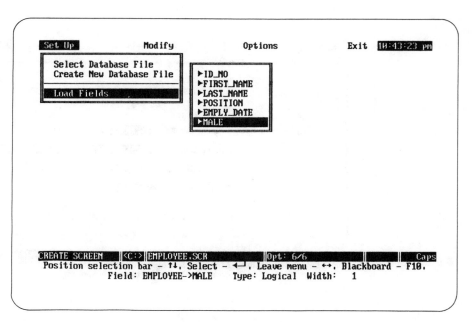

Fig. 4.1. Simultaneously loading all data fields to the blackboard.

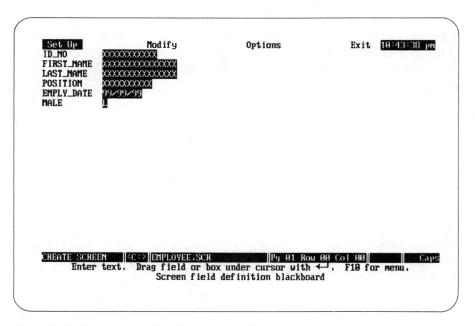

Fig. 4.2. Displaying loaded field on the blackboard.

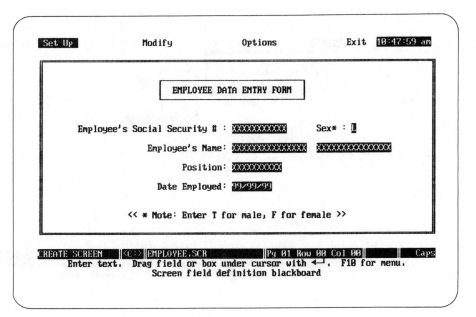

Fig. 4.3. Example of a data-entry form.

Tip:

Use single- or double-line boxes to frame a data-entry form.

While designing a data-entry form with the screen painter, you can draw a single- or double-line box by selecting **Options/ Draw a window or line** from the menu bar.

To draw a box, you first position the cursor at one corner of the box and then press the Enter key. Next, use an arrow key to move the cursor to what will be the opposite diagonal corner of the box. Press Enter.

The data-entry form shown in figure 4.3 is framed by a double-line box; the form's title is framed by a single-line box.

Tip:

Use the arrow keys to adjust the size of an existing box.

After you have drawn a box, you can adjust its size.

To make the box taller, place the cursor at the top line of the box, use the ↑ key to move the line, and then press Enter. Or extend the box downward by placing the cursor at the bottom line of the box and pressing the ↓ key, followed by pressing the Enter key.

To widen the box, position the cursor at either side of the box line, extend the line by using the ← or → keys, and then press Enter.

Tip:

Erase a box by using the Ctrl-U key combination.

To erase a box on the blackboard, place the cursor anywhere on the box line and then press Ctrl-U.

Saving a Screen Layout to a Text File

Before you save your newly designed data-entry form to a screen file, you may want to save the layout of the screen file to a text file. The text file will then contain the attributes of all the data fields in the screen file. This information is especially useful if you need to identify the data fields after you've relabeled them on the data-entry form.

Trick:

Use the text generator to save the layout of a data-entry form to a text file.

To save the layout of the screen file to a text file, select **Options/Generate text file image** from the Set Up menu after you have designed the data-entry form. dBASE III Plus automatically sets up a text file to hold the screen file layout. The name of the text file is the same as that of the screen file, but it is assigned a .TXT file extension (EMPLOYEE.TXT).

You can display the contents of a text file on screen or you can use the TYPE command to print the file. For example, the following command:

. TYPE *EMPLOYEE.TXT* TO PRINT

prints the contents of the EMPLOYEE.TXT file (see fig. 4.4).

Note that attributes of all the data fields on the data-entry form are listed in figure 4.4. The text file identifies the location, name, type, and width of each data field. For example, the form's **Employee's Social Security #** field corresponds to the **ID_NO** field in the EMPLOYEE.DBF database file.

```
Field definitions for Screen : EMPLOYEE.scr

Page  Row  Col  Data Base    Field         Type       Width  Dec
  1     8   39   EMPLOYEE    ID_NO        Character     11
  1    10   39   EMPLOYEE    FIRST_NAME   Character     15
  1    10   56   EMPLOYEE    LAST_NAME    Character     15
  1    12   39   EMPLOYEE    POSITION     Character     10
  1    14   39   EMPLOYEE    EMPLY_DATE   Date           8
  1     8   63   EMPLOYEE    MALE         Logical        1


Content of page :   1




                    EMPLOYEE DATA ENTRY FORM


     Employee's Social Security # : XXXXXXXXXX      Sex* : X

                  Employee's Name: XXXXXXXXXXXXXXX  XXXXXXXXXXXXXXX

                         Position: XXXXXXXXXX

                    Date Employed: XXXXXXXX

              << * Note: Enter T for male, F for female >>
```

Fig. 4.4. The text file containing the screen file layout.

Modifying a Data-Entry Form

Tip:

Use the screen painter to modify an existing data-entry form.

If you want to make changes to the layout or the contents of a data-entry form, you can use the MODIFY SCREEN operation to modify the screen file. To do this from the dot prompt, issue the command:

. MODIFY SCREEN <name of the screen file>

To modify an existing screen file from the Assistant menu, select the following menu options:

^Modify/Format/C:/<name of the screen file>

Trick:

Use the screen painter to create a format file.

When you use the screen painter with the CREATE/MODIFY SCREEN operation, information on your data-entry form is saved in a screen file and a format file.

The data fields and their display locations are written as dBASE III Plus commands and saved in the *format* file automatically.

Information needed to convert these commands to the screen display is stored in the screen file. Format and screen files share the same file name but have different file extensions (.FMT and .SCR).

When the data-entry form shown in figure 4.3 is saved in the screen file (EMPLOYEE.SCR), a format file named EMPLOYEE.FMT is created automatically. This format file contains the dBASE III Plus commands that specify the layout of the data fields and their labels (see fig. 4.5).

```
. TYPE EMPLOYEE.FMT
@  4, 27  SAY "EMPLOYEE DATA ENTRY FORM"
@  8,  8  SAY "Employee's Social Security # :"
@  8, 39  GET  EMPLOYEE->ID_NO
@  8, 56  SAY "Sex* :"
@  8, 63  GET  EMPLOYEE->MALE
@ 10, 22  SAY "Employee's Name:"
@ 10, 39  GET  EMPLOYEE->FIRST_NAME
@ 10, 56  GET  EMPLOYEE->LAST_NAME
@ 12, 29  SAY "Position:"
@ 12, 39  GET  EMPLOYEE->POSITION
@ 14, 24  SAY "Date Employed:"
@ 14, 39  GET  EMPLOYEE->EMPLY_DATE
@ 17, 18  SAY "<< * Note: Enter T for male, F for female >>"
@  1,  0  TO 19, 79    DOUBLE
@  3, 24  TO  5, 53
```

Fig. 4.5. Listing of EMPLOYEE.FMT format file.

As you can see in the figure, every data field in the data-entry form is defined with an @..SAY..GET statement, which may be written as one or two command lines. The locations and labels of these data fields are clearly identified by using the information in the screen file. Using the screen painter to create a format file is often easier than typing in the format statements by way of a text editor.

Trap:

Modifying the format file doesn't affect the screen layout in the screen file.

If you use the CREATE SCREEN or MODIFY SCREEN command to create a format file with the screen painter, dBASE III Plus allows you to modify the text in the format file independently. But doing so is asking for trouble.

The changes you make to the format file will not be used to modify the corresponding screen file. If you try to examine the screen display from screen painter, you won't see any of the formatting changes you've made. And, if you modify the screen file after you change its corresponding format file, all the changes you have made in the format file will be lost when you save the screen file.

Validating Data

When you use the screen painter to create a custom data-entry form, each data field specified in the form is represented by a *field mask* such as *XXXXXX* (for character field), *99/99/99* (for date field), or *L* (for logical field).

For example, the field mask for the ID_NO field (Employee's Social Security #) is displayed (using the template symbol *X*) as XXXXXXXXXXX by the screen painter (refer to fig. 4.3). A value for the field may consist of nine digits and two dashes. With dBASE III Plus, the default *X* can be replaced by any character.

Trap:

You can alter data in the field without realizing it has happened.

Because you can substitute any character for the default *X*, you can make a serious mistake unknowingly. For example, if you mistakenly enter the letter *O* in place of the number *0* to the ID_NO field, no error message or warning will be given.

Trick:

Prevent errors by adding a PICTURE template to format the data field.

You can avoid entering an invalid value if you use a PICTURE template to restrict the types of characters the data field will accept.

To define a PICTURE template on the data-entry form, place the cursor at the data field and then choose the **Modify/ Picture Template** option from the screen painter's menu bar.

For example, you can define a *999-99-9999* PICTURE template for the ID_NO data field, as shown in figure 4.6. Because the template symbol *9* allows only digits to be entered in its place, you can enter only digits and dashes in the ID_NO field.

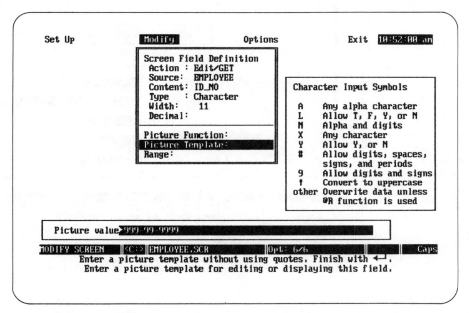

Fig. 4.6. Defining PICTURE template for the ID_NO field.

The PICTURE template also is displayed on the data-entry form (see fig. 4.7).

After you've defined the PICTURE template, if you use the format file to append a new record to the database file:

```
. USE EMPLOYEE
. SET FORMAT TO EMPLOYEE
. APPEND
```

the ID_NO field (labeled **Employee's Social Security # :**) is displayed with the PICTURE template (see fig. 4.8). Notice that two dashes have been inserted in the field. You do not have to enter them yourself.

Now, the ID_NO field will reject any character that is not a digit.

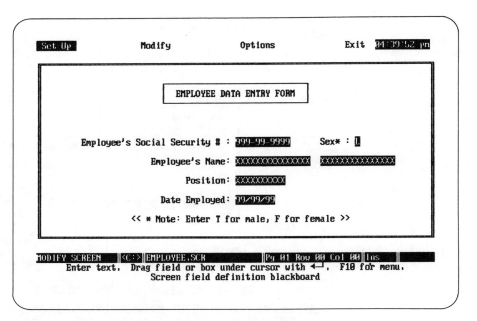

Fig. 4.7. Showing PICTURE template on the data-entry form.

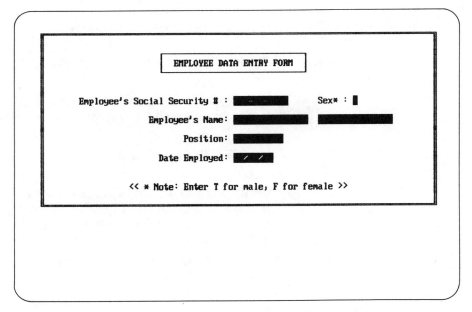

Fig. 4.8. The result of using the PICTURE template with SET FORMAT TO.

Tip:

Use PICTURE template symbols to format data fields in a data-entry form.

The formatting template plays an important role in the PICTURE clause. By using the appropriate template symbols in the clause, you can restrict the type of characters entered in the data field. These template symbols and their uses are

Symbol	Restriction
X	Allows any character
9	Allows only digits for character fields Allows only digits and signs for numeric fields
#	Allows only digits, blanks, and signs in numeric or character fields
A	Allows only letters in a character field
Y	Allows only logical data (T or F, Y or N)
!	Converts letters entered to uppercase

Trick:

Use the screen painter's Picture Function to convert lowercase characters to uppercase.

The **Modify/Picture Function** option in the screen painter menu lets you convert one or more characters in a data field to uppercase letters. Position the cursor at the data field before you select the option.

For example, you can ensure that the last name in the data-entry form for the EMPLOYEE.DBF database file always begins with an uppercase letter. To do so, set the function value for the LAST_NAME data field to the ! picture function symbol (see fig. 4.9).

If you use the PICTURE *!AAAAAAAAAAAA* to define the format of the LAST_NAME field in an @..SAY..GET statement, the first letter you enter in the field is converted automatically to uppercase.

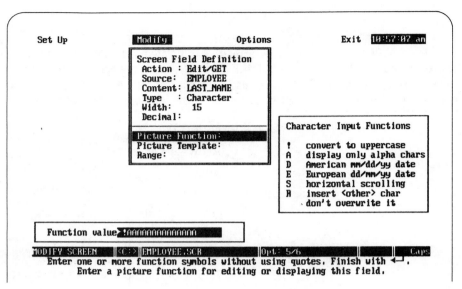

Fig. 4.9. Defining Picture Function on the LAST_NAME field.

Trick:

Use the Picture Function to display a date in different formats.

The standard format for displaying a date is the American format:

mm/dd/yy

in which *mm*, *dd*, and *yy* denote the numeric code for the month, day, and year.

However, by using the screen painter's **Picture Function** option, you can also show a date in European format:

dd/mm/yy

To select the date format, place the cursor at the date field you want to format and press F10. Then select the **Modify/ Picture Function** option from the menu.

As you design an entry form for EMPLOYEE.DBF, for example, you can display the employment date in European format. To do so, position the cursor at the EMPLY_DATE field and press F10 to select **Modify/Picture Function**. At the **Function value** prompt, enter *E* to select European format (see fig. 4.10).

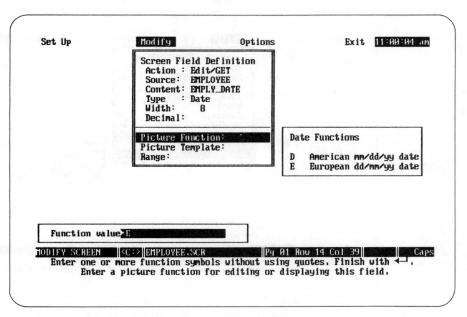

Fig. 4.10. Selecting a European date format for a date field.

Setting Data Ranges

Tip:

Use the Range function of the screen painter to define a valid range for numeric and date fields.

As you design a data-entry form, you can define a valid range for a given data field. For example, you can set the upper and lower limits for a numeric data field. Then only values within those limits will be accepted during data entry. An example of setting the lower and upper limits for the numeric field EXEMPTIONS is shown in figure 4.11.

Notice that the range specified in figure 4.11 for the number of exemptions in the PAYROLL.DBF data file is set between 0 and 6. As a result, the value that can be entered into the EXEMPTIONS field is bounded by that range.

You also can use the screen painter's **Range** option to set a valid range for a date field. For example, by choosing the **Modify/Range** option shown in figure 4.12, you can set the employment date between 1/1/81 and 12/31/87 when you design the data-entry form for the EMPLOYEE.DBF file.

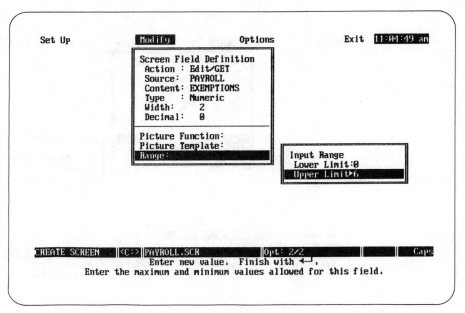

Fig. 4.11. Setting lower and upper limits for a numeric field.

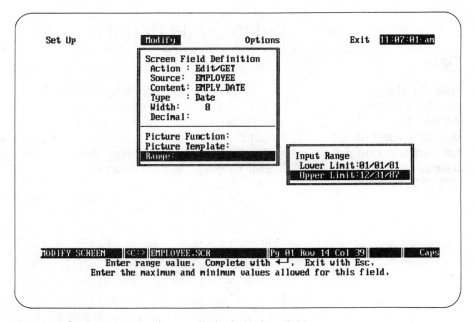

Fig. 4.12. Setting lower and upper limits for a date field.

When you set the range for a date field, the lower and upper limits refer to the earliest and latest dates, respectively.

Trap:

Your keyboard may "lock up" if you enter a value that is not within the specified range.

When you use the Range function in a data-entry screen, all values must fall within the specified range. If you enter a value that is not within the specified range, the keyboard appears to lock up. To clear this condition, press the spacebar. The cursor will then return to the data entry field.

Trick:

You can add new data fields to the database file with the screen painter's Modify **option.**

When you design a data-entry form, you can add new data fields to the active database file without leaving the screen painter. From the screen painter, you first position the field to be added at the desired location on the data-entry form and then select the **Modify/Content** option from the menu.

For example, to add a new field, BIRTHDATE, to the entry form for EMPLOYEE.DBF, you enter the field label on the form and then place the cursor next to the label **Birth Date** (see fig. 4.13).

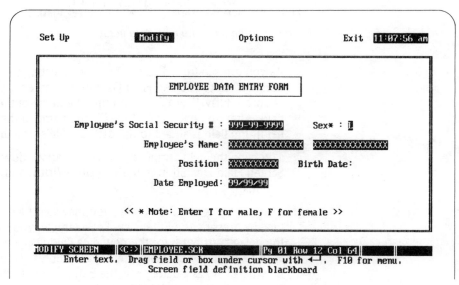

Fig. 4.13. Adding a new data field to the data-entry form.

Then press F10 to switch to the **Modify** option in the menu. Select the following menu options:

Content/<NewField>/**Enter name for new Database Field**

as shown in figure 4.14, and enter the name of the new data field.

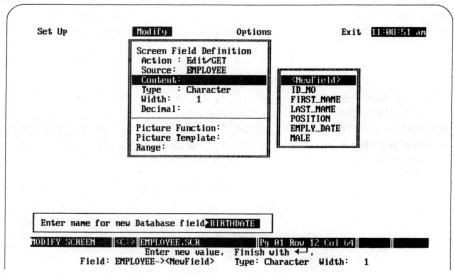

Fig. 4.14. Defining the contents of the new data field.

As you can see from figure 4.14, after selecting the **Content** option from the Screen Field Definition submenu, you can choose <NewField> for entering the name of the new data field. After you enter *BIRTHDATE* (the name of the new data field), the field is added to the database file's structure.

To define the field attributes, move the cursor down to the Screen Field Definition menu's **Type, Width,** and **Decimal** options.

Instead of entering a field type, you may select a given field type by pressing the Enter key. For example, you can change the default attributes for the new data field (a character field with a width of 1 character) by pressing Enter. To define the new data field as a date, press the Enter key until that field type appears (see fig. 4.15).

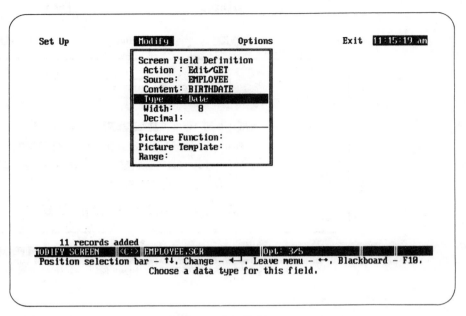

Fig. 4.15. Specifying the new field as a date field.

After you've defined the field attributes, press F10 to return to the blackboard. You now can verify that the new data field has been added to the data-entry form.

As you can see from figure 4.16, the new data field BIRTHDATE is placed at the cursor's current position next to the label **Birth Date**.

Tip:

Use Ctrl-U to delete a data field from the database file.

To remove a data field from the data-entry form you are designing with the screen painter, place the cursor at the field to be removed and then press Ctrl-U.

You will be prompted:

Do you wish to also delete field from database ? [Y/N]

To remove the data field permanently from the data-entry form and the database file, press *Y*. If you simply want to exclude the field from the entry form, press *N*.

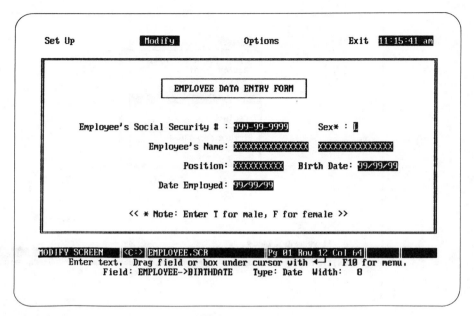

Fig. 4.16. Showing the new field on the data-entry form.

Selecting a Data-Entry Form

Tip:

To select a format file, issue the SET FORMAT TO command.

To select the custom data-entry form you've saved in a format file, select its corresponding database file and then issue the SET FORMAT TO command:

. SET FORMAT TO <name of the format file>

You can, for example, use the data-entry form (EMPLOYEE.FMT) for editing the fifth data record in the EMPLOYEE.DBF database file. Issue the following commands:

. USE EMPLOYEE
. SET FORMAT TO EMPLOYEE
. GOTO 5
. EDIT

The custom data-entry form is displayed and you can edit the data record (see fig. 4.17).

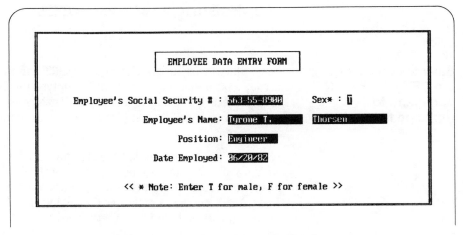

Fig. 4.17. Editing a data record with a custom data-entry form.

Trap:

You can't tell which record you're working on if the status line is not displayed.

If the SET STATUS OFF command is in effect when you use the data-entry form to add a new data record or to edit existing records, no information on the record's status is displayed. In figure 4.10, for example, you can't tell how many records are in the database file or which record you are working on.

Trick:

Use the SET STATUS ON command to show the record number during data entry.

To display the status line, issue the SET STATUS ON command. The status line shows you the current record number and other information about the database file in use.

You also can bring up the custom data-entry form via the Assistant menu before you carry out the EDIT or APPEND operation:

Set Up/Format for Screen/C:/<name of the format file>

The status bar is always displayed in the Assistant menu.

Replicating Data Records

Trick:

Save time by using the SET CARRY ON command to replicate field values.

You ordinarily use the APPEND or INSERT command to display a blank data-entry form and then type the field values for each record you add to an existing database file. This method works well if most of the field values in these records are different.

However, if many of the data fields in the records you are adding share the same values, you can carry the field values from one record to another—without using the keyboard. The CARRY operation replicates the field values of a data record and saves them in another record.

If you first issue the SET CARRY ON command and then execute the APPEND or INSERT operation, field values from the preceding record are carried over in a new record in the existing database file.

If, for example, you want to keep track of all the items sold in your store, you can set up a database file named ITEMSOLD.DBF. Figure 4.18 shows the structure and contents of such a database file.

```
. USE ITEMSOLD
. DISP STRU
Structure for database: C:ITEMSOLD.dbf
Number of data records:       3
Date of last update   : 02/09/87
Field  Field Name  Type       Width    Dec
    1  INVOICE_NO  Numeric        4
    2  DATE_SHIPD  Date           8
    3  CLERK_NO    Numeric        2
    4  DIVISION    Character      2
    5  STOCK_NO    Character      9
    6  UNITS_SOLD  Numeric        3
    7  PRICE       Numeric        8       2
** Total **                     37

. LIST
Record#  INVOICE_NO DATE_SHIPD CLERK_NO DIVISION STOCK_NO UNITS_SOLD    PRICE
      1        1001 01/06/87       10 HW       IBM-AT640          2  4900.00
      2        1001 02/07/87       10 SW       LOT-L0123          1   359.00
      3        1001 02/07/87       10 SW       MIC-WS300          1   269.00
```

Fig. 4.18. The file structure and contents of the ITEMSOLD.DBF.

As you can see from figure 4.19, if you issue the SET CARRY ON *and* APPEND commands after you select the database file (USE ITEMSOLD), the contents of the preceding record (Record No. 3) are carried over to the new record (Record No. 4). The two records now contain the same contents.

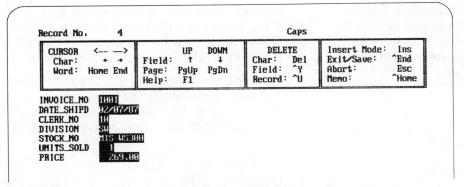

Fig. 4.19. Carrying over to the current record the contents of the preceding record.

At this point, you can edit some of the field values before you save the record.

To replicate the field values of the current record, press the PgDn key. When you press PgDn, the contents of the current record are carried over to the next new record.

Trap:

Leaving CARRY ON after replicating field values can produce unwanted records.

When CARRY ON is in effect, the contents of a record are carried over automatically to the next record when you use the INSERT or APPEND operation. Be sure to issue the SET CARRY OFF command when CARRY is no longer needed.

Appending Data Records from Another Database File

Use only common fields in a filter to append selected records from an existing database file.

Often you need to use a data field in a filtering condition when you append selected records from one file to another. In such cases, the data field must be common to both database files. Otherwise, you will have to use a temporary database file or the COPY FIELDS command to append the records.

Creating a new database file that contains a subset of the records in an existing database file can be desirable when you manipulate data. To create such a file, use the APPEND FROM command to add the records instead of typing them from the keyboard.

When you use the APPEND FROM operation, all the records in the source database file are appended to the target file. To selectively append data records from one database file to another, you can add a qualifier condition to the APPEND FROM command.

For example, to append from the inventory database (INVENTRY.DBF) to the active database file (LOWSTOCK.DBF) the data records for products whose stock levels are near depletion, you can use a qualifier condition (on-hand quantity is two or less) in the APPEND FROM command:

```
. USE LOWSTOCK
. APPEND FROM INVENTRY FOR ON_HAND<=2
```

The operation specified by this command will work properly only if both the LOWSTOCK.DBF and INVENTRY.DBF have the ON_HAND field in their database structure. Otherwise, no records are appended.

Trying to append selected records by using a field that is not shared by both databases results in an error message.

If, as shown in figure 4.20, the data field ON_HAND belongs only to INVENTRY.DBF and not to LOWSTOCK.DBF, executing the APPEND FROM command will cause an error message:

`Variable not found error`

```
. USE INVENTRY
. DISP STRU
Structure for database: C:INVENTRY.dbf
Number of data records:      28
Date of last update   : 02/14/87
Field  Field Name  Type       Width   Dec
    1  STOCK_NO    Character      9
    2  ON_HAND     Numeric        3
    3  ON_ORDER    Numeric        3
** Total **                     16

. USE LOWSTOCK
. DISP STRUC
Structure for database: C:LOWSTOCK.dbf
Number of data records:       5
Date of last update   : 02/14/87
Field  Field Name  Type       Width   Dec
    1  STOCK_NO    Character      9
** Total **                     10
```

Fig. 4.20. File structures of the INVENTRY.DBF and LOWSTOCK.DBF.

The data field ON_HAND, which is missing from the active database file, is considered an undefined memory variable.

Trick:

Use a temporary database file.

One solution to the problem of not having a common field is to copy the structure from the source database file (INVENTRY.DBF) to a temporary working file (TEMP.DBF) and then to append data records from the inventory file to the temporary file:

```
. USE INVENTRY
. COPY STRUCTURE TO TEMP
. USE TEMP
. APPEND FROM INVENTRY FOR ON_HAND <= 2
```

Next, delete the unwanted data fields from the structure of the temporary file and add the remaining records to the original target file (LOWSTOCK.DBF):

```
. USE LOWSTOCK
. APPEND FROM TEMP
. ERASE TEMP.DBF
```

Another solution to the problem is to save the records to be appended to the temporary database file (by using the COPY FIELDS command) and then add them to the target file by using the APPEND FROM command:

```
. USE INVENTRY
. COPY TO TEMP FIELDS STOCK_NO FOR ON_HAND <= 2
. USE LOWSTOCK
. APPEND FROM TEMP
. ERASE TEMP.DBF
```

Editing Selected Records

Trick:

To edit a selected set of records, use a search condition in the EDIT command.

When you issue the EDIT command at the dot prompt or choose the **Update/Edit** option from the Assistant menu, all of the records in the active database file are the subject of the editing command. You can select a record by specifying its record number in the EDIT command:

```
. USE EMPLOYEE
. EDIT RECORD 5
```

or by positioning the record pointer at the record to be edited before you issue the EDIT command:

```
. GOTO 5
. EDIT
```

You also can use the Assistant menu's **Position** option to select the record to be edited:

Position/Goto Record/RECORD/**Enter a numeric value:**5

This approach works adequately if you know the number of the record you want to edit. Otherwise, you may need to find the record (by using the LOCATE, SEEK, or FIND operation) before you use the EDIT command.

As a shortcut, add a search condition to the EDIT command:

```
. EDIT <a search condition>
```

For example, to change those records whose POSITION field value is "Sales Rep" in the EMPLOYEE.DBF database file, issue the following commands:

```
. USE EMPLOYEE
. EDIT FOR POSITION="Sales Rep"
```

The first record to meet the qualifying condition is displayed for editing. Once you've finished editing and passed beyond the last data field or pressed the PgDn key, the next data record to meet the search condition is displayed. All records that do not meet the search condition are ignored.

You can use the .AND. and .OR. operators in the search condition:

    . EDIT FOR MALE .AND.
    DTOC(EMPLY_DATE)>="01/01/86"

And you can filter out the records to be edited by adding a scope condition to the EDIT command:

    . EDIT FOR RECNO()>=5

Editing Selected Data Fields

Tip:

To edit the contents of selected data fields, specify the field list in the EDIT command.

When you edit the contents of an existing database file, you may need to change only the values in selected data fields. Instead of displaying all the data fields, you can specify which fields to edit in the EDIT command:

    . EDIT FIELDS <the fields to be edited>

For example, if you need to change only the price and cost of the products in the PRODUCTS.DBF database file, you can issue the following commands:

    . USE PRODUCTS
    . EDIT FIELDS STOCK_NO,COST,PRICE

Only those data fields specified in the EDIT FIELDS command are displayed for editing. The effect is the same as if you were editing while in the BROWSE FIELDS environment.

And you can edit selected data fields in a subset of data records. Add a search condition to the EDIT FIELDS command:

    . USE PRODUCTS
    . EDIT FIELDS STOCK_NO,COST,PRICE
    FOR TYPE="printer"

Trap:

The EDIT FIELDS command does not work if you use a custom data-entry screen specified in a SET FORMAT TO command.

If you wish to use the selective EDIT function, issue the following command before issuing the EDIT command:

. SET FORMAT TO

This command will cancel any format file specified in an earlier SET FORMAT TO command.

Filtering Data Records to be Edited

Tip:

Use the SET FILTER TO command to select a subset of the data records in a database file to be edited.

To edit a selected group of data records in the database file, single out a subset of the records by using a filtering command:

. SET FILTER TO <filtering condition>

instead of using a search condition in the EDIT command.

Only those records that satisfy the filtering condition will be subjected to the EDIT operation. For example, if you want to edit only those records in the PRODUCTS.DBF database file that contain information on products in the software division, you can set the following filter:

. SET FILTER TO DIVISION="SW"

Only records that meet the filter condition are displayed for editing when you use the BROWSE or EDIT commands.

Trap:

When you are screening data records, dBASE III Plus allows only one filter condition at a time.

You can use the SET FILTER TO command to screen data records. However, you can set only one filter at a time. When you issue a new filter command, the existing filter condition is erased.

If you want to erase the current filter condition without setting another condition, use the SET FILTER TO command without specifying a filter condition.

Editing Multiple Database Files Simultaneously

To design a good database system, store data (according to function) in several database files instead of saving all the information in one large file. Preferably, each of these database files should contain a limited number of data fields.

You may want to be able to use the EDIT or BROWSE operations to modify the records in these database files simultaneously rather than editing the records in each file separately.

Tip:

To edit records in multiple database files, link them with the SET RELATION TO command.

To edit the data records in multiple database files simultaneously, you must first use the SET RELATION operation to link the files. (Chapter 5 contains a detailed discussion on linking database files.)

For example, let's assume that you store information about software products in SOFTWARE.DBF whose structure and records are shown in figure 4.21.

```
Structure for database: C:SOFTWARE.dbf
Number of data records:      10
Date of last update   : 02/15/87
Field  Field Name  Type       Width    Dec
    1  STOCK_NO    Character      9
    2  DSCRIPTION  Character     20
    3  TYPE        Character     20
    4  COST        Numeric        7      2
    5  PRICE       Numeric        7      2
** Total **                      64

. LIST
Record#  STOCK_NO  DSCRIPTION          TYPE                   COST    PRICE
      1  ASH-DB300 dBASE III Plus v1.01 database             395.00  595.00
      2  ANS-DB110 Paradox v1.1         database             525.00  695.00
      3  CLP-DB100 Clipper DB Compiler  database compiler    450.00  595.00
      4  WOR-DB100 WordTech DB Compiler database compiler    469.00  595.00
      5  LOT-LO123 Lotus 1-2-3 Release2 spread sheet         289.00  359.00
      6  MIC-WS330 WordStar v3.30       word processing      229.00  269.00
      7  MIS-WD300 Microsoft Word v3.0  word processing      229.00  289.00
      8  AST-FW200 Framework v2.0       integrated           345.00  395.00
      9  MIC-QB100 Microsoft QuickBasic language              79.00  109.00
     10  BOL-PA300 Turbo Pascal v3.0    language              39.50   69.50
```

Fig. 4.21. File structure and contents of the SOFTWARE.DBF.

You store the inventory level of these software products in another database file named SWSTOCK.DBF (see fig. 4.22).

If you want to modify the data records in SOFTWARE.DBF and SWSTOCK.DBF simultaneously, you must first link the two database files. Figure 4.23 shows the commands for linking the two files with the SET RELATION command. Notice that you link the two database files by using the common data field STOCK_NO with the SET RELATION TO command.

```
. USE SWSTOCK
. DISP STRUC
Structure for database: C:SWSTOCK.dbf
Number of data records:        10
Date of last update   : 02/15/87
Field  Field Name  Type       Width    Dec
    1  STOCK_NO    Character      9
    2  ON_HAND     Numeric        3
    3  ON_ORDER    Numeric        3
** Total **                     16

. LIST
Record#   STOCK_NO  ON_HAND ON_ORDER
       1  ASH-DB300       4        2
       2  ANS-DB110       3        2
       3  CLP-DB100       2        1
       4  WOR-DB100       2        3
       5  LOT-L0123       5        1
       6  MIC-WS330       3        3
       7  MIS-WD300       2        3
       8  AST-FW200       3        2
       9  MIC-QB100       4        1
      10  BOL-PA300       0        2
```

Fig. 4.22. File structure and contents of the SWSTOCK.DBF.

```
. SELE 1
. USE SWSTOCK
. INDE ON STOCK_NO TO SKSTKNO
  100% indexed           10 Records indexed
. SELE 2
. USE SOFTWARE
. INDE ON STOCK_NO TO SWSTKNO
  100% indexed           10 Records indexed
. SET RELATION TO STOCK_NO INTO A
```

Fig. 4.23. Relating the SOFTWARE.DBF and SWSTOCK.DBF.

After you have linked the database files, you can modify some or all of the fields in both files by using the BROWSE FIELDS command:

> . GO TOP
> . BROWSE FIELDS STOCK_NO,DSCRIPTION,COST,PRICE,
> A->ON_HAND,A->ON_ORDER

The BROWSE FIELDS command selects fields from these two database files for display and modification. On the BROWSE screen, you can edit simultaneously the field values common to both database files.

You can see the modified results for Record #2 (STOCK_NO="ANS–DB110") in the example shown in figure 4.24.

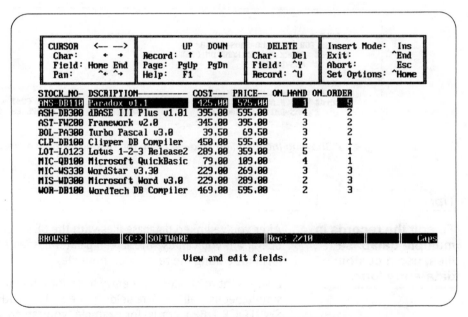

Fig. 4.24. Simultaneously editing fields from the related database files.

The values of the COST, PRICE, ON_HAND, and ON_ORDER fields have been changed as follows:

Field	Original Value	New Value
COST	525.00	425.00
PRICE	695.00	575.00
ON_HAND	3	1
ON_ORDER	2	5

These changes are stored in the data records in both database files when you exit the BROWSE operation by using the Ctrl-End key combination.

At this point, if you display the contents of the STOCK_NO="ANS–DB110" data record, you will see that its field values have been changed (see fig. 4.25).

```
. SELE 1
. DISP FOR STOCK_NO="ANS-DB110"
Record#  STOCK_NO  ON_HAND ON_ORDER
      2  ANS-DB110       1       5

. SELE 2
. DISP FOR STOCK_NO="ANS-DB110"
Record#  STOCK_NO  DSCRIPTION        TYPE          COST   PRICE
      2  ANS-DB110 Paradox v1.1      database      425.00 575.00
```

Fig. 4.25. Showing the modified field values in the related database files.

Tip:

To edit the records in multiple database files, use a custom data-entry form.

After you've linked database files with the SET RELATION operation, you can use the screen painter to create a data-entry form for editing the records in those files.

If you want to create a data-entry form for editing simultaneously all the data fields in the SOFTWARE.DBF and SWSTOCK.DBF records, for example, you can create a screen file.

However, before you issue the CREATE SCREEN command you must link the files with the SET RELATION operation shown in figure 4.23. Then use the SET FIELDS TO command to select the data fields from the two database files:

    . SET FIELDS TO STOCK_NO,DSCRIPTION,TYPE,COST,PRICE,
      A->ON_HAND,A->ON_ORDER
    . CREATE SCREEN MULTEDIT

It's important that you use the SET FIELDS TO command to combine the fields in the two database files you will use in the data-entry form. If you don't use this command, only those data fields in the active work area will be used in the form.

Choose the **Set Up/Load Fields** option from the screen painter's menu to load all the fields in the custom data-entry form (see fig. 4.26).

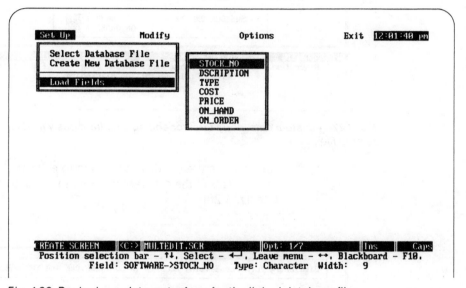

Fig. 4.26. Designing a data-entry form for the linked database files.

Figure 4.27 shows a custom data-entry form that contains all the data fields from the two database files.

After you have saved the data-entry form in a screen file (as MULTEDIT.SCR) and its corresponding format file (as MULTEDIT.FMT), you can use the form to append data records to the two files simultaneously:

    . SET FORMAT TO MULTEDIT
    . EDIT

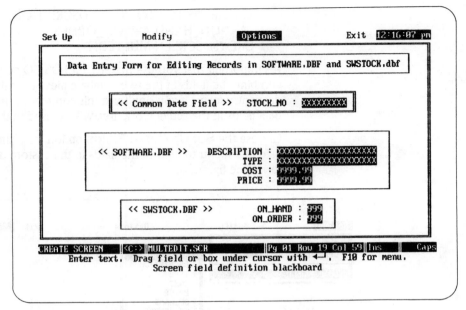

Fig. 4.27. A custom data-entry form for editing simultaneously fields in the related files.

And you can use the data-entry form to edit simultaneously the contents of the data records common to both database files (see fig. 4.28).

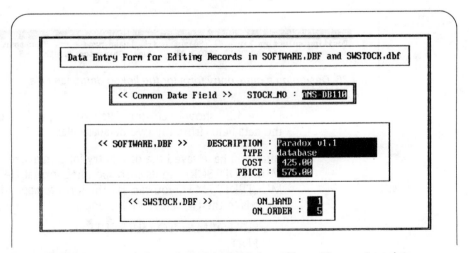

Fig. 4.28. Editing records from the related database files with a custom data-entry form.

Trap:

You can lose some records if you use the INSERT or APPEND command to add new records to database files linked by the SET RELATION operation.

When you link database files with the SET RELATION operation, you can only edit the contents of their records. You cannot add new records to these database files.

If you attempt to add a new record to the files with the INSERT or APPEND operations, the new record's field values will be added only to the database file in the active work area, not to the other database file. The BROWSE operation will not allow you to add new records to the linked files.

Trap:

While multiple files are related on an indexed field, do not edit the index field in an individual file.

When multiple database files are linked with the SET RELATION operation, do not attempt to edit the common (link) data field in an individual database. If you do, records in the database files will be related incorrectly.

When you use a common data field to link multiple database files, you must index the files on the common data field to ensure a correct match of records from these files. Information stored in the index files provides the correct linkage between the records in these database files.

The index field provides the vital link among related files. If you edit the contents of the index field while they are linked, all the related files will be reindexed correctly to preserve the exact record match. However, if you edit the field in one of the files while they are not linked, the records in the other file will not be reindexed correctly. As a result, the records in the files will not match when you attempt to link them up again.

Deleting an Empty Record

Trap:

If you press Ctrl-End at a blank entry screen while appending data, an empty record will be added to the database file.

Frequently, when you append a new record to an existing database file, an empty record is saved by accident. This can occur when you press Ctrl-End at a blank entry screen after a new record has been appended.

A solution to the problem is to exit the blank record by pressing the Esc key. The empty record will not be saved to the database file.

Trick:

To remove empty records, use a blank space surrounded by a pair of quotation marks (" ") as a qualifier in the DELETE command.

If you try to delete blank records in an existing database file by using a blank string enclosed by a pair of quotation marks as the condition in a FOR qualifier of the DELETE command, be sure to include at least one blank space between the quotation marks. Otherwise, any nonblank data fields are considered a match.

If you issue the command:

. DELETE FOR ID_NO=" "

for example, all nonblank records in the database file are marked for deletion.

If this happens, before you pack the records you can recover them by using the RECALL ALL command. However, if you issue the PACK command to remove all records marked for deletion now, all these records will be lost permanently.

5

Organize Data with Catalogs and by Linking Files

dBASE III Plus provides powerful file-management tools. You can group disk files in an applications or project *catalog*. And you can link files by their records and data fields in small, easily managed database files.

Many restrictions are imposed on the use of these functions, however, and traps are hidden in their operations. This chapter provides tips to help you use these tools effectively—and tricks to circumvent the traps and restrictions.

Catalog Files

When you design a sizable database-management system, you work with many data tables and their associated disk files. But you rarely use all the files at the same time. You may need only a subset of these files.

For example, when you work with the invoicing function in your data-management operation, you have to access only the files needed for that particular function. dBASE III Plus provides a catalog file for just such a purpose.

A catalog file is similar in many ways to a regular database file. It is defined with a file structure and consists of a set of records, each holding information about disk files to be included in the catalog. To process the contents of a catalog file, you use most of the commands (such as LIST, DISPLAY, DISPLAY STRUCTURE, EDIT, and APPEND) provided by dBASE III Plus for manipulating a database file.

Structure of a Catalog File

Tip:

To use a catalog file, you need to understand its structure.

Catalog and database files consist of the same types of field attributes: Field Name, Type, and Width. Unlike a regular database file, however, the data structure of the catalog file is not defined by the user. dBASE III Plus specifies the structure of a catalog file with a standard set of data fields and prespecified field attributes. The file structure of the sample SOFTWARE.CAT catalog file is shown in figure 5.1.

```
. SELE 10
. USE SOFTWARE.CAT
. DISP STRUC
Structure for database: C:SOFTWARE.CAT
Number of data records:        12
Date of last update    : 03/25/87
Field  Field Name  Type        Width    Dec
    1  PATH        Character      70
    2  FILE_NAME   Character      12
    3  ALIAS       Character       8
    4  TYPE        Character       3
    5  TITLE       Character      80
    6  CODE        Numeric         3
    7  TAG         Character       4
** Total **                      181
```

Fig. 5.1. The file structure of the SOFTWARE.CAT catalog file.

The attributes of the disk file are saved in data fields in a record of the catalog file:

- The PATH field tells dBASE III Plus where in the directory path to find the disk.

- The fields FILE_NAME and ALIAS are used to identify the disk file. If you do not assign an alias, dBASE III Plus assigns the file name to the ALIAS field.

- The type of disk file is defined in the TYPE field.

- You can save in the TITLE field a label (up to 80 characters long) to describe the disk file.

- The CODE field is used by dBASE III Plus to store an internal file code which is of no significance to most users.

- The last field, TAG, is not used.

Contents of a Catalog File

Tip:

Only certain types of disk files can be included in a catalog.

A catalog file is useful for holding the disk files related to a given database-management application. You can include the following disk files in a catalog:

database files (.DBF)
index files (.NDX)
format files (.FMT)
label files (.LBL)
report files (.FRM)
screen files (.SCR)
view files (.VUE)
query files (.QRY)

Figure 5.2 shows the contents of a sample catalog file (SOFTWARE.CAT).

```
. SELE 10
. USE SOFTWARE.CAT
. LIST FOR RECNO()<=5
Record# PATH
FILE_NAME    ALIAS     TYPE TITLE
                            CODE TAG
      1  C:software.dbf
SOFTWARE.dbf SOFTWARE dbf  Software product description, type, cost and price
                            3
      2  SWINPUT.fmt
SWINPUT.fmt  SWINPUT  fmt  Data entry form for SOFTWARE.DBF
                            3
      3  SWLIST.lbl
SWLIST.lbl   SWLIST   lbl  Software product list
                            3
      4  SWREPORT.frm
SWREPORT.frm SWREPORT frm  Software product report
                            3
      5  SWSEARCH.qry
SWSEARCH.qry SWSEARCH qry  Query to find database compiler software
                            3
```

Fig. 5.2. The contents of the SOFTWARE.CAT catalog file.

Trap:

You can't include a command or program file in a catalog.

Command files (.PRG) that hold programs or procedures written in dBASE III Plus commands cannot be saved in a catalog. They can be accessed in the current directory, however.

Functions of a Catalog File

A catalog file's primary function is to group the data files for a database-management application so that you can better segregate your files. A catalog file also lets you keep track of all the files associated with an open database file.

Trick:

If you forget a file's name, use the query operator (?) to select the file from the catalog.

You can use the query operator (?) when you've forgotten a file's name because the ? can be used in place of the file name. For example, if you need to open a database file in the current catalog (SOFTWARE.CAT), and you do not remember the name of the file, you can use the query operator in the USE command:

        . USE ?

dBASE III Plus then displays a list of all the disk files that are accessible by the command (in this case, all the database files). You select the file you want (see fig. 5.3).

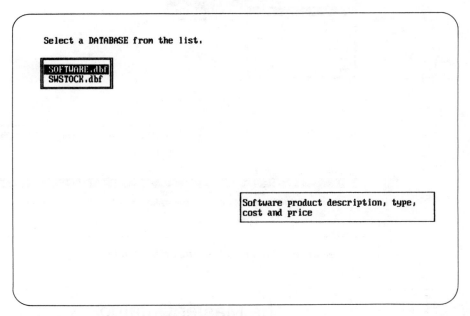

Select a DATABASE from the list.

```
SOFTWARE.dbf
SWSTOCK.dbf
```

Software product description, type, cost and price

Fig. 5.3. Selecting a database file from the active catalog.

As you can see in figure 5.3, a list of database files in the current catalog is shown in the upper left corner of the screen. The title of the highlighted file is displayed in a window in the lower right corner. (Disk file titles are defined when the files are added to the catalog.)

When you attempt to set up a disk file from the Assistant menu, you will see on your screen only the files in the current catalog for that particular setup operation.

For example, you can select the Assistant menu's **Set Up/ Format for Screen** options to select a format file for the active database (SOFTWARE.DBF). Only the format files associated with the active database in the current catalog are displayed (see fig. 5.4).

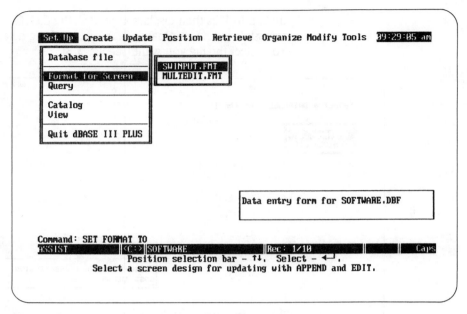

Fig. 5.4. Selecting a format file from the active catalog.

The Master Catalog

Tip:

All catalog files are saved in a master catalog.

When you create your first catalog file, dBASE III Plus automatically sets up a master catalog named CATALOG.CAT. This master file, which organizes all the catalog files in a data-management system, has the same data structure as a regular catalog file. Each record in the master catalog is used to store the attributes of a catalog file.

As you can see from the sample catalog structure shown in figure 5.5, the master catalog contains all the application catalogs.

The disk files related to a particular application (such as an application for processing personnel information) are grouped under a separate catalog (such as EMPLOYEE.CAT).

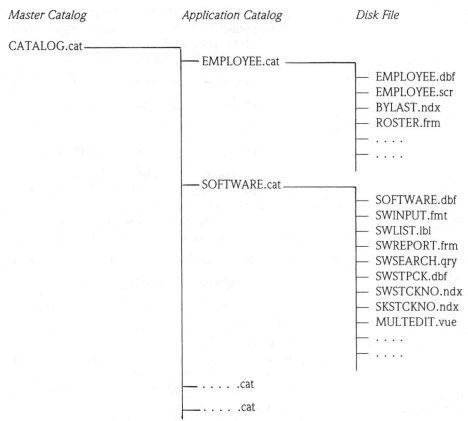

Fig. 5.5. The structure of catalog files.

Creating a Catalog File

Tip:

Use the SET CATALOG TO command to create a catalog file.

As you know, you do not have to create the master catalog (CATALOG.CAT) because dBASE III Plus sets it up automatically.

To create a catalog file, you first assign a name to the file by using the SET CATALOG TO command at the dot prompt:

. SET CATALOG TO <name of the catalog file>

For example, the catalog file SOFTWARE.CAT was created with the following command:

. SET CATALOG TO *SOFTWARE*

Issuing the SET CATALOG TO command activates the master catalog, which will hold the catalog file you are creating. dBASE III Plus sets up the master catalog file (CATALOG.CAT) and places it in work area 10.

When you are asked whether you are creating a new catalog:

> `Create new file catalog? (Y/N)`

type *Y.* You are asked to give a title to the catalog file:

> `Enter title for file SOFTWARE.CAT:`

After you assign the title *Product division, type, cost, and price* to the catalog file, a new record is appended to the master catalog file (CATALOG.CAT) and the new catalog file is loaded into work area 10. Now you can save the data files related to your application in the catalog file.

When you set up a new catalog file, the message:

> `File catalog is empty`

is displayed when you execute the SET CATALOG TO command.

At this point, SOFTWARE.CAT becomes the current catalog in work area 10. If you were to examine the contents of the master catalog, the data record in the master catalog file (CATALOG.CAT) would look like the one shown in figure 5.6.

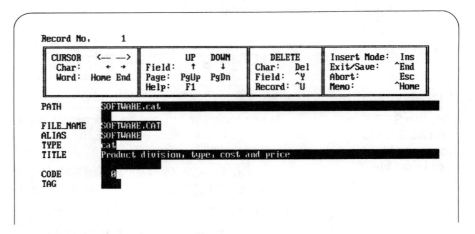

Fig. 5.6. Editing a record in the CATALOG.CAT master catalog.

Activating an Existing Catalog File

Tip:

Use the SET CATALOG TO command to activate and deactivate a catalog.

You can use the SET CATALOG TO command to create a catalog file or to select an existing catalog file.

To activate the catalog file you want, specify the name of the file in the command line. If the catalog file exists, it is loaded in work area 10. Otherwise, a new catalog file is created and added to the master catalog.

If SOFTWARE.CAT is the active catalog in work area 10, for example, you can use the SET CATALOG TO command:

. SET CATALOG TO EMPLOYEE.CAT

to switch to another catalog (EMPLOYEE.CAT).

Because EMPLOYEE.CAT is an existing catalog file, it is loaded into work area 10 and becomes the active catalog.

A catalog remains active until you deactivate it by selecting another catalog or by issuing the SET CATALOG OFF command. Issue the SET CATALOG ON command to activate a catalog that has been selected previously with the SET CATALOG TO command.

Tip:

You can add new disk files to an existing catalog.

One way to build the contents of a catalog file is to add new disk files as you create them.

When you activate a catalog file (by using the SET CATALOG TO or SET CATALOG ON command), any disk files created with the following commands are saved automatically to that catalog file:

```
COPY STRUCTURE TO
COPY TO..STRUCTURE EXTENDED
COPY TO
CREATE FROM
CREATE
CREATE LABEL
CREATE QUERY
CREATE REPORT
```

CREATE SCREEN
CREATE VIEW
IMPORT FROM
INDEX ON..TO
JOIN
SORT ON..TO
TOTAL ON..TO

Tip:

You can add existing disk files to the active catalog.

To load existing disk files into an active catalog, use one of the following commands:

USE
MODIFY LABEL
MODIFY QUERY
MODIFY REPORT
MODIFY SCREEN
MODIFY VIEW
SET FILTER TO FILE
SET FORMAT TO

Disk files invoked with these commands are added to the active catalog in work area 10.

To add the existing database file (SOFTWARE.DBF) and its format file (SWINPUT.FMT) in the SOFTWARE.CAT catalog, for example, you enter the following series of commands at the dot prompt (all file extensions are optional):

. SET CATALOG TO SOFTWARE.CAT
. SELECT 1
. USE SOFTWARE.DBF
. SET FORMAT TO SWINPUT.FMT

Trap:

If you use work area 10 to manipulate data while a catalog is active, the catalog file will be lost.

When you use a catalog, remember that dBASE III Plus holds the active catalog file in work area 10. If you use work area 10 for creating a new disk file or performing other data-manipulation operations, the catalog file will be lost from work area 10.

Trick:

To avoid losing the active catalog file, create a new disk file in another work area.	Select another work area (from 1 to 9) in which to create a new disk file: . SET CATALOG TO SOFTWARE.CAT . SELECT 1 . CREATE ACCOUNT

Trap:

If you try to activate the master catalog file with the SET CATALOG TO CATALOG.CAT command, a new catalog file is created and saved in the master file.	When the first catalog file is created, dBASE III Plus sets up the master catalog CATALOG.CAT to hold the attributes of the catalog files. Whenever you add a new catalog file to the master file, the program appends to the master file a new record describing the new catalog file. Because there is no need to "activate" the master catalog before you create a new catalog file, any name you specify in the SET CATALOG TO command is treated as a catalog file. Therefore, issuing the SET CATALOG TO CATALOG.CAT command at the dot prompt creates a catalog file named CATALOG.CAT and saves it as a new catalog in the master file.

Terminating the Cataloging Operation

Tip:

Selecting a new catalog closes the current catalog automatically.	When you select a new catalog with the SET CATALOG TO command, the active catalog is closed and removed from work area 10.

Trick:

Use the SET CATALOG TO command to close an active catalog.	To terminate the active catalog without selecting another catalog, issue the SET CATALOG TO command without specifying the name of a catalog.

Tip:

Use SET CATALOG OFF to halt the catalog operation temporarily.

If you want to stop adding data files to the active catalog in work area 10, issue the SET CATALOG OFF command at the dot prompt. You can reactivate the catalog by issuing the SET CATALOG ON command.

Displaying the Contents of a Catalog File

Tip:

Use normal display commands to display the contents of a catalog file.

Except for the file structure, which is defined by dBASE III Plus, a catalog file can be treated as a regular database file. To display the contents of a catalog file, use one of the following commands:

DISPLAY STRUCTURE
DISPLAY
LIST
BROWSE

Tip:

Select work area 10 for displaying the contents of a catalog.

Remember that the active catalog file is held in work area 10. If you want to display the contents of the active catalog file, you must select this work area before you issue the display command. To display the catalog, use the following sequence of commands:

. SELECT 10
. DISPLAY STRUCTURE

. . . . .
. LIST
. GOTO 3
. DISPLAY

Editing the Contents of an Existing Catalog

Use normal editing commands to edit the contents of a catalog file.

You can edit the contents of the records in a catalog file with the same procedures you use to modify a database file.

For example, to edit the records in the SOFTWARE.CAT file you could use the EDIT or BROWSE commands:

```
. SELECT 10
. EDIT RECORD 3
. . . . .
. BROWSE
```

Editing Records in the Master Catalog

To change the attributes of an existing catalog, edit its corresponding record in the master catalog.

Each record in the master catalog contains information on the attributes of a catalog file. If you need to modify the attributes of an existing catalog file, you can edit the contents of its corresponding records in the master catalog.

However, you must put the master catalog in work area 10 (by issuing the USE command) before you edit its records.

For example, if the master catalog's third record contains information on the attributes of a given catalog file, the following commands:

```
. SELECT 10
. USE CATALOG.CAT
. EDIT 3
```

allow you to edit the contents of that record after you select the master catalog (. USE CATALOG.CAT) in work area 10 (. SELECT 10).

Trap:

You can lose a file from a catalog if you change the names and the order of fields in the file structure.

Never change the names and order of the fields in the catalog file structure. Even though dBASE III Plus does not prevent you from modifying the structure of a catalog file, you may have your disk files removed from a catalog without warning if you change the names and the order of the fields in the file structure.

Trap:

Do not select work areas 1 through 9 for holding the master catalog.

You must not put the master catalog file in work areas 1 through 9 for editing operations. If you do, any file selected in these areas when an active catalog is in use will be treated as a new catalog file. Work area 10 is reserved for holding catalog files when they are needed.

Deleting an Existing Catalog

Tip:

Delete a catalog file as you would a database file.

To remove an existing catalog from your file directory, simply use the ERASE command.

To remove the SOFTWARE.CAT file from the directory, for example, you would issue the following command at the dot prompt:

. ERASE SOFTWARE.CAT

Trap:

You cannot delete an open catalog file.

If you try to do this, an error message **File is already open** will appear on your screen and the deletion command will be ignored.

Trick:

Close a catalog you intend to delete from the master catalog.

To close a catalog file, use one of the following commands:

SET CATALOG TO (without a file name)
CLOSE ALL
CLEAR ALL

Use the SET CATALOG TO command if you want to close only the catalog file (but not other disk files).

As their names imply, the CLOSE ALL and CLEAR ALL commands close all the disk files and memory variables—not just the catalog file.

When you erase a catalog file, dBASE III Plus automatically deletes from the master catalog (CATALOG.CAT) the data record that describes the catalog file.

Trick:

To erase a catalog file, delete its corresponding record from the master catalog.

One way to remove a catalog file from the master catalog is to delete from the master catalog the record related to that catalog file.

To remove the SOFTWARE.CAT catalog file from the master catalog, for example, use the following commands:

```
. SELECT 10
. USE CATALOG.CAT
. DELETE FOR FILE_NAME="SOFTWARE.CAT"
. PACK
```

You can also delete a record by record number.

Or (from the BROWSE or EDIT commands) delete a record by using the Ctrl-U key combination, followed by the PACK command.

Trick:

To delete all the catalogs from the directory, use the DOS ERASE command.

The dBASE III Plus ERASE command allows you to delete only one file at a time.

To delete a group of catalog files, use the DOS ERASE command:

```
. RUN ERASE *.CAT
```

or

```
. ! ERASE *.CAT
```

Removing Disk Files from a Catalog

Trap:

If you delete a disk file with the ERASE command, the erased file is removed from the catalog file *and* the file directory.

If you want to use a file for other applications, that file must remain in the file directory. *Do not* use the ERASE command if you want to remove a file from the catalog but not from the file directory.

Trick:

To remove a disk file from a catalog, delete its corresponding record from the catalog file.

When you add a disk file to a catalog, a record that describes the disk file is appended to the catalog file.

If you want to remove a disk file from the catalog, simply delete its corresponding record from the catalog file. In this way, the disk file remains in the file directory and can be used for other applications.

Trick:

Use the DISPLAY STATUS command to monitor the program's status.

When you are using more than one work area for data manipulation operations and for setting up a catalog, you can use the DISPLAY STATUS command to monitor the program's status.

To find out which operations are being performed and which database and catalog are active in the work areas, use the DISPLAY STATUS command (see fig. 5.7).

As you can see from figure 5.7, the database and index files currently being used in all the work areas are described when you execute the DISPLAY STATUS command. The status of the printer and function keys is displayed also.

Linking Database Files

Information in two or more database files can be linked in a number of ways. You can link databases *vertically* by adding records from one database file to another. You can also combine data fields from several database files by linking them horizontally, using the dBASE III Plus RELATION operation.

```
. SELE 1
. USE SOFTWARE INDE SWSTCKNO
. SELE 2
. USE SWSTOCK INDE SKSTCKNO
. DISPLAY STATUS

Select area:  1, Database in Use: C:SOFTWARE.dbf    Alias: SOFTWARE
     Master index file:  C:SWSTCKNO.ndx  Key: STOCK_NO

Currently Selected Database:
Select area:  2, Database in Use: C:SWSTOCK.dbf    Alias: SWSTOCK
     Master index file:  C:SKSTCKNO.ndx  Key: STOCK_NO

Select area: 10, Database in Use: C:CATALOG.CAT    Alias: CATALOG

File search path:
Default disk drive: C:
Print destination: PRN:
Margin =      0
Current work area =    2

Press any key to continue...
```

Fig. 5.7. Monitoring program status with the DISPLAY STATUS command.

Combining Data Records in Two Database Files

Tip:

To combine data records in two database files with an identical structure, use the APPEND FROM command.

The simplest way to combine records in two different database files with an identical file structure is to use the APPEND FROM command. This command adds all the records from the source file to the target file.

For example, if sales data for departments A and B is stored in two database files (SALES_A.DBF and SALES_B.DBF), and the two files share the same file structure, you can combine all the records in SALES_A.DBF and SALES_B.DBF by using the APPEND FROM command:

    . USE SALES_A
    . APPEND FROM SALES_B

The APPEND FROM command adds all the records in the source database file (SALES_B.DBF) to the target file (SALES_A.DBF). As a result, the target file holds the combined records while the source file remains unchanged.

Trick:

Use a new database file to hold combined records.

To combine the records of two database files with an identical file structure and save them in a new file, copy the records of one file to the new file and then use the APPEND FROM command.

When you use the APPEND FROM command to combine records from two database files, all the combined records will reside in the target database file.

There are several ways to create a new database file to hold the combined records. The easiest way is to copy the contents of one database file to a new database file. Then use the APPEND FROM command to add records from the other database file to the new file.

For example, to combine all the records in SALES_A.DBF and SALES_B.DBF and save them in a new database file ALLSALES.DBF, issue the following commands:

```
. USE SALES_A
. COPY TO ALLSALES
. USE ALLSALES
. APPEND FROM SALES_B
```

When you use APPEND FROM to add records from the source database file to the target file, you won't have any problems if the two database files share an identical file structure.

However, if the two database files have different file structures, APPEND FROM adds to the target file only records with fields that are common to both files.

Trap:

Use caution when you use the APPEND FROM command to combine two database files with different file structures.

Only records with fields that are common to both files are added from the source file to the target file when you use the APPEND FROM command.

Figure 5.8 shows two database files with different file structures: one (EMPLOYEE.DBF) has six data fields and the other (ROSTER.DBF) has three data fields.

```
, USE EMPLOYEE
, DISP STRUC
Structure for database: C:EMPLOYEE.dbf
Number of data records:       18
Date of last update    : 82/16/87
Field  Field Name  Type        Width    Dec
    1  ID_NO       Character      11
    2  FIRST_NAME  Character      15
    3  LAST_NAME   Character      15
    4  POSITION    Character      18
    5  EMPLY_DATE  Date            8
    6  MALE        Logical         1
** Total **                       61

, USE ROSTER
, DISP STRUC
Structure for database: C:ROSTER.dbf
Number of data records:       18
Date of last update    : 82/16/87
Field  Field Name  Type        Width    Dec
    1  FIRST_NAME  Character      15
    2  LAST_NAME   Character      15
    3  POSITION    Character      18
** Total **
```

Fig. 5.8. File structures of the EMPLOYEE.DBF and ROSTER.DBF files.

Because the structure of the source database file (EMPLOYEE.DBF) and the target file (ROSTER.DBF) is different, only some of the fields from the source file's records are added to the target file when you execute the following commands:

. USE ROSTER
. APPEND FROM EMPLOYEE

In figure 5.9, the records that have been added from the EMPLOYEE.DBF file to the ROSTER.DBF file contain only those data fields that are common to both files.

```
, USE ROSTER
, APPE FROM EMPLOYEE
      18 records added
, LIST
Record#  FIRST_NAME      LAST_NAME        POSITION
      1  Thomas T.       Smith            President
      2  Tina Y.         Thompson         VP
      3  Peter F.        Watson           Manager
      4  Doris Y.        Taylor           Sales Rep
      5  Tyrone T.       Thorsen          Engineer
      6  Cathy J.        Faust            Secretary
      7  Vincent M.      Corso            Sales Rep
      8  Jane W.         Kaiser           Accountant
      9  Tina K.         Davidson         Trainee
     18  James J.        Smith            Trainee
```

Fig. 5.9. Append records from EMPLOYEE.DBF to ROSTER.DBF.

To add records selectively from one database file to another, include a qualifier in the APPEND FROM command, as in the following example:

    . USE OFFICERS
    . APPEND FROM EMPLOYEE FOR POSITION="President" .OR.
    POSITION="VP"

In this example, the data field POSITION is used to select those records in the source file that meet the qualifying conditions for the append operation.

Trap:

If the search field is not common to both database files, no record will be appended and an error message will appear.

You cannot add the records of all the male employees in EMPLOYEE.DBF to ROSTER.DBF (their structures are shown in fig. 5.8) by using the following commands:

    . USE ROSTER
    . APPEND FROM EMPLOYEE FOR MALE

Because the target file (ROSTER.DBF) is active and the field "MALE" is not one of its data fields, the field is treated as an undefined variable. A Variable not found error message appears and the append operation halts.

Trap:

You can't use a logical field as a condition for appending a data record.

When you use a logical field or logical memory variable, the value of the field or variable must be either .T. or .F. Because the value of .T. or .F. is not considered a character string, you cannot use it in a FOR qualifier in a dBASE III Plus command for evaluating a logical field or variable.

For example, the value specified for the logical field MALE in the following APPEND and LIST commands will not be evaluated correctly:

    . USE MALES
    . APPEND FROM EMPLOYEE FOR MALE=.T.
    . LIST FOR MALE=.T.

The correct method is

    . USE MALES
    . APPEND FROM EMPLOYEE FOR MALE
    . LIST FOR MALE

Filtering Out Deleted Records

Trick:

Before appending records from one database file to another, use SET DELETED ON to filter selected records.

With the APPEND operation, one way to screen records in the source file before adding them to a target file is to mark unwanted records temporarily with deletion marks.

To mark selected records, you can use any legitimate qualifying condition in the DELETE command. For example, if you want to add to the ROSTER.DBF database file only the EMPLOYEE.DBF records for male employees, you should first mark with deletion marks the records for female employees. As you can see from figure 5.10, the records are marked with asterisks.

```
. USE EMPLOYEE
. DELE FOR .NOT. MALE
      5 records deleted
. LIST
Record#   ID_NO        FIRST_NAME    LAST_NAME     POSITION    EMPLY_DATE MALE
      1   123-45-6789 Thomas T.      Smith         President   03/01/81   .T.
      2  *254-63-5691 Tina Y.        Thompson      VP          09/22/82   .F.
      3   467-34-6789 Peter F.       Watson        Manager     10/12/82   .T.
      4  *732-08-4589 Doris Y.       Taylor        Sales Rep   08/14/83   .F.
      5   563-55-8900 Tyrone T.      Thorsen       Engineer    06/20/82   .T.
      6  *023-46-6213 Cathy J.       Faust         Secretary   04/15/83   .F.
      7   554-34-7893 Vincent M.     Corso         Sales Rep   07/20/84   .T.
      8  *321-65-9087 Jane W.        Kaiser        Accountant  11/22/82   .F.
      9  *560-56-9321 Tina K.        Davidson      Trainee     05/16/86   .F.
     10   435-54-9876 James J.       Smith         Trainee     01/23/86   .T.
```

Fig. 5.10. Marking with a qualifier those records to be deleted.

Then issue the SET DELETED ON command to filter out the marked records. Because all the marked records will be ignored by most dBASE III commands, including the APPEND FROM command, only the unmarked EMPLOYEE.DBF records are appended to the ROSTER.DBF file (see fig. 5.11).

As you can see from figure 5.11, executing the SET DELETED ON command excludes the marked records from the LIST and APPEND FROM commands. As a result, only the five unmarked records are appended by the APPEND FROM command.

After appending the records, issue the RECALL ALL command to remove the temporary deletion marks.

```
. SET DELETED ON
. LIST
Record#  ID_NO        FIRST_NAME    LAST_NAME    POSITION   EMPLY_DATE MALE
      1  123-45-6789 Thomas T.      Smith        President  03/01/81   .T.
      3  467-34-6789 Peter F.       Watson       Manager    10/12/82   .T.
      5  563-55-8900 Tyrone T.      Thorsen      Engineer   06/20/82   .T.
      7  554-34-7893 Vincent M.     Corso        Sales Rep  07/20/84   .T.
     10  435-54-9876 James J.       Smith        Trainee    01/23/86   .T.

. USE ROSTER
. APPE FROM EMPLOYEE
     5 records added
```

Fig. 5.11. Hiding deleted records from the APPEND operation.

Trap:

If you forget to SET DELETED OFF, marked records cannot be displayed.

After using the SET DELETED ON command, remember to issue the SET DELETED OFF command. Otherwise, the records you marked for deletion will be hidden from view when you issue the LIST, DISPLAY, or BROWSE commands.

Merging Data Fields from Two Database Files

Trick:

To combine data fields from two different databases, use the JOIN command.

If you want to form a new database by combining some or all of the data fields in two database files, use the JOIN command. The JOIN command lets you merge data fields from two database files by using a linking field to find the values common to both database files.

For example, software product information is stored in SOFTWARE.DBF and inventory data is saved in the SWSTOCK.DBF database file. The file structures of these files are shown in figure 5.12. To create an inventory list that contains some of the data fields from both files, use the STOCK_NO as the linking field in the JOIN command.

```
. USE SOFTWARE
. DISP STRUC
Structure for database: C:SOFTWARE.dbf
Number of data records:       10
Date of last update    : 02/15/87
Field  Field Name  Type        Width    Dec
    1  STOCK_NO    Character        9
    2  DSCRIPTION  Character       20
    3  TYPE        Character       20
    4  COST        Numeric          7     2
    5  PRICE       Numeric          7     2
** Total **                       64

. USE SWSTOCK
. DISP STRUC
Structure for database: C:SWSTOCK.dbf
Number of data records:       10
Date of last update    : 02/15/87
Field  Field Name  Type        Width    Dec
    1  STOCK_NO    Character        9
    2  ON_HAND     Numeric          3
    3  ON_ORDER    Numeric          3
** Total **
```

Fig. 5.12. File structures of the SOFTWARE.DBF and SWSTOCK.DBF files.

The method for using the JOIN command follows:

. SELECT 1
. USE <name of file to be joined>
. INDEX <on the linking field> TO <name of index file>
. SELECT 2
. USE <name of the active database>
. INDEX <on the linking field> TO <name of index file>
. JOIN WITH <ALIAS of the file to be joined>
   TO <new file>
   FOR <joining condition>
   FIELDS <list of merged fields>

If the database file has been indexed with an existing index file, you can replace the USE and INDEX commands with one command:

. USE <name of file> INDEX <name of the existing index file>

The joining operation examines each record in the active file and tries to match the records in the joined file according to the value of the linking field. If a match is found, the values in the records of the two files are merged to form a record in the new database file.

The two files you want to join must first be indexed on their linking fields. As you can see from figure 5.13, the database files are indexed on the STOCK_NO linking field. The fields that are to be created in the new database file (SWINVTRY.DBF) are specified with the FIELDS clause.

```
. SELE 1
. INDE ON STOCK_NO TO SWSTCKNO
  100% indexed            10 Records indexed
. SELE 2
. USE SWSTOCK
. INDE ON STOCK_NO TO SKSTCKNO
  100% indexed            10 Records indexed
. JOIN WITH A TO SWINVTRY FOR STOCK_NO=A->STOCK_NO FIELDS STOCK_NO,A->DSCRIPTION
,ON_HAND,COST
      10 records joined
```

Fig. 5.13. Joining records in the SOFTWARE.DBF and SWSTOCK.DBF files.

The two database files are then joined by using the linking field in the JOIN command. The records resulting from the joining operation are saved in the SWINVTRY.DBF file, whose contents are shown in figure 5.14. Notice that SWINVTRY.DBF contains data fields from both the SOFTWARE.DBF and SWSTOCK.DBF files.

```
. USE SWINVTRY
. LIST
Record#  STOCK_NO  DSCRIPTION            ON_HAND    COST
      1  ANS-DB110 Paradox v1.1               1   425.00
      2  ASH-DB300 dBASE III Plus v1.01       4   395.00
      3  AST-FW200 Framework v2.0             3   345.00
      4  BOL-PA300 Turbo Pascal v3.0          3    39.50
      5  CLP-DB100 Clipper DB Compiler        2   450.00
      6  LOT-L0123 Lotus 1-2-3 Release2       5   289.00
      7  MIC-QB100 Microsoft QuickBasic       4    79.00
      8  MIC-WS330 WordStar v3.30             3   229.00
      9  MIS-WD300 Microsoft Word v3.0        2   229.00
     10  WOR-DB100 WordTech DB Compiler       2   469.00
```

Fig. 5.14. Displaying the joined records.

Trap:

To avoid confusion with ALIAS names, do not use the single letters A through M as names for database files to be joined.

When you link database files with the JOIN command, *do not* use the single letters A through M as names for database files to be joined. These letters are reserved for ALIAS names. In general, do not use single-letter names for database files.

Merging Data Fields in Multiple Database Files

Trick:

To merge data fields from more than two database files, perform the join operations in sequence.

Because you can join only two database files at one time, you need to perform the file-joining operation more than once if you want to combine database fields from several database files.

To merge fields in three database files (FILE_A.DBF, FILE_B.DBF, and FILE_C.DBF), for example, follow these steps:

```
. SELECT 1
. USE FILE_A
. INDEX ON . . .
. SELECT 2
. USE FILE_B
. INDEX ON . . .
. JOIN WITH A TO TEMP FOR . . .
. USE TEMP
. INDEX ON . . .
. SELECT 1
. USE FILE_C
. INDEX ON . . .
. JOIN WITH B TO NEWFILE FOR . . .
. CLOSE DATABASE
. ERASE TEMP.DBF
```

Tip:

Allocate sufficient disk space before you join files.

When you join files, the resulting database file may contain many records. Before carrying out the JOIN operations, be sure to provide enough disk space for saving the resulting file.

When you join two database files, the number of records in the resulting database depends on the the number of unique records in the two database files. If each record in the active file matches only one record in the joining file according to the value in the linking field, the new database file that results will contain the same number of records as the active file. However, if a record in the active file matches several records in the joining file, the new database file will contain many more records than the active file.

Relating Data in Two Database Files

Tip:

When you need to access data simultaneously in multiple database files, use the SET RELATION TO command to link the files.

You can save time and disk space when you need to access data simultaneously in multiple database files. Link the files with the SET RELATION TO command instead of joining them in a permanent file.

Because joining two database files is time-consuming and the database file created by the JOIN command may take up a great deal of disk space, the JOIN command may not be appropriate for many applications. Unless you need to create a permanent database file for holding the combined records, the JOIN command is an extremely inefficient way to merge the data fields from two database files.

You may need to access information from more than one database file during a single operation. To access these files simultaneously, you can merge them temporarily with the SET RELATION TO command. The records in the individual files are saved back to the disk rather than to a new database file.

Relating one database file to another is similar to joining files. To relate two database files based on a key field, use the following sequence of commands:

. SELECT 1
. USE <name of file to be related>
. INDEX ON <the key field> TO <name of index file>
. SELECT 2
. USE <name of active file>
. INDEX ON <the key field> TO <name of index file>
. SET RELATION TO <key field>
INTO <ALIAS of file to be related>

If the database file has already been indexed and has an existing index file, you can combine the USE and INDEX commands into one command:

. USE <name of file> INDEX <name of the existing index file>

Use the SET FILTER TO command to specify the condition for record selection. Only records that meet the filter condition are included in the relation operation.

After using the SET RELATION TO command to relate the two files, you can select the data fields you want to access. As shown in figure 5.15, the combined fields are displayed when you list the records.

```
. SELE 1
. USE SOFTWARE INDEX SWSTCKNO
. SELE 2
. USE SWSTOCK INDEX SKSTCKNO
. SELE 1
. SET RELATION TO STOCK_NO INTO B
. SET FIELDS TO STOCK_NO,DSCRIPTION,COST,B->ON_HAND
. SET FILTER TO COST>=200
. LIST
Record#  STOCK_NO  DSCRIPTION              COST ON_HAND
      2  ANS-DB110 Paradox v1.1           425.00      1
      1  ASH-DB300 dBASE III Plus v1.01   395.00      4
      8  AST-FW200 Framework v2.0         345.00      3
      3  CLP-DB100 Clipper DB Compiler    450.00      2
      5  LOT-L0123 Lotus 1-2-3 Release2   289.00      5
      6  MIC-WS330 WordStar v3.30         229.00      3
      7  MIS-WD300 Microsoft Word v3.0    229.00      2
      4  WOR-DB100 WordTech DB Compiler   469.00      2
```

Fig. 5.15. Linking SOFTWARE.DBF and SWSTOCK.DBF with the SET RELATION TO operation.

In addition to LIST, you can use DISPLAY, EDIT, and BROWSE to manipulate the contents of records that contain merged fields.

At this point you can define and invoke a custom data-entry form for the combined data fields by using the SET FORMAT TO command.

Trap:

Because related files are merged temporarily, closing them erases the merged data fields.

It is important to note that when two database files are related in this way, no new data records are created. The data fields are merged only temporarily for the LIST, DISPLAY, EDIT, and BROWSE operations. If you close all the database files in the work areas 1 and 2, records containing the merged data fields are erased.

Trick:

To save information from related database files, create a view file.

Once defined, the relation between the database files can be saved in a view file for later use.

For example, you can save the relation between the SOFTWARE.DBF and SWSTOCK.DBF files by using the CREATE VIEW . . . FROM ENVIRONMENT command:

. CREATE VIEW SWFILES.VUE FROM ENVIRONMENT

Tip:

To relate previously related database files, save time and work by setting up the view file.

Once you save the relation information in a view file, you can repeat the RELATE operation by setting up the view file:

. SET VIEW TO <name of existing view file>

You don't have to enter the commands for selecting, indexing, and relating the files.

For example, when you issue the SET VIEW TO SWFILES command, the SOFTWARE.DBF and SWSTOCK.DBF files are again related according to the procedure described in the view file (see fig. 5.16).

The CLOSE ALL command closes all the database files and clears all the work areas. The LIST command verifies that no database file is in use. By selecting a view file (SWFILES.VUE) with the SET VIEW TO command, you relink the database files from the information contained in the view file. Then, with the LIST command, display the records from the related SOFTWARE.DBF and SWSTOCK.DBF files.

```
. CLOSE ALL
. LIST
No database is in USE. Enter file name:

. SET VIEW TO SWFILES
. LIST
Record#  STOCK_NO  DSCRIPTION              COST  ON_HAND
     2   ANS-DB110 Paradox v1.1           425.00      1
     1   ASH-DB300 dBASE III Plus v1.01   395.00      4
     8   AST-FW200 Framework v2.0         345.00      3
     3   CLP-DB100 Clipper DB Compiler    450.00      2
     5   LOT-L0123 Lotus 1-2-3 Release2   289.00      5
     6   MIC-WS330 WordStar v3.30         229.00      3
     7   MIS-WD300 Microsoft Word v3.0    229.00      2
     4   WOR-DB100 WordTech DB Compiler   469.00      2

.
```

Fig. 5.16. Relinking the database file by activating the view file.

Tip:

To relate database files with no common key field, use RECNO( ) as a key field.

If the two database files do not share a common key field, you can link the files with their record numbers (RECNO()). Simply use the RECNO() function in place of a key field in the SET RELATION TO command:

. SET RELATION TO RECNO() INTO . . .

As a result, because the records from both files are matched by their sequential record numbers, you do not need to index the files before you relate them:

. SELECT 1
. USE FILE_A
. SELECT 2
. USE FILE_B
. SELECT 1
. SET RELATION TO RECNO() INTO B

Relating Multiple Database Files

To relate more than two database files, create a continuous linking chain.

You can simultaneously access data fields from more than two files. To do so, create a relation chain that links the files through a common index field or by record number.

First put the master file in work area 1 and each of the other database files in a separate work area.

If you want to relate the files by a key data field (KEYFIELD), you must first index all but the master file:

```
. USE DBFILE2
. INDEX ON KEYFIELD TO NDXFILE2
. USE DBFILE3
. INDEX ON KEYFIELD TO NDXFILE3

. . . . .

. . . . .
. SELECT 1
. USE DBFILE1
. SELECT 2
. USE DBFILE2 INDEX NDXFILE2
. SELECT 3
. USE DBFILE3 INDEX NDXFILE3

. . . . .

. . . . .

. . . . .
```

The relation chain begins with the master file. Each of the other database files is linked in subsequent steps:

```
. SELECT 1
. SET RELATION TO KEYFIELD INTO DBFILE2
. SELECT 2
. SET RELATION TO KEYFIELD INTO DBFILE3

. . . . .

. . . . .
```

Figure 5.17 shows how to relate three database files: HWLIST.DBF (the master file), HWCOST.DBF, and HWSTOCK.DBF.

As you can see from figure 5.17, the three files are related in two steps. First, the HWLIST.DBF file is linked with the

HWCOST.DBF file. The HWSTOCK.DBF file is then related to the linked files.

After you index the files on the common data field STOCK_NO, you relate the master file HWLIST.DBF in work area 1 to HWCOST.DBF in work area 2 (alias B). Finally, you add the third database file HWSTOCK.DBF in work area 3 (alias C) to the relation chain. You use the LIST command to display the selected fields of the records resulting from the relation operations.

```
. SELE 1
. USE HWLIST
. SELE 2
. USE HWCOST INDE HCSTCKNO
. SELE 3
. USE HWSTOCK INDE HSSTCKNO
. SELE 1
. SET RELATION TO STOCK_NO INTO B
. SELE 2
. SET RELATION TO STOCK_NO INTO C
. SELE 1
. SET FIELDS TO STOCK_NO,DSCRIPTION,B->COST,C->ON_HAND
. LIST
Record#   STOCK_NO  DSCRIPTION                              COST ON_HAND
       1  CPQ-SP256 COMPAQ 256, desk top, 512K RAM       1359.00       3
       2  ZEN-SL181 Zenith Z-181 lap top, 640K RAM       1695.00       5
       3  IBM-AT640 IBM AT 640K, 1.2MB FD + 20MB         3790.00       4
       4  ZEN-MM012 Zenith monochrome monitor              89.00       2
       5  NEC-PC660 NEC 660 printer                        560.00      10
       6  HAY-M1200 Hayes 1200 BAUD internal modem        269.00       5
       7  SEA-HD020 Seagate 20MB internal harddisk        398.00       2
       8  IOM-HD040 Iomega Bernoulli 20+20 system        2190.00       4
       9  PAR-GC100 Paradise CGA graphic card             279.00      10
      10  HER-GC100 Hercules monochrome card              199.00       6
```

Fig. 5.17. Relating more than two database files.

Tip:

To avoid having to index files, link multiple database files by record number.

If you link files by record number, you won't need to index the files before beginning the relation chain.

Link the files with the following sequence of commands:

```
. SELECT 1
. USE DBFILE1
. SELECT 2
. USE DBFILE2
. SELECT 3
. USE DBFILE3
```

```
. . . . .
. . . . .
. SELECT 1
. SET RELATION TO RECNO( ) INTO DBFILE2
. SELECT 2
. SET RELATION TO RECNO( ) INTO DBFILE3
. . . . .
. . . . .
```

Trap:

A circular relation chain is not allowed.

One important point to remember in relating database files is that you are not allowed to create a circular relation chain in which the last database file is linked back to the master file.

Trap:

You can't save records that contain data fields from more than one work area.

When you relate two database files, the contents of these files are held in two different work areas (such as 1 and 2). The active data fields for these files are specified by the SET FIELDS TO command. Because each of these work areas contains only the data fields of *one* database file, you cannot save to a database file the set of records that contains data fields from more than one work area.

Trick:

To relate multiple database files quickly and easily, create a view file from the Assistant menu.

Most users prefer to relate two or more database files by selecting a set of options from the Assistant menu.

Because this approach allows you to view on your screen all the databases, their index files, and data fields, you don't have to remember their names and file structures when you relate them. And you can enter the filter condition and the key field directly from the keyboard.

To merge the data fields in the SOFTWARE.DBF and SWSTOCK.DBF files, for example, you can select a series of menu options from the Assistant menu. (The process is illustrated in detail by the screen displays in figs. 5.18 through 5.25.)

As you can see from figure 5.18, you define the name of the view file (SWFILES.VUE) by choosing the **Create/View** options.

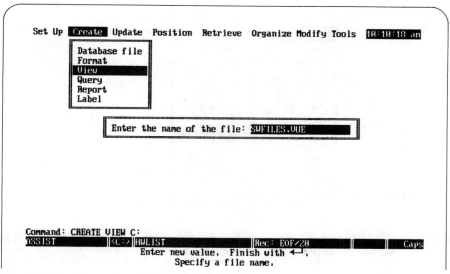

Fig. 5.18. Creating a view file from the Assistant menu.

Then you choose the **Set Up** option to set up and index the database files (see fig. 5.19 and fig. 5.20).

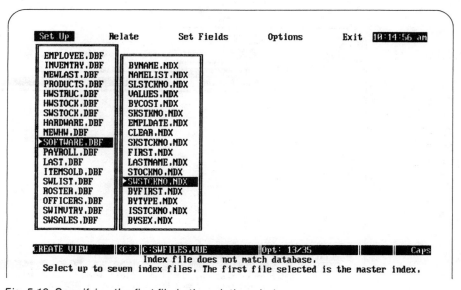

Fig. 5.19. Specifying the first file in the relation chain.

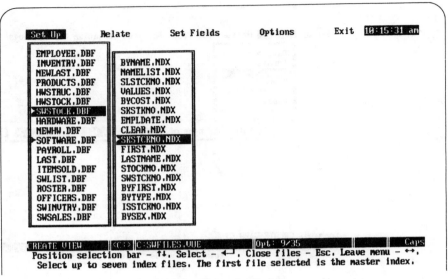

Fig. 5.20. Specifying the file to be related to the first file.

Selecting the Assistant menu's **Relate** option, as shown in
figure 5.21, defines the linking field (STOCK_NO) for relating
the files.

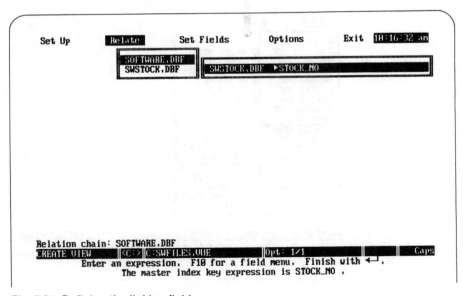

Fig. 5.21. Defining the linking field.

To specify selected data fields from the two database files that are being related, choose the **Set Fields** option (see figs. 5.22 and 5.23).

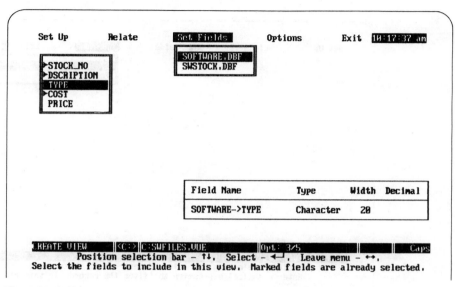

Fig. 5.22. Selecting the fields to be linked from the first file.

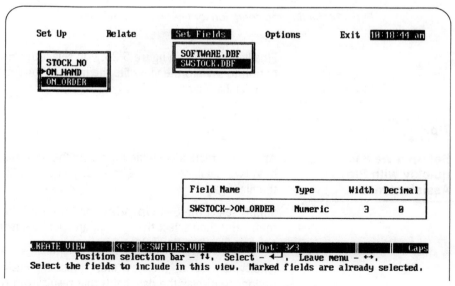

Fig. 5.23. Selecting the fields to be linked from the second file.

You can use a filter condition (such as COST>=200) if you want to select only certain records. Select **Options** and define the filter (see fig. 5.24).

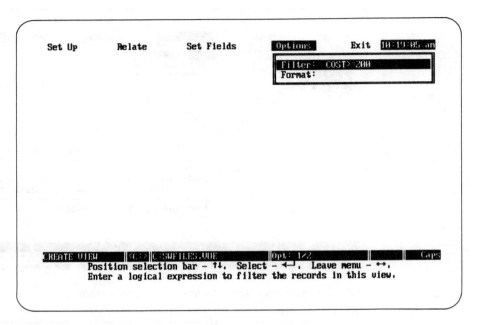

Fig. 5.24. Setting the condition for filtering data records.

Finally, as shown in figure 5.25, you select the **Exit/Save** option to save to the view file the information for relating the two database files.

Tip:

Set up a view file quickly with the Assistant menu.

After you create a view file for saving the information about how two databases files are related, you can set it up to relate the files again.

Simply select the **Set Up/View** options from the Assistant menu and then select the appropriate view file from the list of existing files (see fig. 5.26).

After you've set up the view file, choose the **Retrieve/List** options to display the data fields that result from relating the two database files (see fig. 5.27).

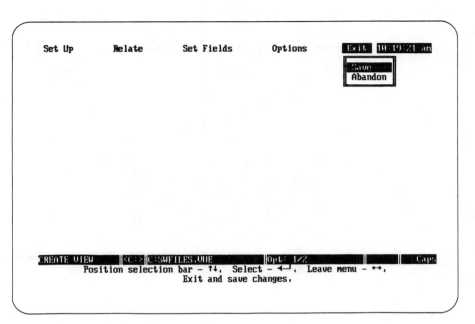

Fig. 5.25. Saving the view file to disk.

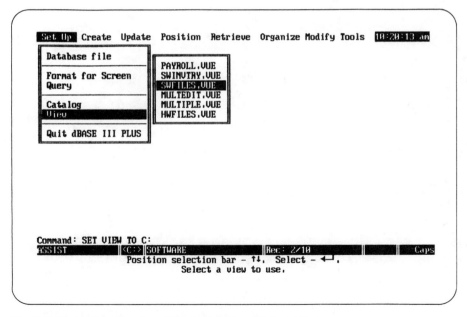

Fig. 5.26. Selecting the view file to relink the database files.

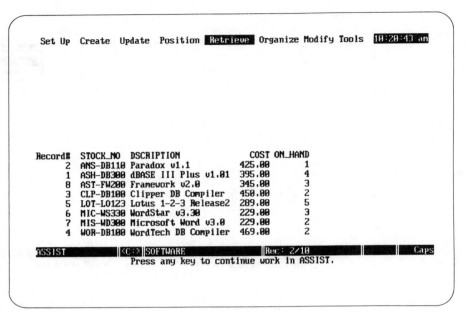

Fig. 5.27. Display records that result from relating the two database files.

6

Sorting and Indexing Data

This chapter focuses on ways to make the most of the sorting and indexing capabilities provided by dBASE III Plus. Although the processes are similar, differences in design philosophy impose different restrictions. Each operation has its own strengths and weaknesses. The tips, tricks, and traps discussed here will help you to take advantage of their strengths and circumvent their restrictions.

Sorting versus Indexing

Tip:

Understand the basic SORT command.

You can use SORT to arrange data records in ascending or descending order, depending on the value of a sorting key. The rearranged or sorted records then are saved in a new database file.

The format of the SORT command is

. SORT ON <key fields> TO <name of sorted file>

or

. SORT TO <name of sorted file> ON <key fields>

Both are used in the following example:

. USE EMPLOYEE
. SORT ON LAST_NAME TO SORTED
. SORT TO ROSTER ON LAST_NAME,FIRST_NAME

Tip:

Understand the basic INDEX command.

Indexing arranges the records in a database file according to the value of the indexing key. The indexing key can be a single key field, a set of key fields, or an expression.

The format of the INDEX command is

. INDEX ON <the indexing key> TO <name of index file>

or

. INDEX TO <name of index file> ON <the indexing key>

Both are used in the following example:

. USE SOFTWARE
. INDEX ON STOCK_NO TO SWSTCKNO
. INDEX ON STOCK_NO+TYPE TO TEMP
. INDEX TO SWCOST ON COST
. INDEX TO SWPROFIT ON (PRICE–COST)

Tip:

Indexing is usually a better approach than sorting for organizing data records.

- Indexing is much faster than sorting. And you can find a record much faster in an indexed file than in a sorted file.

- Index files take up much less disk storage space than sorted files.

- Changes made to records in an indexed database file automatically update its corresponding, active index file.

- Indexed files can be linked with the SET RELATION operation. Their records can be accessed simultaneously with a view file.

- Arithmetic expressions can be used as indexing keys.

Tip:

The sorting operation provides a few functions that indexing does not.

With SORT you can organize your data records by using more than one field as the sorting key (SORT ON PRICE, COST TO . . .). You must specify multiple fields as an expression (INDEX ON PRICE–COST TO . . .) in an indexing operation.

Sorting also creates a database file to hold the sorted records. Indexing does not.

Tip:

To arrange records with a single key field, use the INDEX command.

When you use a single data field as the key for arranging the records in a database file, you can use either SORT or INDEX. Records sequenced by either method are arranged in the same order.

Using STOCK_NO as the key field, you could use the following SORT operation:

. USE SOFTWARE
. SORT ON STOCK_NO TO SORTED

to arrange the records in the SOFTWARE.DBF file.

But the indexing operation:

. INDEX ON STOCK_NO TO SWSTCKNO

takes less time and disk storage space.

The major difference is that SORT saves the sorted records in a .DBF file, which takes up more disk space than an index file.

Trap:

INDEX does not produce a database file for sorted records.

If you need to create such a database file, you can copy the indexed records to a database file.

Trick:

Create a file for indexed records.

To create a database file for indexed records, simply follow these steps:

. USE <name of database file>
. INDEX ON . . . TO . . .
. COPY TO <name of the database file for saving the ordered records>

Using the data from the preceding example:

. USE SOFTWARE
. INDEX ON STOCK_NO TO SWSTCKNO
. COPY TO SORTED

Tip:

Use the INDEX command to sequence records with multiple character key fields.

You can specify several character fields as separate key fields in a SORT command or as an expression in an INDEX command. Either procedure arranges data records in the same order.

If you want to order the records in the EMPLOYEE.DBF file, for example, you can use either method.

Indexing with the following commands:

. USE EMPLOYEE
. INDEX ON LAST_NAME+FIRST_NAME TO BYNAMES

is much faster and takes up less storage space than sorting does:

. USE EMPLOYEE
. SORT ON LAST_NAME, FIRST_NAME TO ROSTER

Sorting Records with Multiple Numeric Key Fields

Trap:

When you use multiple numeric fields as keys for arranging records, the results you get with SORT and INDEX can be quite different.

If you use more than one numeric field as a key for arranging records with SORT, the fields must be specified as separate sorting keys. With INDEX, the fields must be combined as an arithmetic expression.

You can, for example, arrange the records in the SALEITEM.DBF file. Figure 6.1 shows what happens with both sorting and indexing. Each operation arranges the records in a different order.

```
. USE SALEITEM
. SORT ON PRICE,COST TO SORTED
  100% Sorted            4 Records sorted
. USE SORTED
. LIST
Record#   STOCK_NO   PRICE    COST
      1   A1001      100.00   80.00
      2   A1002      100.00   90.00
      3   A1003      110.00   60.00
      4   A1004      120.00   50.00

. USE SALEITEM
. INDEX ON PRICE+COST TO VALUES
  100% indexed           4 Records indexed
. LIST
Record#   STOCK_NO   PRICE    COST
      3   A1003      110.00   60.00
      4   A1004      120.00   50.00
      1   A1001      100.00   80.00
      2   A1002      100.00   90.00
```

Fig. 6.1. Rearranging data records, using multiple numeric fields as a key.

You can sort the records with PRICE as the primary sorting field and COST as the secondary sorting field. You use the following commands:

    . USE SALEITEM
    . SORT ON PRICE,COST TO SORTED

SORT arranges the records in two ways: by the values in the PRICE field and then by the values in the COST field (see fig. 6.1).

To index these same records, you must combine the two fields in the form of an expression. Then use the expression as an indexing key in the INDEX command:

. USE SALEITEM
. INDEX ON PRICE+COST TO VALUES

As you can see in figure 6.1, records are arranged in ascending order by the combined value of PRICE+COST.

Indexing Records in Descending Order with a Numeric Field

INDEX always arranges data records in ascending order (from the smallest to the largest). Unlike the SORT command's /D operator, INDEX provides no means to arrange records in descending order.

Trick:

To arrange data records in descending order with a numeric field, use its negative value as the index key.

If you use a numeric field as the indexing field, you can put the records in descending order. To do so, index the file on the negative value of the key field. The procedure is shown in figure 6.2.

As you can see in figure 6.2, the records are arranged quite differently with COST and −COST as the index keys.

```
. USE SALEITEM
. INDEX ON COST TO BYCOST
    100% indexed           4 Records indexed
. LIST
Record#  STOCK_NO   PRICE     COST
      4  A1004      120.00    50.00
      3  A1003      110.00    60.00
      1  A1001      100.00    80.00
      2  A1002      100.00    90.00

. INDEX ON -COST TO BYCOST
    100% indexed           4 Records indexed
. LIST
Record#  STOCK_NO   PRICE     COST
      2  A1002      100.00    90.00
      1  A1001      100.00    80.00
      3  A1003      110.00    60.00
      4  A1004      120.00    50.00
```

Fig. 6.2. Indexing, using the negative value of a numeric field as a key.

Using a Date Key Field To Arrange Records in Descending Order

You can use a date field as a key for arranging data records with both SORT and INDEX. With SORT, the records can be arranged in either ascending or descending order. With INDEX, however, records are always arranged in ascending order.

Sorting Records Chronologically

Tip:

To arrange data records chronologically in descending order, use the SORT command with the /D option.

When you issue the SORT command with a date field as the sort key field, records in the active database file are arranged in ascending order by default (see fig. 6.3).

To arrange records in descending order according to the values in a date field, include the /D operator in the SORT command (see fig. 6.4).

```
. USE EMPLOYEE
. SORT ON EMPLY_DATE TO SORTED
   100% Sorted          10 Records sorted
. USE SORTED
. LIST ID_NO, LAST_NAME, FIRST_NAME, EMPLY_DATE
Record#  ID_NO        LAST_NAME     FIRST_NAME    EMPLY_DATE
      1  123-45-6789  Smith         Thomas T.     03/01/81
      2  563-55-8900  Thorsen       Tyrone T.     06/20/82
      3  254-63-5691  Thompson      Tina Y.       09/22/82
      4  467-34-6789  Watson        Peter F.      10/12/82
      5  321-65-9087  Kaiser        Jane W.       11/22/82
      6  823-46-6213  Faust         Cathy J.      04/15/83
      7  732-88-4589  Taylor        Doris Y.      08/14/83
      8  554-34-7893  Corso         Vincent M.    07/20/84
      9  435-54-9876  Smith         James J.      01/23/86
     10  560-56-9321  Davidson      Tina K.       05/16/86
```

Fig. 6.3. Sorting records chronologically with a date key field.

```
. USE EMPLOYEE
. SORT ON EMPLY_DATE/D TO SORTED
  100% Sorted          10 Records sorted
. USE SORTED
. LIST ID_NO, LAST_NAME, FIRST_NAME, EMPLY_DATE
Record#  ID_NO        LAST_NAME     FIRST_NAME      EMPLY_DATE
     1   560-56-9321 Davidson      Tina K.         05/16/86
     2   435-54-9876 Smith         James J.        01/23/86
     3   554-34-7893 Corso         Vincent M.      07/20/84
     4   732-08-4589 Taylor        Doris Y.        08/14/83
     5   823-46-6213 Faust         Cathy J.        04/15/83
     6   321-65-9087 Kaiser        Jane W.         11/22/82
     7   467-34-6789 Watson        Peter F.        10/12/82
     8   254-63-5691 Thompson      Tina Y.         09/22/82
     9   563-55-8900 Thorsen       Tyrone T.       06/20/82
    10   123-45-6789 Smith         Thomas T.       03/01/81
```

Fig. 6.4. Sorting records chronologically in descending order.

Indexing Records Chronologically

Trap:

INDEX always arranges records in ascending order.

No matter what type of key you use, INDEX arranges records only in ascending order according to the original value of the key.

For example, when you use a date field as an index key, all the records in the database file are arranged in ascending order. The earliest date is the first record and the most recent date is the last record (see fig. 6.5).

```
. USE EMPLOYEE
. INDEX ON EMPLY_DATE TO EMPLDATE
  100% indexed         10 Records indexed
. LIST ID_NO, LAST_NAME, FIRST_NAME, EMPLY_DATE
Record#  ID_NO        LAST_NAME     FIRST_NAME      EMPLY_DATE
     1   123-45-6789 Smith         Thomas T.       03/01/81
     5   563-55-8900 Thorsen       Tyrone T.       06/20/82
     2   254-63-5691 Thompson      Tina Y.         09/22/82
     3   467-34-6789 Watson        Peter F.        10/12/82
     8   321-65-9087 Kaiser        Jane W.         11/22/82
     6   823-46-6213 Faust         Cathy J.        04/15/83
     4   732-08-4589 Taylor        Doris Y.        08/14/83
     7   554-34-7893 Corso         Vincent M.      07/20/84
    10   435-54-9876 Smith         James J.        01/23/86
     9   560-56-9321 Davidson      Tina K.         05/16/86
```

Fig. 6.5. Indexing records chronologically with a date key field.

Trick:

To arrange records chronologically in descending order with INDEX, convert the date fields to a numeric expression.

After you convert the date field to a numeric expression, use the expression's negative value as the indexing key (see fig. 6.6).

To form the numeric expression used as a key in the indexing operation shown in figure 6.6, follow these steps:

1. Use the DTOC( ) function to convert a date field into a character field.

2. Use the RIGHT( ), LEFT( ), and SUBSTR( ) functions to rearrange and combine the substrings of the character field that correspond to the year, month, and day of the original date fields.

```
. USE EMPLOYEE
. INDEX ON -VAL(RIGHT(DTOC(EMPLY_DATE),2)+LEFT(DTOC(EMPLY_DATE),2)+SUBSTR(DTOC(E
MPLY_DATE),4,2)) TO EMPLDATE
   100% indexed        10 Records indexed
. LIST ID_NO, LAST_NAME, FIRST_NAME, EMPLY_DATE
Record#  ID_NO        LAST_NAME      FIRST_NAME    EMPLY_DATE
      9  560-56-9321 Davidson       Tina K.      05/16/86
     10  435-54-9876 Smith          James J.     01/23/86
      7  554-34-7893 Corso          Vincent M.   07/20/84
      4  732-08-4509 Taylor         Doris Y.     08/14/83
      6  823-46-6213 Faust          Cathy J.     04/15/83
      8  321-65-9087 Kaiser         Jane W.      11/22/82
      3  467-34-6789 Watson         Peter F.     10/12/82
      2  254-63-5691 Thompson       Tina Y.      09/22/82
      5  563-55-8900 Thorsen        Tyrone T.    06/20/82
      1  123-45-6789 Smith          Thomas T.    03/01/81
```

Fig. 6.6. Indexing records chronologically in descending order.

3. Convert the character string into a numeric expression.

4. Use the negative value of the numeric expression as the indexing key.

If you use these steps to convert the date value in record #9 (*05/16/86*) to a key value of *−860516*, for example, and to change the date value of record #10 (*01/23/86*) to *−860123*, INDEX will arrange these records in descending order.

Trick:

To arrange records chronologically in descending order, convert the date to a numeric value.

Another way to arrange records chronologically in descending order is to convert the date to a numeric value that represents the number of days between the date and a future date (such as 12/31/99).

As you can see in figure 6.7, dBASE III Plus lets you compute the number of days between two given dates by taking the difference between these dates. There are 4,977 days between DATE3 (12/31/99) and DATE1 (5/16/86). The figure shows that these dates have been stored as memory variables.

```
. DATE1=CTOD("05/16/86")
05/16/86
. DATE2=CTOD("01/23/86")
01/23/86
. DATE3=CTOD("12/31/99")
12/31/99
. ?"Days between DATE1 and DATE3 =",DATE3-DATE1
Days between DATE1 and DATE3 =        4977
. ?"Days between DATE2 and DATE3 =",DATE3-DATE2
Days between DATE2 and DATE3 =        5090
.
```

Fig. 6.7. Computing the number of days between two dates.

You can arrange the records in EMPLOYEE.DBF chronologically in descending order according to the value in the EMPLY_DATE field. Use the negative value of the number of days between the value in EMPLY_DATE and a future date (see fig. 6.8).

```
. USE EMPLOYEE
. INDEX ON -(EMPLY_DATE - CTOD("12/31/99")) TO EMPLDATE
100% indexed         10 Records indexed
. LIST ID_NO, LAST_NAME, FIRST_NAME, EMPLY_DATE
Record#  ID_NO        LAST_NAME      FIRST_NAME      EMPLY_DATE
     9   560-56-9321 Davidson        Tina K.         05/16/86
    10   435-54-9876 Smith           James J.        01/23/86
     7   554-34-7893 Corso           Vincent M.      07/20/84
     4   732-00-4589 Taylor          Doris Y.        08/14/83
     6   823-46-6213 Faust           Cathy J.        04/15/83
     8   321-65-9087 Kaiser          Jane W.         11/22/82
     3   467-34-6789 Watson          Peter F.        10/12/82
     2   254-63-5691 Thompson        Tina Y.         09/22/82
     5   563-55-8900 Thorsen         Tyrone T.       06/20/82
     1   123-45-6789 Smith           Thomas T.       03/01/81
```

Fig. 6.8. Indexing records chronologically in descending order.

The records in figure 6.8 are ordered according to the negative value of the number of days between December 31, 1999, and the dates in the EMPLY_DATE field. The indexing operation places the record with the earliest employment date at the end of the file because that record has the largest negative value in the index key.

If you use this approach, the expression's future date (*12/31/99*, for example) must be beyond the most recent date in the date field that you index.

Tip:

Use the SET CENTURY ON command to show the century prefix of a date.

If you use *December 31, 2000*, as the future date, be sure to include the century prefix in the future date (*12/31/2000*). Otherwise, as you can see from figure 6.9, the date is treated as *12/31/1900*.

```
. DATEA=CTOD("12/31/1900")
12/31/00
. DATEB=CTOD("12/31/2000")
12/31/00
. ?DATEA, DATEB
12/31/00 12/31/00
. SET CENTURY ON
. ?DATEA, DATEB
12/31/1900 12/31/2000
```

Fig. 6.9. Showing the century prefix in date variables.

Indexing Records in Descending Order on a Character Key

Trick:

To index records in descending order with a character key, use the ASC( ) function to convert the key to a numeric value.

Unfortunately, there is no easy way to convert an alphabetic character string into a numeric value. The only dBASE III Plus function that can be used for this purpose is the ASC( ) function. This built-in function returns the numeric ASCII code of the first character of the string. (Appendix A contains a table of the ASCII codes and characters.)

The numeric value returned by *ASC("Smith")*, for example, is *83*—the ASCII numeric code for the letter *S*.

In some cases, you can arrange data records in descending order with the index operation by using the negative value of the ASC( ) function in the INDEX command (see fig. 6.10).

```
. USE SOFTWARE
. INDE ON -ASC(TYPE) TO BYTYPE
   100% indexed            10 Records indexed
. LIST STOCK_NO,TYPE
Record#  STOCK_NO  TYPE
      6  MIC-WS330 word processing
      7  MIS-WD300 word processing
      5  LOT-LO123 spreadsheet
      9  MIC-QB100 language
     10  BOL-PA300 language
      8  AST-FW200 integrated
      1  ASH-DB300 database
      2  ANS-DB110 database
      3  CLP-DB100 database compiler
      4  WOR-DB100 database compiler
```

Fig. 6.10. Indexing records in descending order with a character key field.

The character strings in the TYPE field shown in figure 6.10 are arranged in descending order.

However, as you can see from figure 6.11, this approach may not always work.

```
. USE EMPLOYEE
. INDEX ON -ASC(FIRST_NAME) TO BYFIRST
   100% indexed            10 Records indexed
. LIST FIRST_NAME
Record#  FIRST_NAME
      7  Vincent M.
      1  Thomas T.
      2  Tina Y.
      5  Tyrone T.
      9  Tina K.
      3  Peter F.
      8  Jane W.
     10  James J.
      4  Doris Y.
      6  Cathy J.
```

Fig. 6.11. Problem of indexing records in descending order with a character key field.

Trick:

Sort the file by using /D in a SORT command.

In figure 6.11, the first names in the EMPLOYEE.DBF file seem to be arranged in descending order if you look only at their first character. But if you study the list, you see that the records are not sorted correctly. For example, *Tina* and *Tyrone* are not in descending order.

The key used in the indexing operation, *−ASC(FIRST_NAME)*, converts only the first character of the string into a numeric value.

To solve this problem, you may have to write a program to index the character field beyond the first character. Writing such a program can be a formidable task.

An easier solution is shown in figure 6.12. Sort the file by using /D in a SORT command.

```
. USE EMPLOYEE
. SORT ON FIRST_NAME/D TO SORTED
  100% Sorted               10 Records sorted
. USE SORTED
. LIST FIRST_NAME
Record#  FIRST_NAME
      1  Vincent M.
      2  Tyrone T.
      3  Tina Y.
      4  Tina K.
      5  Thomas T.
      6  Peter F.
      7  Jane W.
      8  James J.
      9  Doris Y.
     10  Cathy J.
```

Fig. 6.12. Sorting records in descending order.

Indexing a Logical Field

Trick:

To use a logical field as an index key, use the IIF( ) function to convert the key to a character string.

To use a logical field as an indexing key, you must convert the field's value (.T. or .F.) to a character string. Then use that string as a character key in the INDEX command.

To convert the value of a logical field to a character string, use the dBASE III Plus IIF( ) function in the following format:

. IIF(<logical field>, <first expression>,<second expression>)

When the value of the logical field is true (.T.), the IIF( ) function returns the value of the first expression; otherwise, the value of the second expression is returned.

The following function, for example, returns a character string of "Y" if the value of the logical field "MALE" is true:

. IIF (MALE,"Y","N")

If the value of the logical field is false (.F.), the character string "N" is returned.

Figure 6.13 shows how to arrange records in the EMPLOYEE.DBF file. Use the IIF( ) function in the INDEX command, with the logical field MALE in the function argument.

```
. USE EMPLOYEE
. INDEX ON IIF(MALE,"Y","N") TO BYSEX
  100% indexed          10 Records indexed
. LIST ID_NO, LAST_NAME, MALE
Record#  ID_NO       LAST_NAME       MALE
      2  254-63-5691 Thompson        .F.
      4  732-08-4589 Taylor          .F.
      6  823-46-6213 Faust           .F.
      8  321-65-9087 Kaiser          .F.
      9  560-56-9321 Davidson        .F.
      1  123-45-6789 Smith           .T.
      3  467-34-6789 Watson          .T.
      5  563-55-8900 Thorsen         .T.
      7  554-34-7893 Corso           .T.
     10  435-54-9876 Smith           .T.
```

Fig. 6.13. Using a logical field for indexing records.

Or, as shown in figure 6.14, you can use the IIF( ) function to convert the value of the logical field to a numeric value. Then you can use the numeric value to sequence data records with an INDEX command.

```
, USE EMPLOYEE
, INDEX ON IIF(MALE,1,2) TO BYSEX
  100% indexed          10 Records indexed
, LIST ID_NO, LAST_NAME, MALE
Record#  ID_NO        LAST_NAME        MALE
      1  123-45-6789  Smith            ,T,
      3  467-34-6789  Watson           ,T,
      5  563-55-8900  Thorsen          ,T,
      7  554-34-7893  Corso            ,T,
     10  435-54-9876  Smith            ,T,
      2  254-63-5691  Thompson         ,F,
      4  732-88-4589  Taylor           ,F,
      6  823-46-6213  Faust            ,F,
      8  321-65-9887  Kaiser           ,F,
      9  560-56-9321  Davidson         ,F,
```

Fig. 6.14. Another example of using a logical field for indexing records.

Ignoring Case When Sorting or Indexing Character Fields

When you use a character field as a key in a sorting or indexing operation, records in the database file are arranged according to their ASCII order (see Appendix A). The character string's lowercase and uppercase letters are treated differently. As you can see from figure 6.15, first names beginning with a lowercase letter are placed at the end of the list.

```
, USE NAMES
, INDEX ON FIRST_NAME TO FIRST
  100% indexed           10 Records indexed
, LIST
Record#  FIRST_NAME
      6  Cathy J.
      4  Doris Y.
     10  James J.
      8  Jane W.
      3  Peter F.
      1  Thomas T.
      9  Tina K.
      2  Tina Y.
      5  Tyrone T.
      7  Vincent M.
```

Fig. 6.15. Arranging records by lower- and uppercase letters.

Trick:

To ignore case while sorting or indexing a character field, convert the field values to lowercase or uppercase values with the LOWER( ) or UPPER( ) function.

If you want to treat lowercase and uppercase character strings the same, convert the lowercase strings to uppercase by using the UPPER( ) function (see fig. 6.16). Otherwise, your data will be indexed according to case and all lowercase records will follow uppercase records.

When you convert all the characters in the FIRST_NAME field to uppercase letters, case no longer plays a part in the indexing operation. As you can see from figure 6.16, first names are now arranged alphabetically regardless of case.

```
. USE NAMES
. INDEX ON UPPER(FIRST_NAME) TO FIRST
  100% indexed          10 Records indexed
. LIST
Record#  FIRST_NAME
     6  Cathy J.
     4  Doris Y.
    10  James J.
     8  Jane W.
     3  Peter F.
     1  Thomas T.
     9  Tina K.
     2  Tina Y.
     5  Tyrone T.
     7  Vincent M.
```

Fig. 6.16. Arranging records regardless of case.

Ignoring Records with Duplicate Key Field Values

When you index a file with a key field, all the records with key fields that contain the same value are arranged consecutively. As you can see from the first set of records in figure 6.17, for example, records 1 and 4 contain the same name but different addresses.

Trick:

To index records with unique keys, use the SET UNIQUE ON command.

To display each record with unique keys only once, issue the SET UNIQUE ON command before you carry out the indexing operation (see fig. 6.17).

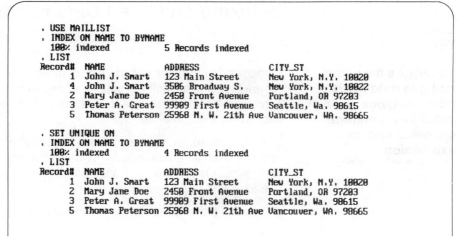

```
. USE MAILLIST
. INDEX ON NAME TO BYNAME
  100% indexed          5 Records indexed
. LIST
Record#  NAME           ADDRESS            CITY_ST
      1  John J. Smart   123 Main Street    New York, N.Y. 10020
      4  John J. Smart   3506 Broadway S.   New York, N.Y. 10022
      2  Mary Jane Doe   2450 Front Avenue  Portland, OR 97203
      3  Peter A. Great  99909 First Avenue Seattle, Wa. 98615
      5  Thomas Peterson 25968 N. W. 21th Ave Vancouver, WA. 98665

. SET UNIQUE ON
. INDEX ON NAME TO BYNAME
  100% indexed          4 Records indexed
. LIST
Record#  NAME           ADDRESS            CITY_ST
      1  John J. Smart   123 Main Street    New York, N.Y. 10020
      2  Mary Jane Doe   2450 Front Avenue  Portland, OR 97203
      3  Peter A. Great  99909 First Avenue Seattle, Wa. 98615
      5  Thomas Peterson 25968 N. W. 21th Ave Vancouver, WA. 98665
```

Fig. 6.17. Indexing records with unique keys with the SET UNIQUE ON command.

Note that when SET UNIQUE ON is in effect, only records with unique values in the key field are displayed.

This approach is handy for eliminating duplicated records from the database and an easy way to update the records in a file. With this method, existing records are ignored when a record with new field values is entered into the file.

Note also that after the SET UNIQUE ON command is executed, the first record with duplicated field values is retained. If you want to use this approach to update your mailing list, for example, be sure to insert the new record at the beginning of the database file.

You can save the updated mailing list to a new file (NEWLIST.DBF) by using the COPY TO command:

. COPY TO NEWLIST

Indexing on Mixed Data Fields

Tip:

To index a file using multiple data fields of different types as an index key, combine the fields into an expression.

If you need to use several data fields of different types as a key for the indexing operation, combine these fields into an expression and then use dBASE III Plus's built-in functions to convert the fields into one type.

In most applications, you can convert all the indexing fields into character fields and include them in a character expression. Or you can use a built-in function to convert a character field into a numeric field.

To convert these fields, use the following built-in functions:

From:	To:	Use:
Numeric	Character	STR( )
Date	Character	DTOC( )
Character	Numeric	VAL( )

To sequence the data records in the SOFTWARE.DBF file in figure 6.18, for example, you can combine a character field (TYPE) and a numeric field (PRICE) as a character expression key in the INDEX command.

```
. USE SOFTWARE
. INDEX ON TYPE+STR(PRICE,6,2) TO BYPRICE
  100% indexed          10 Records indexed
. LIST STOCK_NO, TYPE, PRICE
Record# STOCK_NO  TYPE                    PRICE
      2 ANS-DB110 database               575.00
      1 ASH-DB300 database               595.00
      3 CLP-DB100 database compiler      595.00
      4 WOR-DB100 database compiler      595.00
      8 AST-FW200 integrated             395.00
     10 BOL-PA300 language                69.50
      9 MIC-QB100 language               109.00
      5 LOT-L012: spreadsheet            359.00
      6 MIC-WS330 word processing        269.00
      7 MIS-WD300 word processing        289.00
.
```

Fig. 6.18. Combining character and numeric fields as an index key.

As you can see from figure 6.18, the built-in function STR( ) is used to convert the value of the numeric field PRICE to a character string. Then PRICE is combined with the character field TYPE to form the character expression.

Trap:

Using the YEAR( ), MONTH( ), and DAY ( ) functions to convert a date field into a numeric field causes problems.

Even though you can convert the year, month, and day of a given date to numeric values with the YEAR( ), MONTH( ), and DAY( ) functions, the leading zeros in these values are dropped when you combine these numeric values into a numeric expression (see fig. 6.19).

```
. DATE1=CTOD("04/15/83")
04/15/1983
. ?YEAR(DATE1),MONTH(DATE1),DAY(DATE1)
 1983   4  15
. ?YEAR(DATE1)+MONTH(DATE1)+DAY(DATE1)
  2002
. DATE2=CTOD("10/12/82")
10/12/1982
. ?YEAR(DATE2),MONTH(DATE2),DAY(DATE2)
 1982  10  12
. ?YEAR(DATE2)+MONTH(DATE2)+DAY(DATE2)
  2004
```

Fig. 6.19. Incorrect ways to convert dates to numeric values.

As you can see from figure 6.19, the numeric value *2002* converted from the first date ("04/15/83") is smaller than the value *2004* converted from the second date ("10/12/82"). Therefore, if you use such a numeric expression as a key for indexing, the records in the database file are not arranged correctly (see fig. 6.20).

```
. USE EMPLOYEE
. INDEX ON YEAR(EMPLY_DATE)+MONTH(EMPLY_DATE)+DAY(EMPLY_DATE) TO EMPLDATE
100% indexed         10 Records indexed
. LIST ID_NO, LAST_NAME, FIRST_NAME, EMPLY_DATE
Record#  ID_NO        LAST_NAME      FIRST_NAME     EMPLY_DATE
     1   123-45-6789  Smith          Thomas T.      03/01/1981
     6   823-46-6213  Faust          Cathy J.       04/15/1983
     3   467-34-6789  Watson         Peter F.       10/12/1982
     4   732-08-4589  Taylor         Doris Y.       08/14/1983
     9   560-56-9321  Davidson       Tina K.        05/16/1986
     5   563-55-8900  Thorsen        Tyrone T.      06/20/1982
    10   435-54-9876  Smith          James J.       01/23/1986
     7   554-34-7893  Corso          Vincent M.     07/20/1984
     2   254-63-5691  Thompson       Tina Y.        09/22/1982
     8   321-65-9887  Kaiser         Jane W.        11/22/1982
```

Fig. 6.20. An incorrect way to index records with a date key field.

Tip:

To speed up data manipulation, index a file before using it.

The indexing operation is a powerful tool. If a database file has been indexed on a key field, finding a specific record in that file is much faster than finding the record before you index the file.

Indexing a database file takes time up front, but the amount of time needed to rebuild or reset an index is minimal. And although the index file created by the operation takes up disk and RAM storage space, the amount of space is minimal.

For most applications, the access time saved by using an indexed file is far greater than the time spent indexing the file. Always index a database file before accessing its records.

Using an Index File

Tip:

Always index a database file with an existing index file before accessing the database file.

Before using a database file that has been indexed on a key, use the previously created index file to rearrange the file's records. You don't need to index the file from scratch.

To use an existing index file to rearrange the records in a database file, include the INDEX keyword in the USE command:

. USE <name of database file> INDEX <name of existing index file>

For example, after you have indexed the SOFTWARE.DBF file and created the SWSTCKNO.NDX file, you can use the index file to rearrange the records in the database file:

. USE SOFTWARE INDEX SWSTCKNO

If the database file contains many records, the preceding command is a speedy alternative to the following two commands:

. USE SOFTWARE
. INDEX ON STOCK_NO TO SWSTCKNO

Using the Wrong Index File

If you use the wrong index file to index a database file, some or all of the records in that database file will not be shown.

Before you issue the USE .. INDEX command to index a database file with an existing index file, be careful to identify the correct index file. If you use the wrong index file, two scenarios are possible. In the less severe case, the index operation is not carried out and you are warned with an error message. In the more severe case, some or all data records are excluded without warning. The greatest loss occurs when the indexing key used in the wrong index file is present in the database file you want to index.

For example, if you mistakenly use the index file SWSTCKNO.NDX (created by using the STOCK_NO key field when you indexed SOFTWARE.DBF) to index EMPLOYEE.DBF:

. USE EMPLOYEE INDEX SWSTCKNO

dBASE III Plus returns an error message:

Index file does not match database.

and stops the indexing operation because EMPLOYEE.DBF does not contain the index key field STOCK_NO.

However, if the index key used to create the correct index file happens to have the same name as a field in the file you want to index, you will have problems. dBASE III Plus can't tell which is the right database file. As a result, the information in the wrong index file will be used to sort the records in the database file. The results of such an operation are unpredictable. As you can see in figure 6.21, some records can be lost.

To keep track of the correct index files for a database file, catalog the disk files.

One of the powerful functions of a file catalog is that it keeps track of all database files and their associated index (.NDX), format (.FMT), label (.LBL), and form (.FRM) files.

While you're using a database file, you can use the query operator (?) to find the name of its associated files in a particular operation.

```
. USE SALEITEM
. LIST
Record#  STOCK_NO  DSCRIPTION              TYPE                COST    PRICE
      1  ASH-DB300 dBASE III Plus v1.01 database             395.00  595.00
      2  CLP-DB100 Clipper DB Compiler    database compiler   450.00  595.00
      3  AST-FW200 Framework v2.0         integrated          345.00  349.00
      4  MIC-QB100 Microsoft QuickBasic   language             79.00  109.00
      5  LOT-LO123 Lotus 1-2-3 v2.0       spreadsheet         289.00  359.00
      6  MIC-WS330 WordStar v3.30         word processing     229.00  269.00

. USE SALEITEM INDEX SWSTCKNO
. LIST
Record#  STOCK_NO  DSCRIPTION              TYPE                COST    PRICE
      2  CLP-DB100 Clipper DB Compiler    database compiler   450.00  595.00
      1  ASH-DB300 dBASE III Plus v1.01 database             395.00  595.00

.
```

Fig. 6.21. Effects of using the wrong index file.

To find the names of all index files you've created for indexing a given database file, for example, issue the SET INDEX TO ? command:

. SET CATALOG TO SOFTWARE
. USE SOFTWARE
. SET INDEX TO ?

In response to the query operator (?), all the index files related to the SOFTWARE.DBF file are displayed on-screen. The list of index files is displayed in a box in the upper right corner of the screen (see fig. 6.22). The text in the lower right corner of the screen shows the title of the highlighted index file. To select the index file, simply use a cursor key to highlight the file, and then press Enter.

From the Assistant menu, after you have activated the catalog file and set up a database file, you can select the index file from the screen. You don't have to remember the names of all the index files.

For example, if you attempt to set up a database file by choosing the **Set Up/Database file** options after activating the catalog file:

Set Up/Catalog/C: /SOFTWARE.CAT

a list of the database files in the catalog is displayed (see fig. 6.23). The boxed text in the lower right corner of the screen is the title of the database file in the catalog.

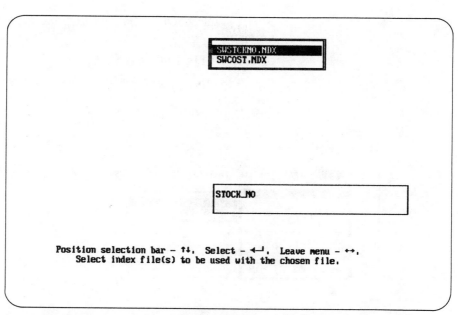

Fig. 6.22. Using the query operator (?) to select an index file.

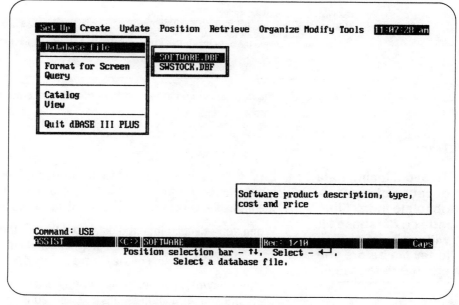

Fig. 6.23. Selecting a database file from the current catalog.

After you select *SOFTWARE.DBF* from the list, you'll see the prompt:

> `Is the file indexed? [Y/N]`

Press *Y* to display a list of the index files associated with the database file (see fig. 6.24). Then select the one you need to index the database file.

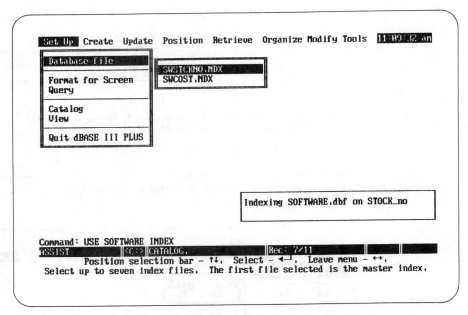

Fig. 6.24. Selecting the corresponding index file from the current catalog.

Trap:

To avoid losing data because of an obsolete index file, index a database file with an existing index file before you edit the database file.

Be sure to activate the index file before adding records to or removing records from an indexed database file. Otherwise, the index file becomes obsolete and data will be lost.

When you select an indexed database file with the USE .. INDEX .. command, the index file is updated automatically whenever the contents of the file are changed.

Therefore, when you set up an existing database file that has been indexed with an indexing key, activating the index file is highly recommended. If you don't activate the index file, it will not reflect any changes you make in the database file. And information stored in the index file won't match the edited contents of the database file. If you then use the index file to rearrange the records in the database file, you may lose access to valuable information.

If the database file has been indexed with more than one index file, you can activate all its index files with the USE command:

. USE SOFTWARE INDEX SWSTCKNO, BYCOST, BYPRICE

The activated index files will be updated automatically whenever you change the contents of the database file.

Selecting the Master Index File

To maintain multiple index files you've created for a given database file, activate them when you select the database file with the USE .. INDEX command:

. USE SOFTWARE INDEX SWSTCKNO, BYCOST, BYPRICE

The first index file (SWSTCKNO.NDX) in the command is used as the master index for arranging the records in the database file.

Tip:

While maintaining multiple indexes, use the SET ORDER TO command to specify the master index file.

If you want to specify a file other than the first as the master index file, use the SET ORDER TO command.

For example, if you want to index the records in the database file and specify the second index file, issue the following command:

. SET ORDER TO 2

The second index file becomes the master index file (see fig. 6.25).

```
. USE SOFTWARE INDEX SWSTCKNO, BYCOST, BYPRICE
. SET ORDER TO 2
Master index: C:BYCOST.ndx
. LIST
Record#  STOCK_NO   DSCRIPTION               TYPE                COST    PRICE
       1 ASH-DB300  dBASE III Plus v1.01 database              395.00  595.00
       2 AMS-DB110  Paradox v1.1             database           425.00  575.00
       3 CLP-DB100  Clipper DB Compiler      database compiler  450.00  595.00
       4 WOR-DB100  Wordtech DB Compiler     database compiler  469.00  595.00
       8 AST-FW200  Framework v2.0           integrated         345.00  395.00
      10 BOL-PA300  Turbo Pascal v3.0        language            39.50   69.50
       9 MIC-QB100  Microsoft QuickBasic     language            79.00  109.00
       5 LOT-LO123  Lotus 1-2-3 Release2     spreadsheet        289.00  359.00
       6 MIC-WS330  WordStar v3.30           word processing    229.00  269.00
       7 MIS-WD300  Microsoft Word v3.0      word processing    229.00  289.00

. SET ORDER TO 1
Master index: C:SWSTCKNO.ndx
. SET ORDER TO 3
Master index: C:BYPRICE.ndx
.
```

Fig. 6.25. Specifying the master index with the SET ORDER TO command.

Tip:

To maintain the integrity of data in an indexed database file, always update your index file.

You need to update the information in your index files regularly. If you're not sure whether an index file has been updated, update it to match the records in the current database file before you use the index file. Use the REINDEX command:

. USE <name of database file>
. SET INDEX TO <name of index file>
. REINDEX

as in the following example:

. USE EMPLOYEE
. SET INDEX TO BYFIRST
. REINDEX
`Rebuilding index - C:BYFIRST.ndx`
`100% indexed          10 Records indexed`

Displaying an Indexing Key

When you index a database file, the index file contains information about the indexing key. But you can't identify the indexing key by listing the contents of the index file.

Trick:

Use DISPLAY STATUS to display the index key of the index file you're using.

If you want to identify the indexing key during a dBASE III Plus session, first activate the index file with the SET INDEX TO command.

After activating the index file, use the DISPLAY STATUS command to display all the information about the active files in the current work area (see fig. 6.26).

```
. USE SOFTWARE
. SET INDEX TO BYCOST
. DISPLAY STATUS

Currently Selected Database:
Select area:  1, Database in Use: C:SOFTWARE.dbf    Alias: SOFTWARE
    Master index file:  C:BYCOST.ndx  Key: TYPE+STR(COST,6,2)

File search path:
Default disk drive: C:
Print destination:  PRN:
Margin =      0
Current work area =    1

Press any key to continue...
```

Fig. 6.26. Displaying current status to identify the index key.

As you can see from figure 6.26, displaying the status identifies both the index key and the master index.

Trap:

Marking records for deletion doesn't exclude them from the indexing operation.

When you index a database file, data records you've marked for deletion (*) are included in the operation.

When the DELETE command is executed, records to be "deleted" are marked with a deletion symbol (*). Until you issue the PACK command, these records will remain in the file. The deletion marks do not affect many dBASE III Plus operations, including the indexing operation (see fig. 6.27).

As you can see in figure 6.27, all the records marked for deletion have been indexed. You can't exclude the "deleted" records from the indexing operation.

```
. USE EMPLOYEE
. DELETE FOR MALE
      5 records deleted
. LIST
Record#   ID_NO        FIRST_NAME       LAST_NAME       POSITION    EMPLY_DATE MALE
       1 *123-45-6789 Thomas T.        Smith           President   03/01/1981 .T.
       2  254-63-5691 Tina Y.          Thompson        VP          09/22/1982 .F.
       3 *467-34-6789 Peter F.         Watson          Manager     10/12/1982 .T.
       4  732-08-4589 Doris Y.         Taylor          Sales Rep   08/14/1983 .F.
       5 *563-55-8900 Tyrone T.        Thorsen         Engineer    06/20/1982 .T.
       6  823-46-6213 Cathy J.         Faust           Secretary   04/15/1983 .F.
       7 *554-34-7893 Vincent M.       Corso           Sales Rep   07/20/1984 .T.
       8  321-65-9087 Jane W.          Kaiser          Accountant  11/22/1982 .F.
       9  560-56-9321 Tina K.          Davidson        Trainee     05/16/1986 .F.
      10 *435-54-9876 James J.         Smith           Trainee     01/23/1986 .T.

. INDEX ON ID_NO TO BYIDNO
  100% indexed            10 Records indexed
```

Fig. 6.27. Deleted records are included in the indexing operation.

Trick:

To hide records you've marked for deletion, use the SET DELETED ON command before issuing the display command.

If you want to hide records you've marked for deletion, issue the SET DELETED ON command before issuing the DISPLAY command (see fig. 6.28).

Figure 6.28 shows that all ten records in the EMPLOYEE.DBF database file were indexed. Although the records marked for deletion (DELETE FOR MALE) are not excluded from the indexing operation, the SET DELETED ON command did hide the deleted records from the LIST operation.

```
. USE EMPLOYEE
. RECALL ALL
      5 records recalled
. DELETE FOR MALE
      5 records deleted
. SET DELETED ON
. INDEX ON ID_NO TO BYIDNO
  100% indexed            10 Records indexed
. LIST
Record#   ID_NO        FIRST_NAME       LAST_NAME       POSITION    EMPLY_DATE MALE
       2  254-63-5691 Tina Y.          Thompson        VP          09/22/1982 .F.
       8  321-65-9087 Jane W.          Kaiser          Accountant  11/22/1982 .F.
       9  560-56-9321 Tina K.          Davidson        Trainee     05/16/1986 .F.
       4  732-08-4589 Doris Y.         Taylor          Sales Rep   08/14/1983 .F.
       6  823-46-6213 Cathy J.         Faust           Secretary   04/15/1983 .F.
```

Fig. 6.28. Use SET DELETED ON to exclude records from the indexing operation.

Trap:

While SET DELETED ON is in effect, you can't recall a record you've marked for deletion.

Although the SET DELETED ON command is very useful for excluding certain "deleted" records from some dBASE III Plus operations, the command may sometimes cause confusion.

Figure 6.29 shows the kind of confusion caused by the SET DELETED ON command. If you forget to issue the SET DELETED OFF command before you issue the RECALL ALL command, you will be told:

```
No records recalled
```

```
. USE EMPLOYEE
. LIST
Record#  ID_NO        FIRST_NAME    LAST_NAME    POSITION    EMPLY_DATE MALE
      1 *123-45-6789 Thomas T.     Smith        President   03/01/1981 .T.
      2  254-63-5691 Tina Y.       Thompson     VP          09/22/1982 .F.
      3 *467-34-6789 Peter F.      Watson       Manager     10/12/1982 .T.
      4  732-08-4589 Doris Y.      Taylor       Sales Rep   08/14/1983 .F.
      5 *563-55-0900 Tyrone T.     Thorsen      Engineer    06/28/1982 .T.
      6  823-46-6213 Cathy J.      Faust        Secretary   04/15/1983 .F.
      7 *554-34-7893 Vincent M.    Corso        Sales Rep   07/20/1984 .T.
      8  321-65-9087 Jane W.       Kaiser       Accountant  11/22/1982 .F.
      9  560-56-9321 Tina K.       Davidson     Trainee     05/16/1986 .F.
     10 *435-54-9876 James J.      Smith        Trainee     01/23/1986 .T.

. SET DELETED ON
. RECALL ALL
No records recalled
```

Fig. 6.29. Effects of the SET DELETED ON command on the RECALL operation.

You may mistakenly interpret this message as meaning that no more "deleted" records remain in the file.

When you no longer need to hide the "deleted" records, you can avoid confusion by issuing SET DELETED OFF.

Running Out of Memory When You Sort and Index Data

Trap:

Sorting or indexing a large database file may cause you to run out of memory.

All the memory (RAM) for dBASE III Plus is allocated with the MAXMEM command in the CONFIG.DB file. If you run out of memory during a sorting or indexing operation, you have to exit dBASE III Plus. You then can allocate additional RAM space in the configuration file and return to the program. (See Chapter 2 for a detailed explanation of how to allocate RAM space in the CONFIG.DB file.)

Trick:

To avoid running out of memory during a SORT or INDEX operation, allocate sufficient RAM space before you begin a dBASE III Plus session.

If you need to sort or index a large database file, be sure to allocate sufficient RAM space for the operation before you begin the dBASE III Plus session.

As you know, the sorting and indexing operations create new files. Before carrying out these operations you need to provide not only sufficient RAM space but also enough disk space to hold these files.

7

Displaying Data

dBASE III Plus commands allow you to display the contents of your database files and information about their structure and directories. You can use the power of these commands to greatly enhance your work.

This chapter focuses on tips and tricks developed from my own work experience. They show you how to make the dBASE III Plus commands more flexible and powerful by using their special features.

Displaying a File Directory

There are several ways to list the files in a directory.

Tip:	
To list only database files in a directory, use the dBASE III Plus DIR command.	The dBASE III Plus DIR command displays the name, number of records, and size (in bytes) of each database file—and the date of each file's most recent update. If you want to interrupt a listing, press Esc.

Tip:

To produce a summary listing of files other than database files, use wild cards (* and ?) in the dBASE III Plus DIR command.

By default, the DIR command lists only the current directory's database files. If you want to list other types of files, you need to specify their file extensions.

To list all the files of a certain type, use an asterisk (*) and the file extension in the DIR command. (The asterisk is a global symbol or wild card that causes all file names to be selected.)

To list all of a directory's index files, for example, use the following command:

. DIR *.NDX

To list certain files in the directory, use the question mark (?) as a wild card in the DIR command. (The question mark is used to denote a character in a file name.)

Figure 7.1 illustrates how to use wild cards in the DIR command to list different types of files with names that share certain common characters.

```
. DIR EMPLOYEE.*
EMPLOYEE.DBF        EMPLOYEE.FMT        EMPLOYEE.DIF        EMPLOYEE.TXT
EMPLOYEE.CAT        EMPLOYEE.BAK        EMPLOYEE.SCR        EMPLOYEE.DAT
EMPLOYEE.WKS        EMPLOYEE.WK1

      9703 bytes in      10 files.
8331264 bytes remaining on drive.

. DIR SW??????.NDX
SWSTCKNO.NDX        SWCOST.NDX

      2048 bytes in       2 files.
8331264 bytes remaining on drive.

. DIR SW????.*
SWLIST.DBF         SWCOST.NDX         SWLIST.LBL

      2620 bytes in       3 files.
8331264 bytes remaining on drive.
```

*Fig. 7.1. Displaying disk files of different types by using the * and ? masking characters.*

The first command, in which an asterisk replaces the file extension, lists all EMPLOYEE files.

In the second command:

. DIR SW??????.NDX

the six question marks cause all the index files whose names begin with *SW* to be displayed.

The third command lists all files with names of up to six letters that begin with *SW*.

Trap:

All files may not be displayed if you use question marks in the dBASE III Plus DIR command.

A command such as:

. DIR SW????.DBF

which uses only four question marks, lists only database files with names beginning with *SW*, followed by up to four characters. This command does not display a file such as SWSTOCK.DBF, even though the file exists.

Tip:

To display a file list in the current directory, use either the LIST FILES command or the DIR command.

You can substitute the LIST FILES command for the dBASE III Plus DIR command. Both commands produce the same result.

Even if you use wild cards (* or ?), the DIR and LIST FILES commands produce only a summary listing of file names (except database files). Other file attributes (such as file size and update information) are not displayed.

Scrolling of the screen display in LIST-type commands can be stopped by pressing the Ctrl-S key combination, and restarted by pressing any key.

Trick:

For a detailed listing of files, use the DOS DIR command with the dBASE III Plus RUN (or !) command.

From within dBASE III Plus, use the RUN command at the dot prompt to issue DOS commands.

With RUN, you can execute a DOS command as if it were part of the dBASE III Plus system. (For a detailed discussion of the RUN command, refer to Chapter 1.)

Note: The RUN command works only if the DOS COMMAND.COM command file is in the root directory when you start the computer.

If you want to list all the screen files in the file directory, issue the RUN DIR *.SCR command at the dot prompt. To list selected disk files, use the ? and * wild cards in the command. As you can see from figure 7.2, the RUN DIR command provides more detailed information than the simple dBASE III Plus DIR command.

```
. RUN DIR *.SCR


 Volume in drive C is DBASE_DISK1
 Directory of   C:\DBASE\DBFILES

 EMPLOYEE SCR     1120    1-26-87   11:00a
 PAYROLL  SCR      649    1-26-87   11:05a
 MULTEDIT SCR     1257    2-15-87   12:16p
          3 File(s)   8323072 bytes free


 . ? DIR SW????.NDX


 Volume in drive C is DBASE_DISK1
 Directory of   C:\DBASE\DBFILES

 SWCOST   NDX     1024    2-28-87    9:05p
          1 File(s)   8323072 bytes free
```

Fig. 7.2. Displaying disk files with the DOS DIR command.

Printing a File Directory

Trap:

To avoid error messages and possible loss of data, be sure to turn on the printer before you send output to it.

If the printer is not turned on when you issue a dBASE III Plus display command that includes the TO PRINT or SET PRINT ON instructions, you'll see a `Printer not ready` error message. The display operation stops.

Sometimes the system hangs and all processing operations are disabled. (This seems to have happened much more often with dBASE III than it does with dBASE III Plus.) You run the risk of losing valuable data when this happens, because you need to reboot the system and reenter dBASE III Plus.

Be sure to turn on the printer before you issue commands that require its use.

Tip:

To print a file directory, use the TO PRINT clause.	Use the dBASE III Plus keywords *TO PRINT* to print the screen display generated by some commands. If you want to print the contents of an active data record, for example, issue the DISPLAY TO PRINT command. You cannot print a file directory by using the DIR..TO PRINT command.

Trick:

To print a file directory, use the LIST FILES..TO PRINT command.	Use the LIST FILES..TO PRINT command: . LIST FILES ∗.NDX TO PRINT to print a listing of the names of all index files in the directory, for example.

Trap:

Using the SET PRINT ON and RUN DIR commands to print a file directory produces an undesirable format.	One way to print a set of files is to turn on the printer (SET PRINT ON) before issuing the DIR and LIST FILES commands. Then turn the printer off after printing: . SET PRINT ON . DIR . SET PRINT OFF But this approach produces listings with an undesirable format. As you can see in figure 7.3, when a listing is too long to fit on one screen, the message `Press any key to continue` is inserted in the list. And when you turn off the printer, the command "SET PRINT OFF" is printed.

Trick:

To direct output to a printer, use the pipe (>) operator in the DOS command.	If you want to print a file directory, using the DOS DIR command from the dot prompt: . RUN DIR . . . >LPT1: is preferable to using the SET PRINT ON and DIR commands. You use the greater-than sign (>), called a *pipe operator*, to specify the destination of the directory list. *LPT1* designates the printer connected to the first printer port. (If you have another

```
Press any key to continue...
CUSTOMER.DBF        6     03/02/87         284
PRODSOLD.DBF       28     03/05/87        1286
ALLSTOCK.DBF       28     03/03/87        1258
HWLIST.DBF         28     03/05/87        1230
HWCOST.DBF         18     03/05/87         512
PRODLIST.DBF       28     03/05/87        1230
PRODSTCK.DBF       28     03/05/87         450
SALARY.DBF         18     04/02/87         708
STAFF.DBF          18     03/14/87         836
JOINFILE.DBF       18     03/30/87         494
BULLETIN.DBF        1     01/06/87         224
SORTLAST.DBF       18     01/06/87         836
SRTFIRST.DBF        8     01/06/87         714
BARDATA.DBF         5     04/15/87         512
PERSONAL.DBF       21     04/23/87        1507
SORTED.DBF         18     02/16/87         836
NAMES.DBF          18     02/16/87         226
SALEITM.DBF         4     02/16/87         250

   27600 bytes in    40 files.
8314000 bytes remaining on drive.

. SET PRINT OFF
```

Fig. 7.3. Press any key to continue displaying a directory.

printer connected to a different printer port, such as LPT2, you would use >*LPT2:* to display the results of the RUN DIR command.)

To print a directory listing of all the index files, for example, enter the command:

    RUN DIR *.NDX >LPT1:

at the dot prompt. The name, size, and update information for each file is included in the printed directory.

Saving a File Directory to a Text File

Trick:

To save the file directory to a text file, use the pipe (>) operator in a DOS DIR command.

You can save the output produced by a DOS DIR command to a text file by including in the command a pipe symbol (>) followed by the name of the text file.

If you want to save the directory of all the index files to a text file named INDEXES.TXT, for example, enter the following command at the dot prompt:

    . RUN DIR *.NDX >INDEXES.TXT

The greater-than ($>$) sign, or *pipe operator*, specifies the destination of output from the RUN DIR command. When you specify a text file as the destination, the results of the command are "piped" to that text file.

To display on-screen the contents of the text file, use the following command:

. TYPE INDEXES.TXT

To print the contents of the text file, use either of the following commands:

. TYPE INDEXES.TXT TO PRINT

or

. RUN TYPE INDEXES.TXT $>$LPT1:

Flushing the Printer's Buffer

Trap:

When you use the TO PRINT option, all of your copy may not be printed.

When you direct output to a printer by using the TO PRINT option in a command, the last line of the output is not always printed.

Sometimes the last line of the output remains in the printer buffer and is printed only with the next batch of output.

Trick:

To flush the printer buffer, use the SET PRINT ON command.

The simplest way to print the last line in the printer buffer is to activate the printer with the SET PRINT ON command. The contents of the printer buffer will be flushed out.

To deactivate the printer, issue the SET PRINT OFF command.

Alternatively, the EJECT command entered at the dot prompt will cause any output held in the print buffer to be printed, and the paper to advance to the top of the next page.

Displaying Data Records

Tip:

Display the contents of active database files by using the LIST, DISPLAY, and BROWSE commands.

The LIST, DISPLAY, and BROWSE commands are commonly used for displaying the contents of data records in an active database file. When combined with the appropriate search and scope conditions, these commands can be used to display the contents of selected records in the database file. You also can display selected records by using a filtering command with a display command.

Filtering Data Records before Displaying Them

Trick:

Use the SET FILTER TO command to screen records that you want to display.

Instead of using a search or scope condition in a display command, use the SET FILTER TO command:

. SET FILTER TO <the filter condition>

to display a subset of the data records in an active database file.

As you can see from the examples in figure 7.4, the filter condition specified in the command instructs dBASE III Plus to filter out records that do not meet the condition.

Trap:

After you impose a filter condition on the data records, only records that match the filter condition are available for additional dBASE III Plus operations.

When you issue the LIST command after imposing a filter condition with the SET FILTER TO MALE command, you will not see all the contents of the file. As you can see in figure 7.4, the contents of EMPLOYEE.DBF are displayed as if the file contained only records of male employees.

```
. USE EMPLOYEE
. SET FILTER TO EMPLY_DATE>=CTOD("1/1/84")
. LIST
Record#  ID_NO        FIRST_NAME    LAST_NAME    POSITION    EMPLY_DATE MALE
      7  554-34-7893  Vincent M.    Corso        Sales Rep   07/20/84   .T.
      9  560-56-9321  Tina K.       Davidson     Trainee     05/16/86   .F.
     10  435-54-9876  James J.      Smith        Trainee     01/23/86   .T.

. SET FILTER TO MALE
. LIST
Record#  ID_NO        FIRST_NAME    LAST_NAME    POSITION    EMPLY_DATE MALE
      1  123-45-6789  Thomas T.     Smith        President   03/01/81   .T.
      3  467-34-6789  Peter F.      Watson       Manager     10/12/82   .T.
      5  563-55-8900  Tyrone T.     Thorsen      Engineer    06/20/82   .T.
      7  554-34-7893  Vincent M.    Corso        Sales Rep   07/20/84   .T.
     10  435-54-9876  James J.      Smith        Trainee     01/23/86   .T.

. SET FILTER TO EMPLY_DATE>=CTOD("1/1/84") .AND. MALE
. LIST
Record#  ID_NO        FIRST_NAME    LAST_NAME    POSITION    EMPLY_DATE MALE
      7  554-34-7893  Vincent M.    Corso        Sales Rep   07/20/84   .T.
     10  435-54-9876  James J.      Smith        Trainee     01/23/86   .T.
```

Fig. 7.4. Screen data records with the SET FILTER command.

Tip:

Use only one filter command at a time.

Filter commands are not cumulative. The most recently entered filter command supersedes those issued earlier.

Displaying Specific Data Records

Tip:

To display the contents of data records based on an exact field value, use the SET EXACT command.

To display CUSTOMER.DBF records in which "Jo" is the value for the FIRST_NAME, issue the following commands:

    . USE CUSTOMER
    . LIST FOR FIRST_NAME="Jo"

As you can see in figure 7.5, the qualifier FOR FIRST_NAME="Jo" did not produce an *exact* match with the field value. Instead, the LIST operation selects all first names that begin with "Jo". dBASE III Plus compares the characters in the qualifying condition with those characters of the file's field values. If all the characters in the condition are present in the field values, they are considered a match.

```
, USE CUSTOMER
, LIST FOR FIRST_NAME="Jo"
Record#  FIRST_NAME       LAST_NAME
      1  John             Smith
      2  Jo               Mason
      3  Jonathan         Walter

, SET EXACT ON
, LIST FOR FIRST_NAME="Jo"
Record#  FIRST_NAME       LAST_NAME
      2  Jo               Mason
```

Fig. 7.5. Listing of data records with "Jo" in the FIRST_NAME data field.

To ensure that only those records that *exactly* match the qualifying condition are listed, use the SET EXACT ON command before you issue the LIST command (see fig. 7.5). When SET EXACT ON is in effect, only the records with a field that exactly matches the qualifying condition are listed.

Storing Complex Search Conditions in a Query File

Trick:

To select records that meet a set of complex search conditions, store the conditions in a query file.

If you define complex search conditions that are tedious to enter from the keyboard, save these conditions in a query (.QRY) file. Then, whenever you need to impose these conditions in a display operation, you can activate the query file with a simple command.

To display the less profitable, over-stocked items in the ALLSTOCK.DBF inventory file, for example, you define the following search conditions for these items:

1. In the hardware division (DIVISION="HW")

2. Less profitable: profit (PRICE–COST) is less than 40% of cost or ((PRICE–COST)/COST)) $<$ 0.4

3. Over-stocked: ON_HAND $>=$ 3 or (ON_HAND+ON_ORDER) $>=$4

Then you incorporate these search conditions in a LIST command with a FOR qualifier:

. LIST FOR (DIVISION="HW".AND.((PRICE−COST)/COST)<.4) .AND. (ON_HAND>=3 .OR. (ON_HAND+ON_ORDER)>=4)

Although this LIST command with its complex search condition produces the appropriate list of records, having to enter the condition whenever you want to examine these selected records will be tedious.

As a shortcut, define the search conditions in a query file and save it on disk. Then recall the file to impose the conditions whenever you choose.

Creating a Query File

You can create a query file by issuing the CREATE QUERY command at the dot prompt:

. CREATE QUERY <name of the query file>

For example, to create a query file named OVRSTOCK.QRY for the previously described set of search conditions, you issue the following command:

. CREATE QUERY OVRSTOCK

Tip:

Use the Assistant menu to create a query file.

Creating a query file is easy if you use the Assistant menu. To create the file, select the **Create/Query** option and then enter the file name *OVRSTOCK.QRY*.

Tip:

Define the filter conditions.

After you name the query file, a form for defining the filter or search conditions appears (see fig. 7.6). Simply fill in each line of the query table with the appropriate condition.

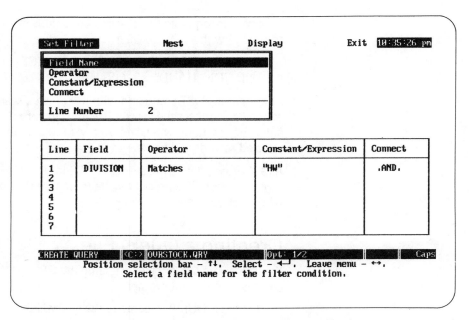

Fig. 7.6. Entering the first search condition into the query table.

For example, to define the first filter condition, select the following menu options:

Set Filter/Field Name/DIVISION
/Operator/= Matches
/Constant/Expression/"HW"
/Connect/Combine with .AND.

Each part of the search condition is entered to the query table as you specify it. Notice that the first line in the query table shown in figure 7.6 defines the query conditions that apply to the DIVISION field.

All the filter conditions are collected in the query table (see fig. 7.7).

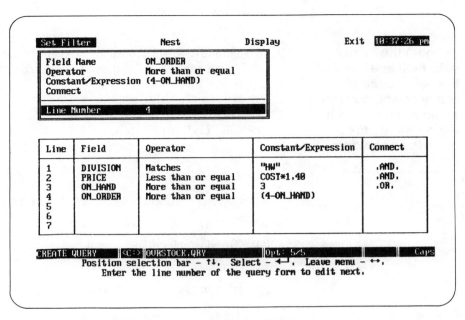

Fig. 7.7. The query table with all the search conditions entered.

Trap:

When you define a filter condition, each line in the query table allows only one data field in the field column.

One of the requirements in defining a search or filter condition is that each line in the query table allows only one data field in the field column.

If the condition involves a formula that requires more than one data field:

$$((PRICE-COST)/COST) < 0.4,$$

you cannot enter (PRICE–COST)/COST as the field name.

Trick:

To meet the "one data field specified in the field column" requirement, convert a condition in which a formula requires more than one data field.

If the condition involves a formula that requires more than one data field, you need to define the condition so that the requirement is met.

Convert the formula:

((PRICE–COST)/COST) < 0.4,

to

PRICE < COST*1.40

so that only one data field is specified in the field column.

Similarly, change the search condition:

(ON_HAND+ON_ORDER) >= 4

to

ON_ORDER >= (4 – ON_HAND)

or

ON_HAND >= (4 – ON_ORDER)

Tip:

To specify priority levels for evaluating the filter conditions, add nesting operators to the conditions.

After defining the query conditions, you need to specify the priority levels in which these conditions are to be evaluated.

To define the priority levels, enclose the conditions in *nesting parentheses*. These parentheses are evaluated as they would be in an algebraic formula.

To specify the priority levels, first select the **Nest** menu option (see fig. 7.8). Then specify an opening parenthesis at the beginning of query line *1* and a closing parenthesis at the end of query line *2*:

Nest/Add Start:1/Add End: 2

As you can see in figure 7.8, a pair of parentheses encloses the first and second query conditions. Use this procedure to add other nesting parentheses.

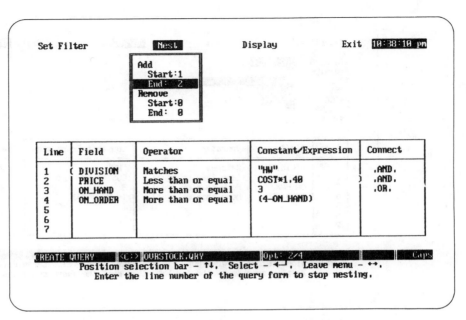

Fig. 7.8. Defining the first nest query condition.

Trick:

If you make a mistake while you're defining the nesting parentheses, select the Nest/Remove option to erase a parenthesis.

To eliminate the parentheses inserted in the previous example, select the Nest option from the Assistant menu and specify:

    Remove Start: 1 / Remove End: 2

Tip:

Test the query conditions before saving them to a file.

Before saving the defined search or filter conditions, test the conditions.

To instruct dBASE III Plus to display the records that meet the defined conditions, choose the Display option. The first record that meets the defined filter conditions is displayed in the upper left corner of the screen (see fig. 7.9).

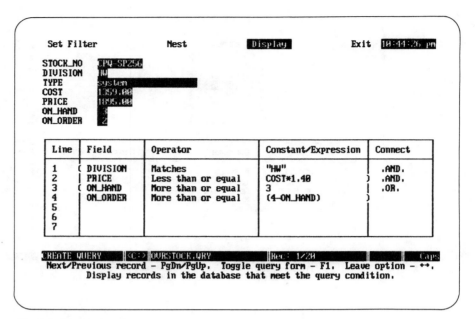

Fig. 7.9. Displaying the first record that meets the query conditions.

Press PgDn to display the next record that meets the conditions.

Tip:

Save the query conditions to a file.

After testing the filter conditions defined in the query table, select the **Exit/Save** options to save the conditions in a query file.

Activating a Query File

Tip:

Use a query file to filter records.

Activate a query file to display the database file records that meet the search condition you defined in the query file. You can use the SET FILTER TO FILE command:

. SET FILTER TO FILE <name of query file>

For example, you can use the SET FILTER TO FILE command to display records in ALLSTOCK.DBF that meet the search or filter conditions defined and saved in the OVRSTOCK.QRY file (see fig. 7.10).

```
. USE ALLSTOCK
. SET FILTER TO FILE OVRSTOCK
. LIST STOCK_NO, DIVISION, COST, PRICE, ON_HAND, ON_ORDER
Record#  STOCK_NO  DIVISION    COST    PRICE  ON_HAND  ON_ORDER
      1  CPQ-SP256 HW        1359.00 1895.00        3         2
      3  IBM-AT640 HW        3798.00 4490.00        5         0
      7  SEA-HD020 HW         398.00  495.00        3         1
      9  PAR-GC100 HW         279.00  389.00        3         2
     10  HER-GC100 HW         199.00  239.00        4         1
```

Fig. 7.10. Displaying data records with the SET FILTER command.

Hiding Deleted Records from Display

When you remove data records from a database file by using the DELETE command, the records are marked with an asterisk (*). Because these "deleted" records remain in the file until you pack the file, they are still accessible by many dBASE III Plus operations.

For example, if you issue the LIST or DISPLAY command after having marked the data records for deletion, the records are still displayed as active records.

Trick:

Use the SET DELETED ON command to hide records.

To exclude marked records from a display operation, issue the SET DELETED ON command. As you can see from figure 7.11, while the SET DELETED ON command is in effect, the records that have been marked for deletion are not displayed by the LIST command.

```
. USE EMPLOYEE
. DELE FOR MALE
      5 records deleted
. LIST
Record#   ID_NO      FIRST_NAME    LAST_NAME      POSITION    EMPLY_DATE MALE
      1 *123-45-6789 Thomas T.     Smith          President   03/01/81   .T.
      2  254-63-5691 Tina Y.       Thompson       VP          09/22/82   .F.
      3 *467-34-6789 Peter F.      Watson         Manager     10/12/82   .T.
      4  732-88-4589 Doris Y.      Taylor         Sales Rep   08/14/83   .F.
      5 *563-55-8900 Tyrone T.     Thorsen        Engineer    06/20/82   .T.
      6  823-46-6213 Cathy J.      Faust          Secretary   04/15/83   .F.
      7 *554-34-7093 Vincent M.    Corso          Sales Rep   07/20/84   .T.
      8  321-65-9887 Jane W.       Kaiser         Accountant  11/22/82   .F.
      9  560-56-9321 Tina K.       Davidson       Trainee     05/16/86   .F.
     10 *435-54-9876 James J.      Smith          Trainee     01/23/86   .T.
. SET DELETED ON
. LIST
Record#   ID_NO      FIRST_NAME    LAST_NAME      POSITION    EMPLY_DATE MALE
      2  254-63-5691 Tina Y.       Thompson       VP          09/22/82   .F.
      4  732-88-4589 Doris Y.      Taylor         Sales Rep   08/14/83   .F.
      6  823-46-6213 Cathy J.      Faust          Secretary   04/15/83   .F.
      8  321-65-9887 Jane W.       Kaiser         Accountant  11/22/82   .F.
      9  560-56-9321 Tina K.       Davidson       Trainee     05/16/86   .F.
```

Fig. 7.11. The effects of SET DELETED ON on listing data records.

Selecting Fields for Display

Trick:

To display selected data fields, use the SET FIELDS TO command.

To select the data fields to be displayed, use the dBASE III Plus SET FIELDS TO command like a filter command:

. SET FIELDS TO <the list of fields to be displayed>

Specify in the command the fields you want to display. Data fields that are not listed are hidden from display (see fig. 7.12).

As you can see from figure 7.12, you can use more than one SET FIELDS TO command to add data fields to the list.

Trap:

The effects of SET FIELDS TO commands are cumulative.

When you issue more than one SET FIELDS TO command, all the data fields specified by these commands remain selected because the effects of SET FIELDS TO commands are cumulative.

```
                                              Caps
, USE EMPLOYEE
, SET FIELDS TO ID_NO, POSITION, LAST_NAME, FIRST_NAME
, LIST
Record#   ID_NO      FIRST_NAME    LAST_NAME    POSITION
      1   123-45-6789 Thomas T.    Smith        President
      2   254-63-5691 Tina Y.      Thompson     UP
      3   467-34-6789 Peter F.     Watson       Manager
      4   732-88-4589 Doris Y.     Taylor       Sales Rep
      5   563-55-8900 Tyrone T.    Thorsen      Engineer
      6   823-46-6213 Cathy J.     Faust        Secretary
      7   554-34-7893 Vincent M.   Corso        Sales Rep
      8   321-65-9087 Jane W.      Kaiser       Accountant
      9   560-56-9321 Tina K.      Davidson     Trainee
     10   435-54-9876 James J.     Smith        Trainee
, SET FIELDS TO EMPLY_DATE
, SET FILTER TO .NOT. MALE
, LIST
Record#   ID_NO      FIRST_NAME    LAST_NAME    POSITION   EMPLY_DATE
      2   254-63-5691 Tina Y.      Thompson     UP         09/22/82
      4   732-88-4589 Doris Y.     Taylor       Sales Rep  08/14/83
      6   823-46-6213 Cathy J.     Faust        Secretary  04/15/83
      8   321-65-9087 Jane W.      Kaiser       Accountant 11/22/82
      9   560-56-9321 Tina K.      Davidson     Trainee    05/16/86
```

Fig. 7.12. Selecting data fields with the SET FIELDS TO command.

Trick:

To remove data fields from the list, repeat the selection process.

To remove selected data fields from the field list, start over. You need to repeat the field-selection process, selecting the database file with the USE command (as in USE EMPLOYEE).

You can clear *all* of the selected fields by issuing the SET FIELDS TO command with no fields specified.

Eliminating Field Headings from Displays

Tip:

To exclude field headings while you display data records, use the SET HEADINGS OFF command.

Whenever you execute the LIST and DISPLAY commands, the field headings are displayed as well as the contents of the records. Because these field headings sometimes clutter the screen, you may prefer to remove them. Issue the SET HEADINGS OFF command before you use the LIST and DISPLAY commands.

Powerful Features of the BROWSE Operation

Trick:

Use the BROWSE menu options to enhance the power of the BROWSE command.

Use options from the BROWSE menu to streamline your work.

To call up the menu, press F10 or Ctrl-Home. To cancel the menu, press Esc.

When you call up the menu, five options are displayed at the top of the screen (see fig. 7.13). The **Bottom** and **Top** options let you place the last and first record of the file being browsed at the top of the screen. Similarly, the **Record No.** option allows you to place a record (by its record number) at the top of the display.

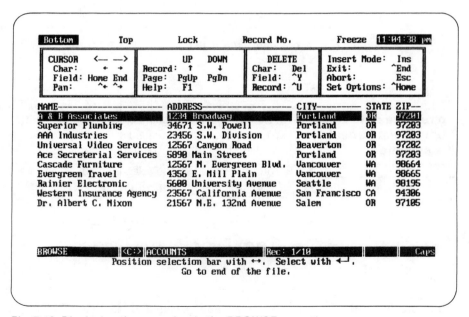

Fig. 7.13. Displaying the menu bar in the BROWSE operation.

Freezing Fields

Trick:

Freeze a data field in the BROWSE operation.

The **Freeze** option is very useful for editing data during a BROWSE operation. When you freeze a field, you can move up and down within the field as you edit. The cursor's movement is restricted within the column that corresponds to the frozen field.

For example, to edit only the ZIP code field of the ACCOUNTS.DBF file during a BROWSE operation, enter *ZIP* as the field to be frozen.

The cursor is placed in the ZIP field so that the movement of the cursor is restricted to that field. By using the ↑ and ↓ keys, you can move up and down the field to make your changes.

Tip:

Use a dot prompt command to freeze a field in the BROWSE operation.

From dot prompt mode, you can select the field to be frozen during the BROWSE operation by including a FREEZE option in the BROWSE command.

For example, to freeze the ZIP field while you browse the records of the ACCOUNTS.DBF file, issue the following commands:

```
. USE ACCOUNTS
. GO TOP
. BROWSE FREEZE ZIP
```

Trick:

Unfreeze a frozen field during the BROWSE operation.

During the BROWSE operation, a frozen field remains frozen until you freeze another field.

To unfreeze a frozen field without freezing another, select the **Freeze** option from the Assistant menu and then press Enter at the prompt:

```
Enter field name to freeze
```

Tip:

Use the F1 function key to toggle the heading off and on in BROWSE mode.

The F1 (Help) function key in BROWSE mode toggles the heading on and off. The BROWSE heading provides details about the functions available while you are in BROWSE mode. Once you become familiar with these functions, press F1 to remove the heading from the screen. This will allow six additional records to be displayed per screen, which may be important if you are dealing with a large database file. Should you need to refresh your memory about the BROWSE functions, press F1 to redisplay the heading.

Displaying Hidden Fields with BROWSE

Tip:

To "pan" data fields in a BROWSE operation, use the Ctrl-← or Ctrl-→ key combinations.

During a BROWSE operation, if the database file you're examining has more fields than can be displayed on the screen, use the Ctrl-← or Ctrl-→ key combinations to "pan" the displayed fields.

When you browse the records in ACCOUNTS.DBF, for example, only the first four fields (ACCOUNT_NO, NAME, ADDRESS, CITY) are shown because not all the data fields fit on the screen. The other five fields (STATE, ZIP, AREA_CODE, PHONE_NO, and MAX_CREDIT) are hidden from view.

If you want to display the hidden data fields, use the Ctrl-→ key combination to pan the fields. Each time you press the Ctrl-→ key combination, one of the hidden data fields on the right is revealed.

For example, press Ctrl-→ three times to pan three data fields to the right (see fig. 7.14). Now the leftmost data fields are hidden and the rest of the data fields are displayed.

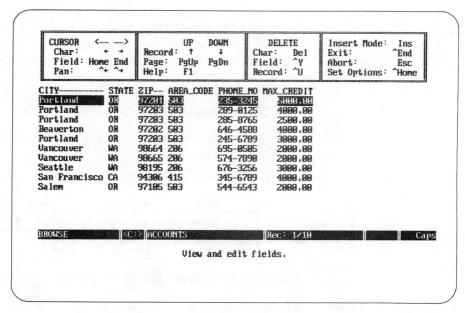

```
┌──────────────────────────────────────────────────────────────────────────────┐
│  CURSOR    <── ──>  │          UP   DOWN  │   DELETE        │ Insert Mode:  Ins │
│  Char:      ←   →   │ Record:    ↑    ↓   │   Char:   Del   │ Exit:        ^End │
│  Field: Home End    │ Page:    PgUp PgDn  │   Field:  ^Y    │ Abort:        Esc │
│  Pan:    ^←  ^→     │ Help:      F1       │   Record: ^U    │ Set Options: ^Home│
└──────────────────────────────────────────────────────────────────────────────┘

CITY───────── STATE ZIP── AREA_CODE PHONE_NO MAX_CREDIT
Portland      OR    97201 503       235-3245   5000.00
Portland      OR    97203 503       289-0125   4000.00
Portland      OR    97203 503       285-8765   2500.00
Beaverton     OR    97202 503       646-4588   4000.00
Portland      OR    97203 503       245-6789   3000.00
Vancouver     WA    98664 206       695-0505   2000.00
Vancouver     WA    98665 206       574-7890   2000.00
Seattle       WA    98195 206       676-3256   3000.00
San Francisco CA    94306 415       345-6789   4000.00
Salem         OR    97105 503       544-6543   2000.00


BROWSE          |<C:> ACCOUNTS            |Rec: 1/10              Caps
                    View and edit fields.
```

Fig. 7.14. Showing the last six data fields in the BROWSE operation.

Locking Data Fields in a BROWSE Operation

Trap:

If fields are hidden from view, knowing which record you are looking at is difficult.	One of the problems associated with using Ctrl-← or Ctrl-→ in the BROWSE operation is that panning hides data fields.
	As you saw from figure 7.14, panning to the right hid the ACCOUNT_NO and NAME fields. It's difficult to tell which record you're examining or editing.

Trick:

To create a window effect while browsing data, lock certain data fields.	You can create a window effect by locking certain data fields (to exclude them from panning) so that they remain displayed.
	Choose the **Lock** option from the BROWSE menu and indicate the number of columns to be locked. (If you need to call up the menu, press F10.)

For example, you can lock the first two data fields (ACCOUNT_NO and NAME) so that they are displayed at all times. Use the Ctrl-← key combination to pan the data fields to the left. When the two fields appear in the first and second columns, press F10. Then choose the **Lock** option from the menu. At the prompt:

Change number of columns to lock to:

enter *2* as the number of data fields to be locked (see fig. 7.15).

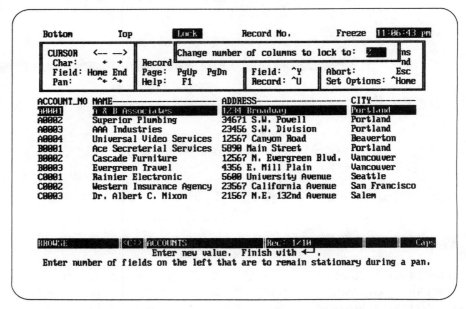

Fig. 7.15. Using the Lock option to lock data fields in the BROWSE operation.

Now the two locked fields will remain on the screen when you pan left or right. In our example, if you press Ctrl-→ twice, the file's fifth data field (STATE) now appears as the third column. And the last four data fields are also revealed on the screen (see fig. 7.16).

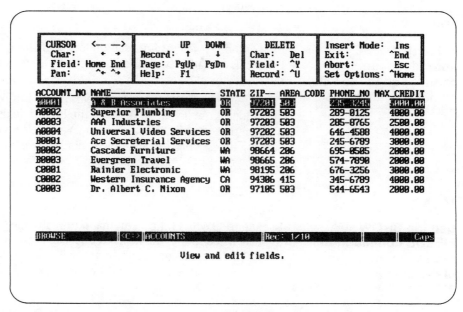

CURSOR	<— —>		UP	DOWN	DELETE		Insert Mode:	Ins
Char:	← →	Record:	↑	↓	Char:	Del	Exit:	^End
Field:	Home End	Page:	PgUp	PgDn	Field:	^Y	Abort:	Esc
Pan:	^← ^→	Help:	F1		Record:	^U	Set Options:	^Home

ACCOUNT_NO	NAME	STATE	ZIP—	AREA_CODE	PHONE_NO	MAX_CREDIT
A0001	A & B Associates	OR	97201	503	235-3245	5000.00
A0002	Superior Plumbing	OR	97203	503	289-0125	4000.00
A0003	AAA Industries	OR	97203	503	285-8765	2500.00
A0004	Universal Video Services	OR	97202	503	646-4588	4000.00
B0001	Ace Secreterial Services	OR	97203	503	245-6789	3000.00
B0002	Cascade Furniture	WA	98664	206	695-0505	2000.00
B0003	Evergreen Travel	WA	98665	206	574-7890	2000.00
C0001	Rainier Electronic	WA	98195	206	676-3256	3000.00
C0002	Western Insurance Agency	CA	94306	415	345-6789	4000.00
C0003	Dr. Albert C. Nixon	OR	97105	503	544-6543	2000.00

BROWSE   <C:> ACCOUNTS   Rec: 1/10   Caps

View and edit fields.

Fig. 7.16. Panning the unlocked data fields in the BROWSE operation.

Trap:

When you lock a number of columns, you lock the displayed data fields.

If you specify *2* as the number of columns to be locked, the first two data fields that are currently displayed are locked. These two data fields may not be the very first two fields in the database file.

Trick:

Place data fields to the left of your screen before locking them.

To avoid hiding data fields pan the fields so that they appear in the screen's left most columns. You then can lock all of the data fields.

Trap:

In the BROWSE operation, you cannot pan to the left of locked data fields.

One of the restrictions imposed on locking fields in the BROWSE operation is that you cannot pan to the left beyond the locked data fields.

When you lock a number of data fields in the BROWSE operation, those fields to the left of the locked fields will be hidden from the BROWSE operation. You can't reveal them by panning unless you rearrange the order of the fields before applying the BROWSE operation.

Trick:

Use the BROWSE FIELDS command to rearrange the order of the data fields.

Use the BROWSE FIELDS command to rearrange the order of the data fields so that the fields to be locked appear in the screen's leftmost columns. Then you will be able to pan the data fields that appear to the right of the locked fields.

Tip:

Use the BROWSE FIELDS command to select and arrange the data fields to be browsed.

If a database file contains more data fields than can be displayed simultaneously, use the BROWSE FIELDS command to browse selected fields.

For example, you can select and rearrange the fields in the ACCOUNTS.DBF file for the BROWSE operation. Issue the following command:

```
. BROWSE FIELDS MAX_CREDIT,ACCOUNT_NO,NAME,AREA_CODE
  PHONE_NO,ADDRESS,CITY,STATE,ZIP
```

The data fields are displayed in the order specified in the command.

Displaying Data in Color

Depending on the type of monitor you have, you can display data on the screen in either monochrome or color mode. If you have a color monitor with the appropriate graphics adapter card, you can use the SET COLOR TO command to choose a number of colors for displaying data.

Text, lines, and graphics symbols are displayed in one color (foreground color) over another (background color). There are two types of text: standard and enhanced.

Use *standard* text to display:

- the dBASE III Plus command at the dot prompt
- the direction of cursor movement in the navigation line
- information on the message line
- field labels
- double- and single-line boxes
- menu options in the Assistant menu (except the highlighted option)
- contents of data records displayed with DISPLAY and LIST commands
- listing of data records in the BROWSE operation (except the current record)

Other items are displayed in *enhanced* text:

- the text in the status bar
- the highlighted option on the menu bar of the Assistant menu
- contents of the current record displayed with the BROWSE operation
- contents of the data record under edit in the EDIT or APPEND operations

The foreground and background colors for standard and enhanced text can be set independently, as can the color of the screen's border. There are two ways to specify colors: in the CONFIG.DB file or with a dot prompt command.

Tip:

Use a one- or two-letter code to define the foreground, background, and border colors.

To specify the colors you want in a screen display, use the following letter codes:

Color	Letter Code
Black	N
White	W
Blue	B
Green	G
Cyan	BG
Red	R
Magenta	RB
Brown	GR
Blank	X

To display text in blinking color, add an asterisk after the letter code. For example, specify *B** for blinking blue text.

To display a color in high intensity, add a plus (+) sign after the letter code. Specify *R+* for bright red, for instance.

It is important to note that not all the colors listed here are available to all graphic adapters and color monitors.

Tip:

Set screen colors in the CONFIG.DB file.

To specify colors in the CONFIG.DB file, include a configuration line:

COLOR=<color of standard text/background color>,
        <color of enhanced text/background color>,
        <border color>

as in the following example:

COLOR=W/B,R+/W,G

Tip:

Use the SET COLOR TO command to set foreground, background, and border colors.	You can select the screen color at the dot prompt by issuing the SET COLOR TO command in the following format: . SET COLOR TO <color of standard text/background color>, <color of enhanced text/background color>, <border color>

Tip:

Foreground and background colors must be defined in pairs.	You must define foreground and background colors in pairs. Specify the code for the foreground color, then type a slash (/) followed by the code for the background color. For example, to display standard text as white letters on a blue background, enhanced text as bright red letters on a white background with a green border, issue the following command at the dot prompt: . SET COLOR TO W/B, R+/W, G

Trick:

To eliminate the border, set the border color to the background color of the standard text.	If you prefer not to show a border, set the border color to match the background color of the standard text: . SET COLOR TO W/B, R+/W, B

Tip:

To select the default colors, do not specify colors in the SET COLOR TO command.	The default color setting is W/N, N/W, N. In this default setting, standard text is displayed as white letters on a black background, enhanced text as black letters on a white background (in *reverse video*) with no border. To switch to the default color setting at any point during processing, issue the SET COLOR TO command without specifying colors: . SET COLOR TO

Tip:

Use SET COLOR ON/OFF to switch from a monochrome to a color monitor.

The color combinations described here can be displayed only on a color monitor. If you have both a monochrome monitor and a color monitor, you can switch from one to the other with the following commands:

. SET COLOR ON

or

. SET COLOR OFF

On a color monitor, the whole screen may go blank if you issue the SET COLOR OFF command. If this happens, use the SET COLOR ON command to return to the default color setting.

Because of the differences among the variety of color monitors and their adapter cards, these outcomes can be unpredictable. Experiment with your equipment.

8

Generating Reports and Mailing Lists

The report generator provided by dBASE III Plus lacks the power and flexibility you may need to produce complex reports with sophisticated formats. This chapter presents tips and tricks to help you make the most of the dBASE III Plus report generator. With these tips and tricks, you can add extra power and flexibility to the report generator.

Producing Mailing Lists

dBASE III Plus provides one of the most useful functions a database can offer: the capability of producing mailing lists. You can easily format and produce a mailing list with a label file.

Tip:

Design a mailing label with the CREATE LABEL command.

The simplest way to design a mailing label is to use the label form generated by the CREATE LABEL command. Use this command after you've set up the database file.

To produce a mailing list from the names and addresses in the ACCOUNTS.DBF file, for instance, create a label file (MAILING.LBL) with the following dot prompt commands:

```
. USE ACCOUNTS
. CREATE LABEL MAILING
```

and then use the resulting two-screen label design form to format the label.

After you've specified the label's dimensions and left margin, you can define the contents of the label. Define each line with an expression, which may include data fields and symbols.

You can combine different types of data fields in an expression. But you must convert these fields to the same type before combining them. Use the TRIM( ) function to trim off trailing spaces in an address or name.

After you've formatted and defined the contents of the label, save the information in a label file by choosing the **Exit/Save** options from the Assistant menu. You will use this label file to produce your mailing list.

Tip:

Display names and addresses as a mailing list with the LABEL FORM command.

To display names and addresses from your label file, use the LABEL FORM command:

```
. USE ACCOUNTS
. LABEL FORM MAILING
```

to select the label file and display the output on your screen.

Tip:

To align labels on the printer, test the label before producing the mailing list.

Before you produce a mailing list, it is good practice to print a sample label. Then use this sample to align the labels correctly on the printer. There are two ways to produce a sample label.

Tip:

Use the SAMPLE option to produce a sample label.

One way to produce a sample mailing label for aligning the printer is to use the SAMPLE option of the LABEL FORM command:

    . USE ACCOUNTS
    . LABEL FORM MAILING SAMPLE TO PRINT

The contents of the mailing label are displayed and printed as a set of asterisks rather than as normal characters (see fig. 8.1).

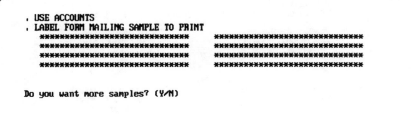

Fig. 8.1. Sample mailing labels.

If, after you print one row of labels and adjust the printer, you need to see other sample labels, press *Y* at the prompt:

    Do you want more samples? (Y/N)

Press *N* to print the mailing list. (You can interrupt printing at any time by pressing Esc.)

Adding Qualifier Conditions to a LABEL FORM Operation

Tip:

To produce a mailing list of selected records, use a qualifier in the LABEL FORM command.

To produce a small set of sample labels, set the record range to only a few data records by using a qualifying condition (FOR . . .) in the LABEL FORM command:

    . USE ACCOUNTS
    . LABEL FORM MAILING FOR RECNO( )<=4 TO PRINT

These commands print only the first four records.

To include only the names and addresses of certain data records, use an appropriate qualifier in the LABEL FORM command to select the records.

Tip:

To facilitate handling mail, index your data records by ZIP code.

To produce a mailing list for specific ZIP codes, specify those ZIP codes as a search condition in the LABEL FORM command (see fig. 8.2).

```
. USE ACCOUNTS
. LABEL FORM MAILING FOR ZIP="97203" .OR. ZIP="9866"
                        A0002                              A0003
        Superior Plumbing            AAA Industries
        34671 S.W. Powell            23456 S.W. Division
        Portland, OR  97203          Portland, OR  97203


                        B0001                              B0002
        Ace Secreterial Services     Cascade Furniture
        5890 Main Street             12567 N. Evergreen Blvd.
        Portland, OR  97203          Vancouver, WA  98664


                        B0003
        Evergreen Travel
        4356 E. Mill Plain
        Vancouver, WA  98665
```

Fig. 8.2. Printing a mailing list with selected ZIP codes.

As you can see in figure 8.2, the search condition ZIP="9866" will find and include all ZIP codes that begin with *9866*. If you want to search for a specific ZIP code, use the SET EXACT ON command.

Tip:

Use a scope condition as a shortcut in a LABEL FORM command.

You can use a search condition (such as FOR . . .) in a LABEL FORM command to select the records you want to display. But this may not be the best method. When you include a search condition in the LABEL FORM command, each record in the file is checked to see whether the condition is met. If you have a large set of records, processing the file is slow and cumbersome.

You can use a shortcut. After you've indexed the file, position the record pointer at the beginning of the correct record. Then specify a scope condition (with the WHILE operator) in the command.

For example, you can display a mailing list for all the ACCOUNTS.DBF records with "OR" as the STATE code. First, index the file on the STATE field. This groups together all records with the same STATE codes. Next, skip unwanted records by using the FIND command to place the record pointer at the beginning of the records you need. Then issue the LABEL FORM command with the scope condition (WHILE . . .). Records will be selected until the condition is no longer satisfied (see fig. 8.3).

```
. USE ACCOUNTS
. INDEX ON STATE TO BYSTATE
  100% indexed            10 Records indexed
. FIND OR
. LABEL FORM MAILING WHILE STATE="OR"
                       A0001                              A0002
    A & B Associates              Superior Plumbing
    1234 Broadway                 34671 S.W. Powell
    Portland, OR  97201           Portland, OR  97203


                       A0003                              A0004
    AAA Industries                Universal Video Services
    23456 S.W. Division           12567 Canyon Road
    Portland, OR  97203           Beaverton, OR  97202


                       B0001                              C0003
    Ace Secreterial Services      Dr. Albert C. Nixon
    5890 Main Street              21567 N.E. 132nd Avenue
    Portland, OR  97203           Salem, OR  97105
```

Fig. 8.3. Grouping data records with the INDEX operation.

Eliminating Duplicate Entries from a Mailing List

Trick:

To exclude duplicate records, use the SET UNIQUE ON command.

If you suspect that more than one record in the database file may belong to the same subject (an individual or a company account, for instance), you need to print only one of these records in the mailing list. To do so, index the database file with the SET UNIQUE ON function in effect.

You can ensure, for example, that each company is listed only once in the mailing list. To do so, index the database file on the company's name before printing the list:

```
. USE ACCOUNTS
. SET UNIQUE ON
. INDEX ON NAME TO ACCTNAME
. LABEL FORM MAILING TO PRINT
```

Trap:

Duplicate-key records become unavailable for manipulation.

After you've executed the SET UNIQUE ON and INDEX ON NAME TO ACCTNAME commands, you will not be able to manipulate the records excluded by this operation—even though those records are still part of the file. Because the active index file controls which records are available for manipulation, you can issue the following commands to retrieve the hidden records:

```
. SET UNIQUE OFF
. REINDEX
```

The first command removes the unique-key restriction and the REINDEX command causes *all* records in the database to be indexed in the active index file (ACCTNAME.NDX) according to the currently specified key (NAME).

Excluding Inactive Records from the Mailing List

Trick:

Use the SET DELETED ON command to exclude inactive records from the mailing list.

When you produce a mailing list, you frequently need to exclude entries that are considered inactive. But you may not want to remove these records permanently from the database file. In such a case, you can mark the inactive records by pressing the Ctrl-U key combination in the EDIT or BROWSE operation. After these records have been "deleted," issue the SET DELETED ON command to exclude them from the LABEL FORM command.

When the mailing list has been produced, you may want to reactivate the "deleted" records. Recall them with a RECALL ALL command.

Producing Reports

A basic report format you can create with the dBASE III Plus report generator is shown in figure 8.4. The contents of the specified data fields of each record are listed horizontally in a table.

```
Page No.     1
05/29/87
                             MONTHLY SALES REPORT
                        Hardware and Software Divisions
                          Month ending March 31, 1987

Stock No     Product Type        Units Sold      Price      Total Sales

--------     --------------------  ----------    --------   ------------------


CPQ-SP256  system                       2      1895.00         3790.00
ZEN-SL181  system                       1      2399.00         2399.00
IBM-AT640  system                       3      4490.00        13470.00
ZEN-MM012  monitor                      2       159.00          318.00
NEC-PC660  printer                      3       820.00         2460.00
HAY-M1200  modem                        4       389.00         1556.00
SEA-HD020  hard disk                    3       495.00         1485.00
IOM-HD040  hard disk                    2      2790.00         5580.00
PAR-GC100  graphic card                 2       389.00          778.00
HER-GC100  graphic card                 3       239.00          717.00
ASH-DB300  database                     3       595.00         1785.00
ANS-DB110  database                     4       695.00         2780.00
CLP-DB100  database compiler            2       595.00         1190.00
WOR-DB100  database compiler            1       595.00          595.00
LOT-LO123  spreadsheet                  4       359.00         1436.00
MIC-WS330  word processing              2       269.00          538.00
MIS-WD300  word processing              2       289.00          578.00
AST-FW200  integrated                   2       395.00          790.00
MIC-QB100  language                     1       109.00          109.00
BOL-PA300  language                     2        69.50          139.00
*** Total ***
                                       48                     42493.00
```

Fig. 8.4. A sample horizontal tabulating report.

The first four columns of this report are values in the data fields of PRODSOLD.DBF. (Fig. 8.5 shows the PRODSOLD.DBF file's structure and contents.) The report's fifth column (Total Sales) is computed by multiplying the values of the UNITS_SOLD and PRICE data fields.

```
. list stru
Structure for database: A:Prodsold.dbf
Number of data records:       20
Date of last update   : 03/05/87
Field  Field Name  Type        Width     Dec
    1   STOCK_NO    Character       9
    2   DIVISION    Character       2
    3   TYPE        Character      20
    4   COST        Numeric         7        2
    5   PRICE       Numeric         7        2
    6   UNITS_SOLD  Numeric         3
** Total **                       49

. list all
Record#  STOCK_NO  DIVISION  TYPE                    COST    PRICE  UNITS_SOLD
      1  CPQ-SP256  HW       system              1359.00  1895.00           2
      2  ZEN-SL181  HW       system              1695.00  2399.00           1
      3  IBM-AT640  HW       system              3790.00  4490.00           3
      4  ZEN-MM012  HW       monitor               89.00   159.00           2
      5  NEC-PC660  HW       printer              560.00   820.00           3
      6  HAY-M1200  HW       modem                269.00   389.00           4
      7  SEA-HD020  HW       hard disk            398.00   495.00           3
      8  IOM-HD040  HW       hard disk           2190.00  2790.00           2
      9  PAR-GC100  HW       graphic card         279.00   389.00           2
     10  HER-GC100  HW       graphic card         199.00   239.00           3
     11  ASH-DB300  SW       database             395.00   595.00           3
     12  ANS-DB110  SW       database             525.00   695.00           4
     13  CLP-DB100  SW       database compiler    450.00   595.00           2
     14  WOR-DB100  SW       database compiler    469.00   595.00           1
     15  LOT-LO123  SW       spreadsheet          289.00   359.00           4
     16  MIC-WS330  SW       word processing      229.00   269.00           2
     17  MIS-WD300  SW       word processing      229.00   289.00           2
     18  AST-FW200  SW       integrated           345.00   395.00           2
     19  MIC-QB100  SW       language              79.00   109.00           1
     20  BOL-PA300  SW       language              39.50    69.50           2
```

Fig. 8.5. File structure and contents of PRODSOLD.DBF.

Creating a Report

Tip:

Learn the operations of the report generator.

The report generator's menu options offer a number of operations for designing a custom report:

Menu Option	*Operation*
Options	Defining report heading and layout specifications (page width, margins, line spacing, instructions on printer paging, etc.)
Groups	Defining and labeling data groups and subgroups
Columns	Defining column labels and contents
Locate	Finding the specification of an existing report column or skipping to a given column

Exit   Saving the report form and exiting from the report generator

Options, Columns, and **Exit** are the three menu options required for producing a report. You need the **Groups** option only if you want to summarize data in groups or subgroups. The **Locate** option is handy. You can determine the specification of a particular column by moving quickly to a specific column.

Tip:

Design a report form with the CREATE REPORT command.

The first step in creating a new report form is to assign a name to the report (.FRM) file. This .FRM file will store the format and contents of the report.

To create a new report form, issue the CREATE REPORT command at the dot prompt:

. CREATE REPORT SALERPT1

or select the Assistant menu's **Create/Report** options:

Create/Report/C:/Enter the name of the file: *SALERPT1*

The report generator displays a menu of options. You then can select a suitable option for the report form you are designing.

Tip:

Define the report title.

To design a report heading (called the *page title*), choose **Options** from the menu (see fig. 8.6). You can specify a heading of up to four lines, each as many as 60 characters long. Each line of the heading is centered automatically and displayed at the top of every page.

Tip:

Define report columns.

Select the **Columns** option to define the contents and heading of each column. Column width is determined by the width of the data field in the column or the column heading, whichever is greater. The program automatically adjusts the width whenever you change a column's contents or heading.

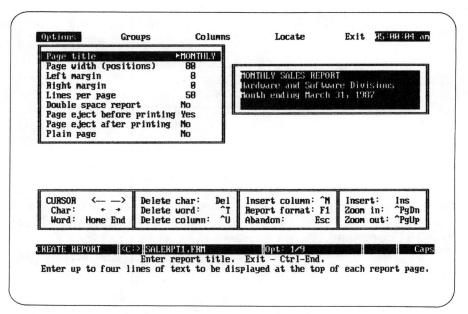

Fig. 8.6. Defining a report heading with the Page title *option.*

You can change the width of a column by specifying it in the **Width** option. But specifying a width narrower than the column's heading or contents causes them to be displayed in a wraparound format.

If the report column consists of one or more character fields, all you have to provide are the column's contents, headings, and width.

You may have a report column that consists of a numeric data field (see fig. 8.7) or an arithmetic expression that includes more than one numeric data field (see fig. 8.8). If so, specify the number of decimal places to be displayed for these values. And indicate whether the values in this column are to be totaled.

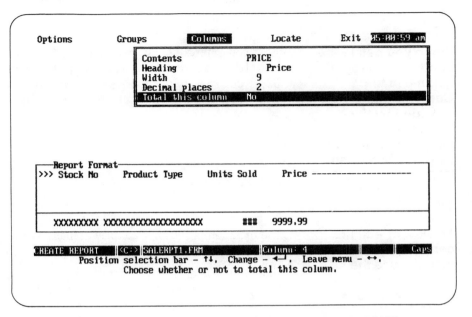

Fig. 8.7. Defining report column with a single numeric data field—PRICE.

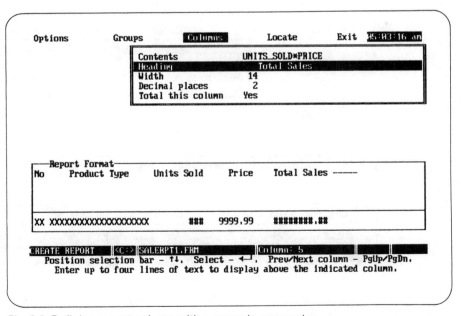

Fig. 8.8. Defining report column with a numeric expression.

Trap:

When you define the contents of a report column in the Contents line provided by the Columns option, a long expression will be partially hidden.

After you enter a long expression in the Contents line and press Enter, only the first portion of the expression is displayed. To view the entire expression, you have to use the arrow keys to scroll back and forth on the Contents line.

Trick:

To view or edit the contents of a report column, use the zoom action instead of the arrow keys.

Use the zooming action to display as many as 80 characters of an expression in the Contents line.

After you have entered an expression in the Contents line and pressed Enter, press Ctrl-PgDn. The expression is displayed at the bottom of the screen (see fig. 8.9) where you can view and edit it.

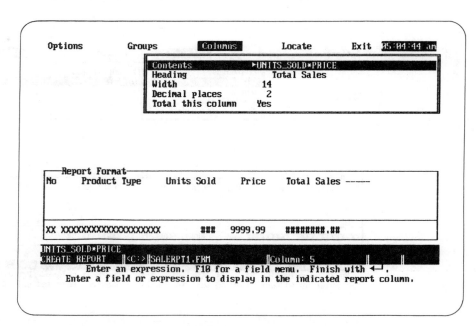

Fig. 8.9. Editing Column contents with the zooming action (by pressing Ctrl-PgDn).

Modifying a Report Form

For safety's sake, make a backup copy of your report file before modifying it.

To change the layout or contents of a report, you can either issue the MODIFY REPORT command or choose the Assistant menu's **Modify/Report** options.

Because changes made to the report file are permanent, make the changes in a *copy* of the report file (a *backup* file). Then you can go back to the original report file if you make any mistakes in the backup file. When you are satisfied with the modified report, delete the original file and rename the backup file.

To copy a report file, use the COPY FILE command:

. COPY FILE SALERPT1.FRM TO SALERPT2.FRM

Be sure to include the file extension (.FRM).

Formatting a Numeric Value

A numeric value is displayed as a series of digits and decimal point editing symbols.

When you specify a numeric value (either the value of a numeric field or a formula) that value is displayed as a series of digits and decimal points, such as *123456.78*. The report generator doesn't place a dollar sign in front of a monetary value nor does it add commas to conform to the format of a business report (123,456.78).

To display a numeric or monetary value in conventional business format, use the TRANSFORM( ) function.

You can display as currency the Price column of the report shown in figure 8.10. To do so, change the contents of the column from `PRICE` to `"$"+TRANSFORM(PRICE,"9,999.99")` (see fig. 8.10).

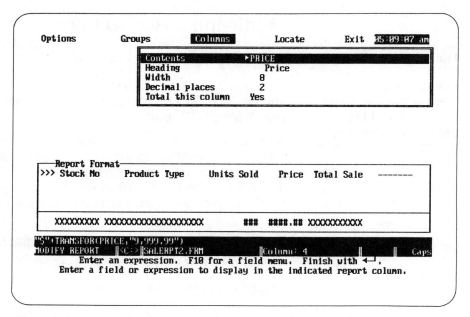

Fig. 8.10. Formatting a numeric value with the TRANSFORM() function.

With the TRANSFORM( ) function, you define a picture format for displaying the value of a numeric or character expression. Specify this picture format within a pair of quotation marks in the function argument:

TRANSFORM(<a numeric or character expression>, "<the picture format>")

Similarly, you can format the report's Total Sales column shown in figure 8.10 by defining its contents as:

"$"+TRANSFORM(UNITS_SOLD*PRICE, "999,999.99")

The modified report form (SALERPT2.FRM) is shown in figure 8.11.

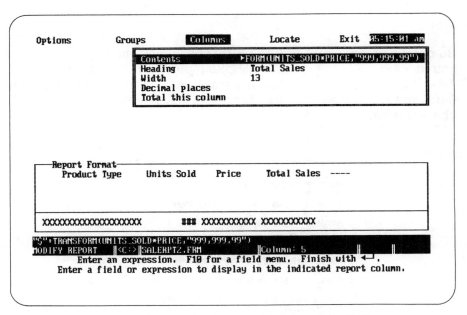

Fig. 8.11. Displaying a monetary value in conventional format with the TRANSFORM() function.

Trap:

If you use TRANSFORM( ) to format an expression, you can't total the contents of that column.	Because the TRANSFORM( ) function always converts a numeric expression into a character string, the contents of the formatted column will not be totaled. And because dollar signs are concatenated to the expression, a single dollar sign cannot be placed directly in front of a monetary value.

If you include a dollar sign in the picture clause, as in *"$9,999.99"*, the dollar sign replaces every leading blank:

```
$1,234.56
$$$123.45
$$$$$1.23
```

Tip:

Use the TRANSFORM( ) function to format character strings.	To display the character string in a PHONE_NO field (such as *123 456 7890*) in a conventional format ((123) 456-7890), use the TRANSFORM( ) function:

```
TRANSFORM(PHONE_NO,"(999)999-9999")
```

Trap:

Be careful when you use the TRANSFORM( ) function to format a character string.

Each symbol or blank space in the picture clause of a TRANSFORM( ) function requires a matching blank space or the same symbol in the character string. Otherwise, some of the characters in the string are not displayed (see fig. 8.12).

```
. PHONE_NO="1234567890"
1234567890
. ?TRANSFORM(PHONE_NO,"(999)999-9999")
(234)678-0
. PHONE_NO=" 123 456-7890"
 123 456-7890
. ?TRANSFORM(PHONE_NO,"(999)999-9999")
(123)456-7890
. ?TRANSFORM(PHONE_NO,"(999) 999-9999")
(123) 56--890
. PHONE_NO=" 123   456-7890"
 123   456-7890
. ?TRANSFORM(PHONE_NO,"(999) 999-9999")
(123) 456-7890
```

Fig. 8.12. Using the TRANSFORM() function to format a character string.

Selecting Printers

Tip:

Use the SET PRINTER TO command to select a printer.

If your computer system has only one printer port, issuing the SET PRINT ON or REPORT FORM . . . TO PRINT commands directs the report (by default) to the LPT1: printer port. But if you have more than one printer connected to different printer ports, you can direct the report to any printer port. Use the SET PRINTER TO command, as in:

. SET PRINTER TO LPT2:

Setting Printer Control Codes

Most printers are capable of printing a report in different type fonts (such as italic and boldface), with different character and line spacing. Text also can be printed in different modes (emphasized, double-strike, or underlined, for example).

To select and designate these printer functions, you print a control code specified by the printer manufacturer. After a control code has been printed, the printer will print the report with that particular function in effect.

Trick:

To issue printer control characters, use the SET PRINT ON command and a ? command.

If you are using an EPSON printer, for example, and you want to print a report in italic font, use the SET PRINT ON command to activate the printer and print the appropriate control code:

```
. SET PRINT ON
. ?CHR(27)+CHR(52)
. USE PRODSOLD
. REPORT FORM SALERPT2 TO PRINT
. EJECT
```

After printing the report, you can deactivate the printer function and return to the original status by issuing the following commands:

```
. SET PRINT ON
. ?CHR(27)+CHR(53)
. SET PRINT OFF
. EJECT
```

This approach has one minor drawback—all the control codes and commands issued when SET PRINT ON is in effect are printed. You need to advance the page manually so that the control codes and commands will not be printed on the same page as the report.

Printing Wide Reports in Compressed Mode

Trick:

To save space, print wide reports in compressed mode.

Most dot-matrix printers allow you to print text in compressed mode, a very useful option for printing wide reports. A report printed in compressed mode takes up much less space than a normal report.

The control code for condensed-print mode may differ for different types of printers. (For example, the control code for an EPSON printer is *CHR(27)+CHR(15)*.) After printing the report in compressed mode, use the *CHR(27)+CHR(18)* control code to return the printer to normal print mode.

To print the report shown in figure 8.13 on an EPSON printer, issue the following commands:

```
. SET PRINT ON
. ?CHR(27)+CHR(15)
. SET PRINT OFF
. USE PRODSOLD
. REPORT FORM SALERPT3 TO PRINT
. SET PRINT ON
. ?CHR(27)+CHR(18)
. SET PRINT OFF
```

Page No.   1
02/21/87

MONTHLY SALES REPORT
Hardware and Software Divisions
Month ending March 31, 1987

Stock No	Product Type	Units Sold	Unit Price	Unit Cost	Unit Profit	Total Sales	Total Profit
CPQ-SP256	system	2	$1,895.00	$1,359.00	$ 536.00	$ 3,790.00	$1,072.00
ZEN-SL181	system	1	$2,399.00	$1,695.00	$ 704.00	$ 2,399.00	$ 704.00
IBM-AT640	system	3	$4,490.00	$3,790.00	$ 700.00	$ 13,470.00	$2,100.00
ZEN-MM012	monitor	2	$ 159.00	$ 89.00	$ 70.00	$ 318.00	$ 140.00
NEC-PC660	printer	3	$ 820.00	$ 560.00	$ 260.00	$ 2,460.00	$ 780.00
HAY-M1200	modem	4	$ 389.00	$ 269.00	$ 120.00	$ 1,556.00	$ 480.00
SEA-HD020	hard disk	3	$ 495.00	$ 398.00	$ 97.00	$ 1,485.00	$ 291.00
IOM-HD040	hard disk	2	$2,790.00	$2,190.00	$ 600.00	$ 5,580.00	$1,200.00
PAR-GC100	graphic card	2	$ 389.00	$ 279.00	$ 110.00	$ 778.00	$ 220.00
HER-GC100	graphic card	3	$ 239.00	$ 199.00	$ 40.00	$ 717.00	$ 120.00
ASH-DB300	database	3	$ 595.00	$ 395.00	$ 200.00	$ 1,785.00	$ 600.00
ANS-DB110	database	4	$ 695.00	$ 525.00	$ 170.00	$ 2,780.00	$ 680.00
CLP-DB100	database compiler	2	$ 595.00	$ 450.00	$ 145.00	$ 1,190.00	$ 290.00
WOR-DB100	database compiler	1	$ 595.00	$ 469.00	$ 126.00	$ 595.00	$ 126.00
LOT-LO123	spreadsheet	4	$ 359.00	$ 289.00	$ 70.00	$ 1,436.00	$ 280.00
MIC-WS330	word processing	2	$ 269.00	$ 229.00	$ 40.00	$ 538.00	$ 80.00
MIS-WD300	word processing	2	$ 289.00	$ 229.00	$ 60.00	$ 578.00	$ 120.00
AST-FW200	integrated	2	$ 395.00	$ 345.00	$ 50.00	$ 790.00	$ 100.00
MIC-QB100	language	1	$ 109.00	$ 79.00	$ 30.00	$ 109.00	$ 30.00
BOL-PA300	language	2	$ 69.50	$ 39.50	$ 30.00	$ 139.00	$ 60.00
*** Total ***							

48

Fig. 8.13. Printing a report in compressed mode.

Grouping Data in a Report

Use the dBASE III Plus report generator to group data in up to
two levels—a subgroup within a given group.

You can modify the report shown in figure 8.13, for example,
to group by product division (DIVISION) all the products sold.
Then products in a given division can be divided by product
type (TYPE) into subgroups.

If you use the **Groups** option to define how you want to
group data, the field values will be summarized in the
modified report. For example, you can group product prices in
two levels: by product division (Hardware and Software) and,
within each product division, by product type. Subtotals are
computed for each group and subgroup, with a grand total at
the end of the report.

Displaying Multiple-Line
Report Columns

In most reports, the content of each character data field or
expression is shown horizontally in a report column, with one
line for each record. But you may want to display the contents
of several character fields or expressions vertically in a
multiple-line format.

If you need to show a set of character data fields or expressions
in a report column as multiple lines, separate these fields or
expressions by using a semicolon (;) in the Contents column.

To illustrate the process, data from the SALARY.DBF file
shown in figure 8.14 is used to create a report (see fig. 8.15).

```
Structure for database: C:SALARY.dbf
Number of data records:      10
Date of last update   : 04/02/87
Field  Field Name  Type       Width    Dec
    1   ID_NO       Character     11
    2   LAST_NAME   Character     10
    3   FIRST_NAME  Character     10
    4   POSITION    Character     10
    5   SALARY      Logical        1
    6   BASE_PAY    Numeric        8       2
    7   EXEMPTIONS  Numeric        2
** Total **                      53

Record#  ID_NO       LAST_NAME  FIRST_NAME  POSITION   SALARY BASE_PAY EXEMPTIONS
      1  123-45-6789 Smith      Thomas T.   President   .T.   39500.00          3
      2  254-63-5691 Thompson   Tina Y.     VP          .T.   32900.00          4
      3  467-34-6789 Watson     Peter F.    Manager     .T.   26000.00          2
      4  732-08-4589 Taylor     Doris Y.    Sales Rep   .F.      10.00          3
      5  563-55-8900 Thorsen    Tyrone T.   Engineer    .T.   29000.00          2
      6  823-46-6213 Faust      Cathy J.    Secretary   .T.   19500.00          1
      7  554-34-7893 Corso      Vincent M.  Sales Rep   .F.      12.00          2
      8  321-65-9087 Kaiser     Jane W.     Accountant  .T.   28900.00          3
      9  560-56-9321 Davidson   Tina K.     Trainee     .F.       9.50          2
     10  435-54-9876 Smith      James J.    Trainee     .F.       7.50          1
```

Fig. 8.14. The file structure and contents of SALARY.DBF.

```
Page No.      1
02/21/87
                ****************************************
                **          PAYROLL REPORT           **
                **         March 31, 1987            **
                ****************************************

Social Security #  Employee Name              Base Pay        Number of
                   Position                                   Exemptions


** Type of Compensation: Hourly Wage
732-08-4589        Taylor, Doris Y.        $      10.00/Hour           3
                   Sales Rep
554-34-7893        Corso, Vincent M.       $      12.00/Hour           2
                   Sales Rep
560-56-9321        Davidson, Tina K.       $       9.50/Hour           2
                   Trainee
435-54-9876        Smith, James J.         $       7.50/Hour           1
                   Trainee
** Subtotal **
                                                                       8


** Type of Compensation: Salary
123-45-6789        Smith, Thomas T.        $39,500.00/Year            3
                   President
254-63-5691        Thompson, Tina Y.       $32,900.00/Year            4
                   VP
467-34-6789        Watson, Peter F.        $26,000.00/Year            2
                   Manager
563-55-8900        Thorsen, Tyrone T.      $29,000.00/Year            2
                   Engineer
823-46-6213        Faust, Cathy J.         $19,500.00/Year            1
                   Secretary
321-65-9087        Kaiser, Jane W.         $28,900.00/Year            3
                   Accountant
** Subtotal **
                                                                      15

*** Total ***
                                                                      23
```

Fig. 8.15. A report showing multiple lines in a column.

You can see that the report's second column displays vertically two lines of characters from the SALARY.DBF file's records. The contents of these two lines are defined with two expressions:

TRIM(LAST_NAME)+", "+TRIM(FIRST_NAME)

and

POSITION

each of which is formed by using character strings from the data fields:

LAST_NAME, FIRST_NAME
POSITION

Because the contents of a report column can be defined by only one expression, you must combine the two expressions in a single expression.

If you use a concatenation operation (+) to join the two expressions:

TRIM(LAST_NAME)+", "+TRIM(FIRST_NAME)+POSITION

all the character strings in the expression will be displayed on one line.

To show the strings as two lines in the report column, use a semicolon (;) to separate the character strings (see fig. 8.16).

Note: The semicolon must be enclosed in quotation marks and treated as a character string.

Displaying Multiple Numeric Values in a Report Column

Trap:

The semicolon can only be used to separate character strings, not numeric expressions.

The semicolon is an extremely powerful tool. With it, you can separate character strings to display them vertically on separate lines in a report column. But you cannot use semicolons to separate numerical values or expressions.

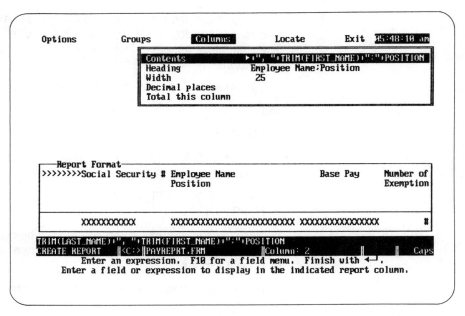

Fig. 8.16. Defining multiple lines in report column with a semicolon separator.

Trick:

Use the STR( )
function to convert
numeric expressions
to character strings.
Then use semicolons
to join them.

For example, to display the values of four numeric
expressions:

UNITS_SOLD
PRICE
COST
(PRICE–COST)*UNITS_SOLD

stacked vertically in a report column, use the STR( ) function
to convert the numeric expressions to character strings and
combine the strings with semicolons:

STR(UNITS_SOLD,10,0)+";"+STR(PRICE,10,2)+";"
+STR(COST,10,2)+";"+STR((PRICE–COST)*UNITS_SOLD,10,2)

Using Logical Fields in a Report

Trap:

A logical field rarely provides adequate descriptive information because its value can be only .T. or .F.

If you use the field "SEX" in a database to describe the sex of an employee, a .T. can represent either a male or a female. When you display the logical value in a report, a .T. may not clearly describe the data field.

Trick:

Use the IIF( ) function to display the value of a logical data field in a report.

To define the contents of a report column that involves a logical data field, use the IIF( ) function. This function can convert the logical value to different expressions, depending on the value.

For example, to display "Male" when the value of the logical field "SEX" is .T. and "Female" when the value is .F., use the IIF( ) function:

. IIF(SEX,"Male","Female")

Similarly, by using the logical field *SALARY* in the SALARY.DBF file (see fig. 8.14) to indicate employee compensation (.T. for a salaried employee, .F. for an hourly worker), you can use IIF( ) to convert the logical values in the SALARY field to labels ("/Hour" or "/Year") in the Base Pay column.

Grouping Data with a Logical Data Field

Trap:

You cannot use a logical data field to group data in a report.

Although logical fields play an important role in data management, many restrictions are imposed on how they are used. One of the major restrictions is that you cannot use a logical field as a key for indexing a database file. To use a logical field to group data in a report, you must perform an extra operation. You must convert the logical value to a character string expression with the IIF( ) function.

Trick:

To group data in a report, use the IIF( ) function to convert the logical value to a character string expression.

For example, the payroll report shown in figure 8.15 groups the data records in the SALARY.DBF file by the value of the logical field *SALARY* (.*T.* for *Salary*, .*F.* for *Hourly Wage*). This grouping is done according to the character string returned by the IIF( ) function:

IIF(SALARY,"Salary","Hourly Wage")

using the **Groups** option to group on the expressions "Salary" and "Hourly Wage."

The IIF( ) function returns the string "Salary" if the value of the logical field SALARY is .*T.*, or "Hourly Wage" if the value is .*F.*

Trick:

When using a logical field to group data in reports, index the file before producing the report.

dBASE III Plus does not index the records based on the string returned by the IIF( ) function when you use the function to group records. You must index the data file on the character string derived from a logical field *before* you issue the REPORT FORM command.

For example, the report shown in figure 8.15 was produced with the following commands:

```
. USE SALARY
. INDEX ON IIF(SALARY,"Y","N") TO PAYTYPE
. REPORT FORM PAYREPRT TO PRINT
```

Figure 8.17 was produced without indexing the database file on the string produced by the IIF(SALARY,"Y","N") function. As you can see, the records are not summarized in groups.

```
02/21/87
                    *************************************
                    **        PAYROLL REPORT         **
                    **        March 31, 1987         **
                    *************************************

Social Security #  Employee Name                 Base Pay       Number of
                   Position                                     Exemptions


** Type of Compensation: Salary
   123-45-6789     Smith, Thomas T.          $39,500.00/Year         3
                   President
   254-63-5691     Thompson, Tina Y.         $32,900.00/Year         4
                   VP
   467-34-6789     Watson, Peter F.          $26,000.00/Year         2
                   Manager
** Subtotal **
                                                                     9

** Type of Compensation: Hourly Wage
   732-08-4589     Taylor, Doris Y.          $    10.00/Hour         3
                   Sales Rep
** Subtotal **
                                                                     3

** Type of Compensation: Salary
   563-55-8900     Thorsen, Tyrone T.        $29,000.00/Year         2
                   Engineer
   823-46-6213     Faust, Cathy J.           $19,500.00/Year         1
                   Secretary
** Subtotal **
                                                                     3

** Type of Compensation: Hourly Wage
   554-34-7893     Corso, Vincent M.         $    12.00/Hour         2
                   Sales Rep
** Subtotal **
                                                                     2

** Type of Compensation: Salary
   321-65-9087     Kaiser, Jane W.           $28,900.00/Year         3
                   Accountant
** Subtotal **
                                                                     3

** Type of Compensation: Hourly Wage
   560-56-9321     Davidson, Tina K.         $     9.50/Hour         2
                   Trainee
   435-54-9876     Smith, James J.           $     7.50/Hour         1
                   Trainee
** Subtotal **
                                                                     3
*** Total ***
                                                                    23
```

Fig. 8.17. Payroll report grouped by using a logical data field.

Adding Report Headings at Time of Reporting

Trap:

When you specify a report heading in a report form, that heading remains fixed for all subsequent reports. Whenever you want to change it, you need to modify the report form.

When you create a new report form with the report generator, you are given up to four lines for defining the report heading under the **Options/Page title** menu option. Text entered in the page title box is displayed at the top of every report page. And this text can be changed only by using the MODIFY REPORT command. If you need a different heading every time you produce the report, you must modify the report form before you issue the REPORT FORM command.

When you generate a sales report at the end of every month, for example, you need to add the reporting period (such as *For the month of March, 1987*) to the report form. This task can be tedious and time-consuming.

Trick:

Use the HEADING option to display dynamic report headings.

To display a dynamic report heading at the time of reporting, use the HEADING option in the REPORT FORM command. Then you can display a new heading without modifying the report form.

To enter the heading, use the HEADING option in the REPORT FORM command. You can add multiple lines to the report heading by using semicolons as line separator characters:

```
. USE PRODSOLD
. REPORT FORM SALERPT1 HEADING "MONTHLY SALE
REPORT"+";"+
"Hardware and Software Divisions"+";"+
"For the month of March, 1987"
```

When the report is produced, these lines of text are added above the report heading specified in the report form's **Page title** option. Each line is centered automatically.

You also can use the HEADING option in the REPORT FORM command to include character memory variables or data field values as part of the report heading:

```
. LINE1="THE GREAT NORTHWEST COMPUTER STORE"
. LINE2="SALE SUMMARY REPORT"
. LINE3="Period Ending "
. RPTDATE="4/30/87"
. USE SALEDATA
. REPORT FORM SALERPRT HEADING LINE1+";"+LINE2+";"+
LINE3+";"+RPTDATE
```

Trick:

Store dynamic report headings in memory variables.

You can store the values of memory variables in a memory file and recall whenever you need them.

To save memory variables to a file (REPTVARS.MEM), use the SAVE TO command after you have entered the values for the variables.

```
. LINE1="THE GREAT NORTHWEST COMPUTER STORE"
. LINE2="SALE SUMMARY REPORT"
. LINE3="Period Ending "
. RPTDATE="4/30/87"
. SAVE TO REPTVARS
```

When you need to recall the variables from the memory file, issue the RESTORE FROM . . . ADDITIVE command:

```
. RESTORE FROM REPTVARS ADDITIVE
```

After recalling the memory variables from the memory file and adding them to memory, use the DISPLAY MEMORY command to examine their values. If you need to change the value of a specific memory variable, you can alter the variable's value and save it back to the memory file (see fig. 8.18).

Trick:

To eliminate page numbers and system dates from reports, use the Plain page **option.**

dBASE III Plus generates a standard report form. In this report form, the page number and the current system date are displayed in the upper left corner. If you don't want them on your report, choose **Options/Plain page** from the menu when you define the report layout in the report generator.

To select the **Plain page** option, move the cursor to the option and press Enter to change the status of the option from *No* to *Yes*. Or use PLAIN in the REPORT FORM command.

```
, RESTORE FROM REPTVARS ADDITIVE
, DISP MEMORY
LINE1      pub   C   "THE GREAT NORTHWEST COMPUTER STORE"
LINE2      pub   C   "SALE SUMMARY REPORT"
LINE3      pub   C   "Period Ending "
RPTDATE    pub   D   04/30/87
    4 variables defined,        82 bytes used
    252 variables available,   5918 bytes available

, RPTDATE=CTOD("5/31/87")
05/31/87
, SAVE TO REPTVARS
REPTVARS.mem already exists, overwrite it? (Y/N) Yes
,
,
```

Fig. 8.18. Recalling memory variables from a memory file.

Processing Data Before Reporting

The dBASE III Plus report generator has limited power and
imposes a number of restrictions. Because of these restrictions,
many data-manipulation operations must be performed outside
the report generator.

Trick:

**To produce complex
reports and shorten
reporting time,
process the data
before reporting.**

One of the program's serious limitations is that you can use
data records from only one database file in a report. To
produce a report with records from multiple database files, you
need to combine the records before performing the reporting
operation.

Similarly, the report generator has extremely limited power
for sorting data records in a report. If you need to arrange the
records by using one or more key fields, for example, you
have to presort the data records before producing the report.

Filter conditions for screening data records cannot be specified
in the report generator. You must specify these conditions
before using the report form if only a selected set of records is
to be included in the report.

Trick:

To use data records from multiple database files, combine the records with the APPEND operation.

If you need to produce a report using data records from more than one database file, combine the records in a database file. Then use that file to produce your report.

To combine these records, create a new database file and then use the APPEND operation to add records from the existing database files.

For example, to produce a report for the sales of two regional offices (REGION1.DBF and REGION2.DBF), create a database file (ALLSALES.DBF) for the combined records of the two database files. Then append records from the regional database files:

```
. USE ALLSALES
. APPEND FROM REGION1
. APPEND FROM REGION2
```

Now, using the records in the ALLSALES.DBF file, you can design a custom report form.

Trick:

To use data fields from multiple database files, link the files with the SET RELATION operation.

The dBASE III Plus report generator allows the use of only one database file for a report. If you want to combine data fields from multiple database files in the same report, you must first link the files.

One way to link several data fields from different database files is to use the SET RELATION operation.

For example, to use selected data fields from the SOFTWARE.DBF and SWSTOCK.DBF database files, link the files with the following SET RELATION commands:

```
. SELECT 1
. USE SOFTWARE
. INDEX ON STOCK_NO TO SWSTCKNO
. SELECT 2
. USE SWSTOCK
. INDEX ON STOCK_NO TO SKSTCKNO
. SELECT 1
. SET RELATION TO STOCK_NO INTO B
```

You can select data fields from the linked files by using the SET FIELDS command.

For example, you can select STOCK_NO, PRICE, and COST from SOFTWARE.DBF in active work area 1, and ON_HAND and ON_ORDER from SWSTOCK.DBF in work area 2 (alias B), with the following command:

. SET FIELDS TO STOCK_NO,COST,PRICE,B->ON_HAND,B->ON_ORDER

At this point, you can invoke the report generator (CREATE REPORT) to design a report form based on the data fields specified with the SET FIELDS command:

. CREATE REPORT INVREPRT

If you expect to link the two database files again, save (in a view file) the information about relating the files. You can create such a view file while the files are being related. To do so, use the CREATE VIEW <name of the view file> FROM ENVIRONMENT command:

. CREATE VIEW INVREPRT FROM ENVIRONMENT

Whenever you need to produce the report, you can relink the database files by using the SET VIEW TO command before selecting the report form:

. SET VIEW TO INVREPRT
. REPORT FORM INVREPRT

Trick:

To use records from multiple database files with different file structures in a report, create a joined database file.

You can use data fields from more than one database file in a report. One way is to link the fields with the JOIN operation before producing the report. A JOIN operation combines selected data fields from two database files, using a common field as a linking key field.

For example, you can join the data fields from SOFTWARE.DBF and SWSTOCK.DBF by using the common STOCK_NO data field:

```
. SELECT 1
. USE SOFTWARE
. SELECT 2
. USE SWSTOCK
. JOIN WITH A TO JOINFILE FOR STOCK_NO=A->STOCK_NO
FIELDS STOCK_NO,A->COST,A->PRICE,ON_HAND,ON_ORDER
```

Then use the report generator to design a custom report form with the records in JOINFILE.DBF, which combines the data fields from the two database files:

```
. USE JOINFILE
. CREATE REPORT
```

Trick:

Rearrange data records with the SORT or INDEX operation before producing reports.

The report generator does not allow you to alter the order of records in the database when you display the report.

If you want to display the records in a specific order in a report, use the SORT or INDEX operation to rearrange the records in the database file.

To list products in ascending order according to their prices in a monthly sales report, for example, index the file on the PRICE field before issuing the REPORT FORM command:

```
. USE PRODSOLD
. INDEX ON PRICE TO BYPRICE
. REPORT FORM SALERPT1 TO PRINT
```

Trick:

Perform complex mathematical operations on data fields before producing reports.

Although the dBASE III Plus report generator allows you to perform certain mathematical operations on data fields, these operations are limited to only a few basic functions. Performing mathematical operations on a large number of records while you produce a report greatly hampers processing speed.

Performing these operations outside the report generator and saving the results to a database file is highly recommended. You can use that database file to produce your report.

Trick:

You can use an external report generator to produce custom reports.

You can produce reports by using a number of different report generators, such as Quickreport© for dBASE by Fox & Geller.

Quickreport for dBASE allows you to connect as many as six database files in one report. The program also lets you use special printer features anywhere on the report to display fields and titles in different print styles.

Another powerful feature of Quickreport for dBASE is that it allows you to include your own computed fields in the report and to summarize any data field with a family of statistical functions (such as TOTAL, COUNT, AVERAGE, MAX, and MIN).

9

Programming in dBASE III Plus Command Language: Program Editing, Memory Variables, and Screen Design

Although not developed to be a general-purpose language, the dBASE III Plus command language offers many powerful programming tools. Using these tools, you can design and develop a powerful yet user-friendly data-management system.

This chapter focuses on tips and tricks for program design. It focuses also on how to maximize the flexibility and power of your data-management system. For example, you can use commands in a program file to write sophisticated statistical and graphics programs.

Creating and Editing a Program

A *program* or *command* file (with a *.PRG* file extension) consists of a set of instructional text. It can be created and edited with a text editor.

You can create and edit a text file with the dBASE III Plus text editor (invoked by CREATE COMMAND or MODIFY COMMAND). But the program's text editor lacks the power and features (including many convenient editing functions) of other word-processing programs. And because the dBASE III Plus text editor can process only a small text file (up to 5,000 characters), you cannot use it to create a large program.

Trap:

You may lose part of your program if you use the dBASE III Plus text editor to edit a large program.

Do not attempt to edit a large program with the dBASE III Plus text editor. With the internal text editor, you are limited to 5,000 characters. If you extend an existing program beyond the 5,000-character limit while you are in the text editor, you may lose part of the program.

Use a more powerful word processor or text editor when you want to write a relatively large, complex program.

Trick:

Use an external text editor or word processor for creating and editing your programs.

To use an external text editor or word processor, you must specify the external program's name in the TEDIT command of the CONFIG.DB file:

TEDIT=<name of the text editor or word processor>

If, for example, you want to use WordStar as the text editor within dBASE III Plus, include the following line in the CONFIG.DB file:

TEDIT=*WS.COM*

Most text editors or word processors (WordStar, WordPerfect, Microsoft Word, and MultiMate, to name a few) can be used to edit a program file within dBASE III Plus.

If you decide to use an external word processor (such as WordStar) as the text editor, all of the programs related to the word processor must be accessible by the disk operating system (DOS).

Trap:

Special embedded characters used by a word processor for formatting cannot be used in a program file.

The special embedded characters used by some word processors to format documents and type fonts are not allowed in program files.

Trick:

To use external word-processing programs, you need to strip special characters from the program files before storing the files.

For example, if you are using WordStar as a text editor, choose the **Non-document** option for editing your program file. The paging and special characters will be excluded.

Trap:

The TEDIT command will not recognize a directory path.

When you identify an external text editor or word processor to be used in dBASE III Plus (by using the TEDIT command in the CONFIG.DB file), you should enter only the name of the editor or word processor. You cannot specify a directory path.

Setting Paths

Trick:

Use the PATH command to tell DOS where the external word processor resides.

To ensure that all the programs related to an external word processor are accessible by DOS, save and install the related program files in a separate directory. Then use a PATH command to tell DOS where to find the directory.

A PATH is a list of drive/directory specifications separated by semicolons. DOS searches in order from the top level directory through the other levels for program and command files.

If you save all the WordStar files in the WORDPROC directory, for example, you can instruct DOS where to search for the word-processing program by issuing the following PATH command:

C>*PATH C:\WORDPROC*

To specify multiple paths in the PATH command, use semicolons to separate the paths:

C> *PATH C:\WORDPROC; C:\DOSFILES;*
C:\DBASE\SYSPROGS

Trap:

You cannot use the SET PATH TO command within dBASE III Plus to locate word-processing programs.

The dBASE III Plus SET PATH TO command can be used only to search for database-related files.

If you save all the program files related to an external word-processing program in a separate directory, you cannot use the SET PATH TO command to inform DOS where these programs are located.

Using a Memory-Resident Text Editor

Trick:

Use a memory-resident text editor to edit program files.

Instead of using an external word processor (such as WordPerfect, Microsoft Word, or MultiMate), use a memory-resident program such as SideKick to create and edit a program file within dBASE III Plus.

A memory-resident program such as SideKick is a very convenient way to create and edit a program file within dBASE III Plus. SideKick's notepad feature offers many advantages over other text editors or word processors for editing a dBASE III Plus program file.

You can edit a text file of 1,000 to 50,000 characters with SideKick's notepad. If you intend to write a large program in dBASE III Plus and have enough memory space, set the notepad size by using the notepad File size ("F") option in the SKINST.COM installation program.

You needn't specify a memory-resident text editor like SideKick in the CONFIG.DB file. You simply load the program before using it. Once installed, SideKick can be invoked by pressing Ctrl-Alt.

When you use more than one memory-resident program (SideKick and Superkey, for example), the order in which these programs are loaded can be important. Unless the programs are loaded in the proper order, errors caused by memory overlap may occur.

Normally, you load SideKick before entering dBASE III Plus by issuing the *SK* command at the DOS prompt. However, if you forget to do so, you can load the program by using the RUN command at the dot prompt:

. RUN SK

If the SK.COM program is not in the current directory, specify its location in a directory path in the RUN command. (Refer to Chapter 1 for a discussion of how to use the RUN command to execute a DOS command within dBASE III Plus.)

Viewing a Program

Trick:

Use the TYPE command to view a program.

An easy way to view a program is to issue the TYPE command at the dot prompt.

If the program is more than one screen long, use the Ctrl-S key combination to halt the listing temporarily. Press any key to resume the listing operation.

Tip:

Use the TYPE .. TO PRINT command to print a program listing.

If you want to direct a program listing to the printer, add the TO PRINT option to the TYPE command at the dot prompt:

. TYPE MAIN.PRG TO PRINT

Programming Conventions

Tip:

Standardize the representation of data fields, memory variables, and command words in a program.

A program is a set of instructions that include dBASE III Plus commands and keywords. Memory variables are used for storing values (which may be entered from the keyboard) or for saving the intermediate results of computations.

To make these program elements easily identifiable, you need to standardize the way in which commands, memory variables, and keywords are represented in your program. dBASE III Plus has no universal rules, or *conventions*. Just be consistent. In this book, for example, the following program elements are represented in uppercase letters:

- dBASE III Plus commands (USE, INDEX, DISPLAY, IF . . . ENDIF)

- names of database files (EMPLOYEE.DBF, SOFTWARE.NDX)

- names of programs or procedures (MAIN.PRG, FINDRECD.PRG)

- names of data fields (LAST_NAME, COST, PRICE)

The names of *memory variables* begin with *m*, followed by an assigned name in both upper- and lowercase letters, as in *mTotalCost* and *mChoice*.

Comment and *remark* lines begin with an asterisk (∗) on a separate line or double ampersands (&&) following an instruction:

```
* This is a remark line
USE EMPLOYEE    && Select the database file
```

Tip:

Use comments and remarks to make a program more readable.

When you're developing a program for data management, using remarks or comments is good practice.

Remarks and comments describing the nature of the program and the important components and procedures you've used make it easier to read and understand the program.

Include (at the beginning of the program) a general description
of the program task. Also, define the important memory
variables you use in the process, and add blank spaces in
command lines to make them more readable. The following
program illustrates how you might develop a program to find
and display a record in a database file:

```
*** FINDRECD.PRG
* Find and display a data record in a given database file
*
* Use mDBF, mNDX to store name of .DBF and .NDX files
* mKeyValue stores the searching key value
PARAMETERS mDBF,mNDX, mKeyValue
*
* Display parameters passed from LOCATE.PRG
CLEAR          && clear the screen
@5,20 SAY ">> Search parameters specified <<"
@7,10 SAY "Name of the database file (.dbf) : " GET mDBF
@9,10 SAY "   Name of the index file (.ndx) : " GET mNDX
@11,10 SAY "      Value for the key field  : " GET mKeyValue
*
USE &mDBF INDEX &mNDX     && select and index .dbf file
SEEK mKeyValue              && find the record by the key value
IF FOUND( )
   @15,10 SAY "The record found:"
   ?
   DISPLAY
ELSE
   @15,30 SAY "No such record!"
ENDIF
@22,1
WAIT           && pause
RETURN         && return to the calling LOCATE.PRG
```

Excessive remarks and blank spaces can be costly. Storing
them takes up disk space and execution time is slightly slower,
even though they are ignored during execution. But the
benefits of these remarks may outweigh the cost in time and
space.

Using Memory Variables

Tip:	

Understand the basic functions of a memory variable.

A memory variable represents a memory location that is used for storing a piece of information. Depending on the type of memory variable, that piece of information can be a character string, a numerical value, a date, or a logical value.

The basic functions of memory variables are

- storing the values of variables in a formula
- storing the result of a computation
- passing values among different program modules and procedures
- storing the value of a counter or an accumulator
- storing parameters for controlling a program loop
- storing values for branching operations

These basic functions are discussed in separate sections in this chapter.

Naming Memory Variables

Tip:	

Name memory variables properly.

When you name a memory variable, try to assign a descriptive, easily identified name. To store the value of the unit cost, for example, use *unit_cost* instead of *x*.

A memory variable's name can be as many as 10 characters long. But many punctuation marks and special symbols (such as @, #, $, %, &, *, ?, /, and \) are not allowed.

Use only the letters *A* through *Z* (and *a* through *z*) and the numerals *0* through *9* to name a memory variable. The name must begin with a letter.

You can use both uppercase and lowercase letters (as in *TotalCost*) because case is ignored in a memory variable name. If you need to group characters in a name, use the underscore symbol (_), as in *Total_Cost*.

Trap:

When you use a large set of memory variables in a program, searching for and identifying all of them may be time-consuming.

If you adopt a convention for naming variables, however, you can locate them quickly. Use the search-and-find features offered by most text editors or word processors.

Trick:

To minimize search time, begin all memory variable names with an *m*.

You can minimize search time by beginning all memory variable names with the letter *m*, as in:

mTotalCost
mHourlyPay
mQty_Sold
mUnitPrice

and then asking the text editor or word processor to search the program for all strings that begin with *m*.

Trap:

Do not use reserved words, dBASE III Plus commands, or the single letters A through J for naming memory variables.

When you name memory variables, be sure not to use any reserved words or dBASE III Plus commands as names. For example, using any of the following summary commands as a memory variable:

Total
Count
Sum
Average

may result (without warning) in erroneous answers.

Do not use the single letters *A* through *J* as memory variable names because these letters are reserved as aliases for database files in the work areas.

Trick:

Use the STORE command to initialize the value of a memory variable, and the equal (=) assignment operator to change it.

The value of a memory variable can be assigned by the STORE command or by using the equal (=) arithmetical operator.

If you are using a large set of memory variables in a program, you may want to find out where and when they were set up in the program. To do so, adopt a convention for assigning values to these variables.

Use STORE to initialize the memory variables and use the equal (=) operator to change their values as needed. Then use the search-and-find features provided by a text editor or word processor to identify the STORE command easily.

For example, values are assigned to mAnswer, mCost, mBirthDate, and mPaid by the following STORE commands:

```
STORE "Yes" TO mAnswer
STORE 299.50 TO mCost
STORE CTOD("07/04/87") TO mBirthDate
STORE .T. TO mPaid
```

The same set of values may be assigned to the memory variables by the following commands:

```
mAnswer="Yes"
mCost=299.50
mBirthDate=CTOD("07/04/87")
mPaid=.T.
```

Trick:

Do not change a variable from one type to another.

In many programming languages, different syntax rules are used for naming different types of variables. When you program in BASIC, for instance, numeric and alphanumeric (character) variables are named differently.

In the dBASE III Plus command language, however, all variables are named with the same syntax rules. The variable type is determined by the value assigned to it.

For example, a character string (such as "John") assigned to a memory variable (mVar) becomes a character variable. It remains a character variable until you assign a different type of value to it. (In other words, if you assign a numeric value to the variable it becomes a numeric variable.)

Although dBASE III Plus allows you to change a variable's type within a program, it is not good practice and should be avoided.

Using one variable to store different types of data in the same program is quite confusing because the variable type may be different depending on its location in the program.

Allocating Memory for Memory Variables

dBASE III Plus allocates (by default) 6,000 bytes of memory space for storing the contents of memory variables. You can use a maximum of 256 memory variables in dBASE III Plus. Different types of variables occupy different amounts of memory space.

Date and numeric variables each use nine bytes; logical variables occupy two bytes. The amount of space occupied by a character variable is the length of the string it holds (up to 254 characters) plus two bytes.

For example, if you assign the string *"JOHN"* (four characters, or bytes) to the *mFirstName* variable, the variable consumes six bytes of memory.

Tip:

Reserve additional memory if you need to use a large set of memory variables.

The memory space allocated by dBASE III Plus for storing the contents of memory variables is set by default at 6,000 bytes.

If you anticipate using more memory space than the default 6,000 bytes, you can specify in the CONFIG.DB file the additional memory you need.

MVARSIZ=<memory in increments of 1 kilobyte>

Memory space in this case is measured by kilobytes. (A kilobyte is equivalent to 1,024 bytes.) To reserve ten kilobytes (10,240 bytes) of space for storing your memory variables, for example, add the following line to the CONFIG.DB file:

MVARSIZ=10

You can allocate from one to 31 kilobytes (or 1,024 to 31,744 bytes) of space for memory variables.

Tip:

When you reserve additional memory space for memory variables, also allocate additional space for dBASE III Plus.

If you set a large value in the MVARSIZ command in the CONFIG.DB file, you take memory away from other dBASE III Plus operations. You will need to allocate additional memory space for dBASE III Plus by using the MAXMEM command in the CONFIG.DB file.

If you have a large amount of RAM in your computer system, for example, allocate 384K or more to dBASE III Plus.

    MAXMEM=384

Chapter 2 discusses in detail how to allocate memory space in the configuration file for dBASE III Plus.

Entering Values for Memory Variables

Tip:

Use the WAIT command to assign a single keystroke value to a memory variable.

When you design an interactive program, you frequently need to add prompts to tell the user how to proceed. Use the dBASE III Plus WAIT command at these times.

Executing the WAIT command causes a prompt:

    Press any key to continue...

to appear. As its name implies, the WAIT command waits for a key to be pressed at the prompt. As soon as that key is pressed, the program proceeds to the next instruction.

Use a WAIT command to display a prompt message and save the keystroke to a memory variable:

    WAIT "<prompt message>" TO <name of memory variable>

For example, you may want to ask "Is the item entered correct [Y/N] ? " after processing a data item. To save a single-key answer (Y or N) to a memory variable (mAnswer) to determine the next processing step, use the following command:

WAIT "Is the item entered correct [Y/N] ?" TO *mAnswer*

As soon as a keystroke is entered, it's assigned to the memory variable specified in the WAIT command. The command accepts only the first keystroke entered; subsequent keystrokes are ignored.

Tip:

Use the INPUT command to assign a value to a memory variable at program execution.

When you need to get a value from keyboard entry at the time of program execution and assign that value to a memory variable, use the INPUT command. The INPUT command can be used with a prompt describing the value to be entered:

INPUT <prompt> TO <name of memory variable>

The following program illustrates the use of INPUT commands for assigning values to memory variables:

```
*** INPUTDAT.PRG
* Assign values to memory variables from keyboard entry
SET TALK OFF
SET ECHO OFF
CLEAR
* Get variable values from keyboard entries
  @5,1
  INPUT SPACE(5)+"Enter:   Account number . . . "  TO mAcctNo
  ?
  INPUT SPACE(5)+"         Invoice date . . . . . "  TO mInvDate
  ?
  INPUT SPACE(5)+"         Amount of sale . . . "  TO mSale
  ?
  INPUT SPACE(5)+"         A COD sale [T/F] ? "  TO mCOD
* Display contents of these memory variables
  @15,10 SAY ">> Values assigned to memory variables <<"
  @17,15 SAY " mAcctNo : " GET mAcctNo
  @18,15 SAY "mInvDate : " GET mInvDate
  @19,15 SAY "    mSale : " GET mSale
  @20,15 SAY "     mCOD : " GET mCOD
RETURN
```

Any type of data can be stored in a memory variable with the INPUT command. The variable type is determined by the type of data entered in response to the INPUT command.

The values to be assigned to the memory variables by using INPUTDAT.PRG are shown in figure 9.1. In the figure, you will notice that the character string to be assigned to mAcctNo is enclosed in a pair of quotation marks. A date value must be entered by using the CTOD( ) function to assign it to the date variable mInvDate. The numeric variable mSale is assigned a value, while the .T. logical value is stored in the mCOD logical variable.

```
Enter:   Account number ...  "A123-4567"

         Invoice date .....  CTOD("7/4/87")

         Amount of sale ...  895

         A COD sale [T/F] ?  .T.

      >> Values assigned to memory variables <<

             mAcctNo :  A123-4567
            mInvDate :  07/04/87
               mSale :        895
                mCOD :  T
```

Fig. 9.1. Assigning data to memory variables with INPUT commands.

Trap:

To store a character string in a memory variable with an INPUT command, be sure to enclose the string in a pair of quotation marks.

Using the INPUT command, any type of data can be assigned to a memory variable. The variable type is determined by the type of data you enter in response to the INPUT command. If you intend to assign a character string to a memory variable, you must enclose the string in a pair of quotation marks. Otherwise, the character string will be considered a variable.

For example, you can use the following INPUT command to get a first name from keyboard entry and assign it to the memory variable mFirstName:

INPUT "Enter customer's first name . . ." TO mFirstName

If the first name to be assigned to the variable is "JOHN", you must enter it (enclosed in quotation marks) at the INPUT prompt:

`Enter customer's first name ...` *"JOHN"*

If you enter the character string without the quotation marks:

`Enter customer's first name ...` *JOHN*

the error message `Variable not found` will be displayed.

This happens because you can enter the name of another memory variable at the INPUT prompt. Because the character string is not enclosed in quotation marks, the string is interpreted as the name of a variable.

Tip:

Use the ACCEPT command to assign a character string to a memory variable.

The ACCEPT command is used primarily to assign (with or without a prompt) a character string or the contents of another character variable to a memory variable:

ACCEPT <prompt> TO <name of memory variable>

The command is designed to assign a character string to a memory variable from keyboard entry at the time of program execution. It functions like the INPUT command, except that only character data can be used with the ACCEPT command.

For example, the following command can be used in a program file to get the name of a customer and assign it to the memory variable mCustomer:

ACCEPT "Enter name of customer : " TO mCustomer

Be sure to enclose in quotation marks the character string to be assigned to the memory variable mCustomer:

`Enter name of customer :` *"John J. Smith"*

Without the quotation marks, the first character string (*John*) will be mistakenly interpreted as the name of another variable.

Tip:

**Use the @ .. SAY ..
GET command for
storing a value in a
memory variable.**

You can store a value in a memory variable in a number of ways. One way is to use the INPUT or ACCEPT command to assign a value to a memory variable.

A better approach is to use the @ .. SAY .. GET command for getting the value that is entered from the keyboard. This command gives you the freedom to place an input prompt anywhere on the screen. In addition, the command allows you to select the type of data (character, numeric, date, or logical) you want to assign to the variable.

For example, the following commands display, at the screen's 5th row and 10th column, a message requesting that a character string be entered:

```
STORE SPACE(10) TO mAcctName
@5,10 SAY "Enter name of the account : " GET mAcctName
READ
```

When these commands are executed, the memory variable's current contents are displayed in reverse video following the prompt (see fig. 9.2).

Fig. 9.2. Entering account name in a reverse video prompt.

Because the memory variable mAcctName has been initialized with 10 blank spaces (SPACE(10)) by using the STORE command, an entry block of 10 blank characters is displayed for data entry.

As you can see from figure 9.3, the contents of date, logical, and numerical memory variables are displayed in the appropriate format.

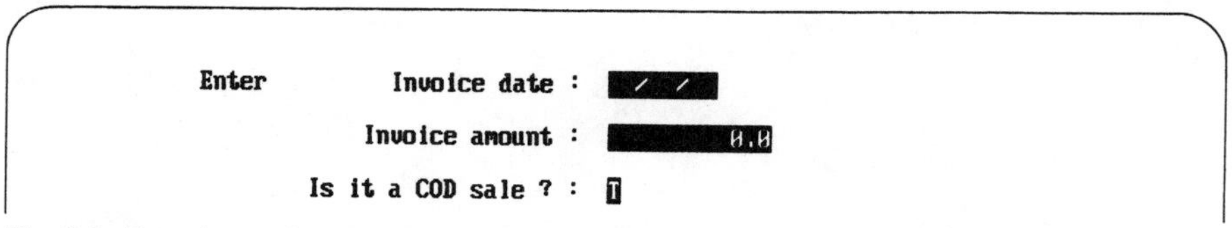

Fig. 9.3. Entering values to different memory variables.

The screen shown in figure 9.3 was generated by executing the commands in the following program:

```
*** PROMPTS.PRG
* Prompt for different types of memory variables
CLEAR
STORE CTOD(" / / ") TO mInv_Date
STORE 0.0 TO mAmount
STORE .T. TO mCOD
@5,10 SAY "Enter          Invoice date : " GET mInv_Date
@7,10 SAY"           Invoice amount : " GET mAmount
@9,10 SAY"        Is it a COD sale ? : " GET mCOD
READ
```

Trick:

Add PICTURE template to @ .. SAY .. GET to format the input value of a memory variable.

While you're using the @ .. SAY .. GET command to store a value in a memory variable, you can also add a PICTURE template. This will ensure that the data is entered in the format you want.

For example, when the following program is executed, the data values to be stored in the memory variables must conform to the formats specified by the PICTURE templates:

```
*** PICTURE.PRG
* Format input values in picture templates
CLEAR
STORE SPACE(11) TO mId_No
STORE SPACE(10) TO mFirst
STORE SPACE(2) TO mInit
STORE SPACE(10) TO mLast
STORE 0 TO mSalary
@5,10 SAY "Employee's Id. No. : " GET mId_No
PICTURE "###- ##-####"
@7,10 SAY "     First Name : " GET mFirst PICTURE
"!AAAAAAAAA"
@9,10 SAY "  Middle Initial : " GET mInit PICTURE "!."
@11,10 SAY "        Last Name : " GET mLast PICTURE
"!!!!!!!!!!"
@13,10 SAY "     Annual Salary : " GET mSalary PICTURE
"##,###.##"
READ
```

The program produces prompts that request values for the memory variables (see fig. 9.4).

Employee's Id. No. :

First Name :

Middle Initial :

Fig. 9.4. Formatting input values with PICTURE templates.

In figure 9.4, you will notice that the symbols (dashes, commas, and period) in the employee's identification number, salary, and middle initial are inserted in the entry block.

The masking symbols (!, #, A) specified in the PICTURE templates determine the types of characters allowed in their places.

For example, the *"A"* symbol permits only a letter of the alphabet to be entered in its place. Only numbers are allowed where a *"#"* is specified. A letter entered in place of an *"!"* symbol will be converted to uppercase.

As a result, an employee's identification number is entered at the prompt as a series of digits separated by two dashes. Only letters are accepted for the middle initial and last names, and they are converted to uppercase. All first names will begin with an uppercase letter. The salary figure is displayed in conventional business format, with each three digits separated by a comma (see fig. 9.5).

Employee's Id. No. : 123-45-6789

First Name : James

Middle Initial : J.

Last Name : SMITH

Annual Salary : 39,590.00

Fig. 9.5. Displaying formatted input values on the entry form.

Tip:

Use a macro function with a memory variable as a file name at the time of program execution.

One way to select a database file is to specify the name of the file in the USE command.

For example, to display the structure and records in EMPLOYEE.DBF, select the file by including the USE command in your program before you display the contents of the file:

```
USE EMPLOYEE
DISPLAY STRUCTURE
LIST
```

This program segment can be used only to select EMPLOYEE.DBF, but you can convert it to a general-purpose program.

You can display the contents of any database file by specifying the name of the file at the time of execution. To do this, add a command that requests the name of the database file before you execute the DISPLAY and LIST commands. The name of the file can be stored in a memory variable such as mFileName:

```
STORE SPACE(8) TO mFileName
@10,5 SAY "Enter name of the file : " GET mFileName
READ
```

After the name of the file has been saved in the memory variable, use the & macro function to supply the name to the USE command:

```
USE &mFileName
```

The & macro function tells dBASE III Plus to use the contents of the variable (instead of the actual string "mFileName") in place of the file name in the USE command.

You can use the & macro function also (with a memory variable) as a name for other types of disk files, as in the following examples:

```
USE &mDBF INDEX ON &mNDX
SET FORMAT TO &mFMT
LABEL FORM &mLBL
REPORT FORM &mFRM
TYPE &mTXT
MODIFY COMMAND &mPRG
SET VIEW TO &mVUE
MODIFY SCREEN &mSCR
```

Screen Control

Trick:

Use @ and SPACE( ) to position a WAIT prompt at a given location on the screen.

When you execute the WAIT command, the prompt message is displayed at the beginning of the line in which the cursor is located. If you want to reposition the prompt message, use the @ command to specify a row position for the prompt message.

To display the prompt message at line 10, for example, use the following @ command:

```
@10,1
WAIT "Is the item entered correct [Y/N] ? " TO mAnswer
```

The prompt message will always be displayed at the beginning of the specified line, regardless of the column number specified in the @ command. Even if you specify @*10,20*, the message will be displayed at the beginning of line 10.

If you want the WAIT command's prompt message to appear in a specific column position on the screen, you need to add the appropriate number of blank spaces to the message. An easy way to do this is to use the SPACE( ) function. This function, with a numeric argument in the parentheses, will return a specified number of blank spaces.

For example, the following commands display a prompt message for the WAIT operation at the 21st column of the 10th line on the screen:

```
@10,1
WAIT SPACE(20)+"Is the item entered correct [Y/N] ? "
TO mKey
```

It is important to note that because the first row of the screen is designated as line 0, line 10 is actually the 11th row on the screen. However, the screen is divided into 80 columns that are designated as 1 through 80. The first display position is column 1, not 0.

Trick:

Eliminate status messages from the screen.

When you are working in dBASE III Plus, messages describing the processing status are shown on the status line (line 22) or at the top of the screen, depending on whether STATUS is on or off. When you display program output, you may want to blank out these messages in certain applications.

To eliminate the status line (line 22) from the screen, issue the SET STATUS OFF command before displaying output.

However, even when STATUS is off, certain messages (such as the status of the Insert and Caps Lock keys) will be displayed at the top (line 0) of the screen. To eliminate the messages from line 0, issue the SET SCOREBOARD OFF command.

Displaying Output in Colors

Tip:

Use the SET COLOR TO command to display color output.

If you have a color monitor that is connected to a color graphics card, you can display text and graphic symbols in a number of colors. The command for setting the screen color is

SET COLOR TO <color of standard text/background color>,
                  <color of enhanced text/background color>,
                  <border color>

Colors are defined in pairs by using such color letter codes as:

SET COLOR TO W/B,R/W,B

(Refer to Chapter 7 for a detailed discussion of setting screen colors with the SET COLOR TO command.)

dBASE III Plus uses colors for enhanced text to display data and text in operations such as DISPLAY, EDIT, APPEND, and so on.

When you are writing a program to display output in color text and graphs, you're concerned mainly with the colors for standard text and its background. Specify the colors in the first pair:

```
SET COLOR TO W/B
SET COLOR TO R/G
SET COLOR TO RB/BG
```

Some of the basic colors you can use for displaying text and graphic symbols are

Color	Letter Code
Red	R
Blue	B
Cyan	BG
Green	G
Brown	GR
Magenta	RB
White	W
Yellow	GR+
Black	N

To display a color in high-intensity, add a plus (+) sign after the color letter. For example, displaying brown (GR) in high-intensity (GR+) creates yellow.

If you want to display the text or a graphic symbol in blinking color, add an asterisk (✴) to the end of the color letter. For example, R✴ allows you to display text in blinking red.

After you set the standard text and its background to a given color combination (such as *W/B* for white text on blue background), any text or graphics symbols will be displayed in that color combination. You will have to reset the colors when you want something different.

You can display sections of text or graphs in different colors by resetting the text and its background colors for each section.

To produce a color text screen, use the following program:

```
✴✴✴ COLRTEXT.PRG
✴ Program to display sample colored text
SET TALK OFF
SET ECHO OFF
CLEAR
SET COLOR TO W/B
?"Text in white on blue background          "
```

```
SET COLOR TO R/B
?"Text in red on blue background              "
SET COLOR TO G/B
?"Text in green on blue background            "
SET COLOR TO RB/B
?"Text in magenta on blue background          "
SET COLOR TO BG/B
?"Text in cyan on blue background             "
SET COLOR TO GR/B
?"Text in brown on blue background            "
SET COLOR TO B/W
?"Text in blue on white background            "
SET COLOR TO R/W
?"Text in red on white background             "
SET COLOR TO G/W
?"Text in green on white background           "
SET COLOR TO RB/W
?"Text in magenta on white background         "
SET COLOR TO BG/W
?"Text in cyan on white background            "
SET COLOR TO B/R
?"Text in blue on red background              "
SET COLOR TO W/R
?"Text in white on red background             "
SET COLOR TO BG/R
?"Text in cyan on red background              "
SET COLOR TO GR/R
?"Text in brown on red background             "
SET COLOR TO B/BG
?"Text in blue on cyan background             "
SET COLOR TO R/BG
?"Text in red on cyan background              "
SET COLOR TO RB/BG
?"Text in magenta on cyan background          "
SET COLOR TO W/G
@1,41 SAY "Text in white on green background      "
SET COLOR TO R/G
@2,41 SAY "Text in red on green background        "
SET COLOR TO RB/G
@3,41 SAY "Text in magenta on green background    "
SET COLOR TO GR/G
@4,41 SAY "Text in brown on green background      "
SET COLOR TO R/GR
```

```
@5,41 SAY "Text in red on brown background          "
SET COLOR TO G/GR
@6,41 SAY "Text in green on brown background         "
SET COLOR TO RB/GR
@7,41 SAY "Text in magenta on brown background       "
SET COLOR TO BG/GR
@8,41 SAY "Text in cyan on brown background          "
SET COLOR TO W/RB
@9,41 SAY "Text in white on magenta background       "
SET COLOR TO G/RB
@10,41 SAY "Text in green on magenta background       "
SET COLOR TO BG/RB
@11,41 SAY "Text in cyan on magenta background        "
SET COLOR TO GR/RB
@12,41 SAY "Text in brown on magenta background       "
SET COLOR TO W/GR+
@13,41 SAY "Text in white on yellow background        "
SET COLOR TO R/GR+
@14,41 SAY "Text in red on yellow background          "
SET COLOR TO G/GR+
@15,41 SAY "Text in green on yellow background        "
SET COLOR TO RB/GR+
@16,41 SAY "Text in magenta on yellow background      "
SET COLOR TO BG/GR+
@17,41 SAY "Text in cyan on yellow background         "
SET COLOR TO GR/GR+
@18,41 SAY "Text in brown on yellow background        "
SET COLOR TO W/B
@19,1
?"Color      Letter Code      Color      Letter Code "
?"Blue          B             Green         G        "
?"Cyan          BG            Red           R        "
?"Magenta       RB            Brown         GR       "
?"Yellow        GR+           White         W        "
SET COLOR TO R/B
@19,47 TO 23,79
@20,48 SAY "    Poor color combinations:"
@21,48 SAY "GR/W, RB/R, G/BG, R/RB, GR/BG"
@22,48 SAY "BG/G, W/GR, BG/W, GR/G"
SET COLOR TO W/B
RETURN
```

Menu Design

Trick:

Design a menu program to execute your program modules.

When you develop a complete database management system, organize the system into a number of program modules—each to perform a specific task. Once you've designed and tested the programs, you can link them as a complete system by using a set of menus. Figure 9.6 shows a sample menu.

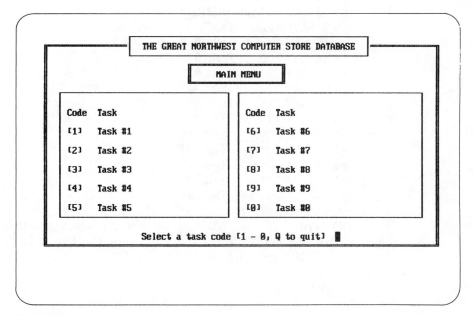

Fig. 9.6. A typical menu design.

As you can see, you select a specific task by entering a task code (0 through 9). Depending on the task code you enter, a specific program module is called and executed from the MAINMENU.PRG program:

```
*** MAINMENU.PRG
* A typical main menu
SET STATUS OFF
SET SCOREBOARD OFF
SET TALK OFF
SET ECHO OFF
```

```
STORE " " TO mChoice
* Set up loop to display menu choices
DO WHILE UPPER(mChoice) <> "Q"
   CLEAR
   @2,0 TO 23,79 DOUBLE      && draw a double-line box
   @4,29 TO 6,48 DOUBLE
   @1,17 TO 3,65             && draw a single-line box
   @7,3 TO 20,37
   @7,39 TO 20,76
   @2,18 SAY "  THE GREAT NORTHWEST COMPUTER STORE DATABASE  "
   @5,35 SAY "MAIN MENU"
   @9,5 SAY "Code    Task"
   @11,5 SAY "[1]     Task #1"
   @13,5 SAY "[2]     Task #2"
   @15,5 SAY "[3]     Task #3"
   @17,5 SAY "[4]     Task #4"
   @19,5 SAY "[5]     Task #5"
   @9,41 SAY "Code    Task"
   @11,41 SAY "[6]     Task #6"
   @13,41 SAY "[7]     Task #7"
   @15,41 SAY "[8]     Task #8"
   @17,41 SAY "[9]     Task #9"
   @19,41 SAY "[0]     Task #0"
   mChoice=SPACE(1)
   DO WHILE .T.       && program loop for selecting a task code
      @22,20 SAY "Select a task code [1 - 0, Q to quit] ";
         GET mChoice
      READ
      DO CASE
         CASE mChoice="Q" .OR. mChoice="q"
            EXIT
         CASE mChoice="1"
            DO TASK1
            EXIT
         CASE mChoice="2"
            DO TASK2
            EXIT
         CASE mChoice="3"
            DO TASK3
            EXIT
         CASE mChoice="4"
            DO TASK4
            EXIT
```

```
                        CASE  mChoice="5"
                           DO  TASK5
                           EXIT
                        CASE  mChoice="6"
                           DO  TASK6
                           EXIT
                        CASE  mChoice="7"
                           DO  TASK7
                           EXIT
                        CASE  mChoice="8"
                           DO  TASK8
                           EXIT
                        CASE  mChoice="9"
                           DO  TASK9
                           EXIT
                        CASE  mChoice="0"
                           DO  TASK0
                           EXIT
                     ENDCASE
                  ENDDO              && end of task selection loop
               ENDDO                 && end of menu display loop
               RETURN
```

As you can see from MAINMENU.PRG, a memory variable
(mChoice) is used to store the task code. The task code is
entered and assigned to the memory variable by the
@ .. SAY .. GET command within a program loop (between
the *DO WHILE .T.* and *ENDDO* commands).

The program loop is set up by using CASE statements to get a
valid task code. In other words, if the task code meets one of
the conditions specified in the CASE statements, a specified
program module is called. Otherwise, the prompt is displayed
repeatedly until a valid task code is entered.

After you enter a valid task code, the code is used to
determine which program module is to be called. For
example, pressing *1* at the task selection prompt causes the
command DO TASK1 to be executed. At this point, program
control is transferred to the TASK1.PRG program module.
After the instructions in TASK1.PRG are executed and the
RETURN command is encountered, program control is
returned to the calling program:

```
*** TASK1.PRG
* A program module called from MAINMENU.prg
. . . . .
. . . . .
RETURN          && pass control back to the calling program
```

When you return from TASK1.PRG, program execution begins from the MAINMENU.PRG command immediately following DO TASK1 (in this case, the EXIT command). As a result, the program exits the task-selection program loop and returns you to MAINMENU.PRG. The menu screen is displayed and you can select another task.

Tip:

Use RETURN TO MASTER to return to the main program.

The RETURN command is used in a program module to transfer control back to the immediate calling program. Each time you execute a RETURN command, program control is passed back to the program module that called the current module. Use a series of RETURN commands to return to the main program from a module several levels below it.

If you don't need to pass data values to these intermediate program modules, you can return directly to the main program. To do so, use the RETURN TO MASTER command in the program module. Whenever the RETURN TO MASTER command is executed, program control is passed directly to the main calling program, regardless of which program module you are in.

Tip:

Group menu options by applications.

As you plan your menu layout on the screen, you may want to group in one area the menu options related to a given application. These options can be framed by a single- or double-line box for better visual presentation. If you're using a color monitor, you can display menu boxes in different colors. Figure 9.7 shows a sample menu design.

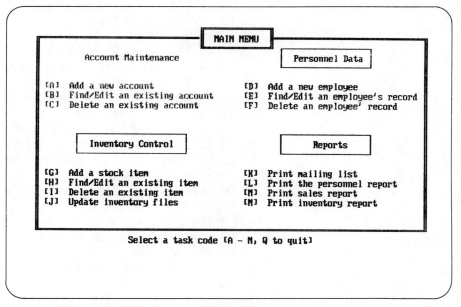

Fig. 9.7. Grouping menu options by application.

The following program produced the menu layout:

```
**  MENU.PRG
*  Group menu options by applications
SET STATUS OFF
SET TALK OFF
SET ECHO OFF
SET SCOREBOARD OFF
STORE " " TO mChoice
DO WHILE UPPER(mChoice)<>"Q"      && displaying menu
CLEAR
    SET COLOR TO R+/B,,B
    @2,1 TO 22,79 DOUBLE     && frame the menu screen
    @1,34 TO 3,48 DOUBLE     && frame main menu heading
    @2,35 SAY "  MAIN MENU  "
    SET COLOR TO G/B,,B
    @4,2 TO 11,39     && frame account maintenance options
    @4,41 TO 11,78     && frame personnel data options
    @13,2 TO 21,39     && frame inventory control options
    @13,41 TO 21,78   && frame reports options
    SET COLOR TO GR/B,,B
```

```
@3,9 TO 5,31       && frame account maintenance heading
@4,10 SAY " Account Maintenance "
@7,3 SAY "[A]   Add a new account"
@8,3 SAY "[B]   Find/Edit an existing account"
@9,3 SAY "[C]   Delete an existing account"
SET COLOR TO BG+/B,B
@3,50 TO 5,68          && frame personnel data heading
@4,51 SAY "   Personnel Data "
@7,43 SAY "[D]   Add a new employee"
@8,43 SAY "[E]   Find/Edit an employee's record"
@9,43 SAY "[F]   Delete an employee' record"
SET COLOR TO W/B,,B
@12,9 TO 14,31     && frame inventory control heading
@13,10 SAY " Inventory Control   "
@16,3 SAY "[G]   Add a stock item"
@17,3 SAY "[H]   Find/Edit an existing item"
@18,3 SAY "[I]   Delete an existing item"
@19,3 SAY "[J]   Update inventory files"
SET COLOR TO RB/B,,B
@12,50 TO 14,68   && frame reports heading
@13,51 SAY "        Reports       "
@16,43 SAY "[K]   Print mailing list"
@17,43 SAY "[L]   Print the personnel report"
@18,43 SAY "[M]   Print sales report"
@19,43 SAY "[N]   Print inventory report"
STORE " " TO mChoice
DO WHILE .T.       && loop for task code selection
   SET COLOR TO R+/B,R+/B,B
   @23,20 SAY "Select a task code [A – N, Q to quit] ";
      GET mChoice PICTURE "!"
   READ
   DO CASE
      CASE mChoice="Q"
         EXIT
      CASE mChoice="A"
         DO ADDACCT
         EXIT
      CASE mChoice="B"
         DO EDITACCT
         EXIT
      CASE mChoice="C"
         DO DELTACCT
         EXIT
```

```
            CASE mChoice="D"
               DO  ADDEMPL
               EXIT
            CASE mChoice="E"
               DO  EDITEMPL
               EXIT
            CASE mChoice="F"
               DO  DELTEMPL
               EXIT
            CASE mChoice="G"
               DO  ADDITEM
               EXIT
            CASE mChoice="H"
               DO  EDITITEM
               EXIT
            CASE mChoice="I"
               DO  DELTITEM
               EXIT
            CASE mChoice="J"
               DO  UPDATINV
               EXIT
            CASE mChoice="K"
               DO  MAILLIST
               EXIT
            CASE mChoice="L"
               DO  EMPLREPT
               EXIT
            CASE mChoice="M"
               DO  SALEREPT
               EXIT
            CASE mChoice="N"
               DO  INVNREPT
               EXIT
         ENDCASE
      ENDDO                && end of task selection loop
   ENDDO                && end of menu display loop
   RETURN
```

10

Programming in dBASE III Plus Command Language: Branching, Looping, Subprograms, and Debugging

Using the dBASE III Plus command language to design the programs you need can help you speed up and simplify your work. This chapter presents tips and tricks to help you make the most of dBASE III Plus command language programming.

Conditional Branching

One of the most important programming tools is a logical branching operation, using the value of a variable to determine the next processing step.

In computing weekly wages, for example, the formula you use depends on whether overtime pay is involved:

Wage = Hours worked * Wage rate

or

Wage = 40 Hours * Wage rate
+ Overtime hours * Wage rate * 1.5

The overtime wage rate in this case is assumed to be one and one-half times the regular rate.

Tip:

Use the IF .. ELSE .. ENDIF command for a two-branch decision operation.

To direct the program to use one of the two formulas, you need a decision branching statement. An IF..ENDIF is one of these types of statements. The format of the IF..ENDIF command is

IF <a condition>

The program segment to be executed if the condition
is met
. . . . .
. . . .

ENDIF

Two approaches can be used to compute wages with IF..ENDIF commands.

First, you can compute the wage for all cases and then revise the wage if you encounter an overtime case. In the following examples, the number of hours worked in a week and the normal wage rate are saved in the memory variables mHours and mWageRate. The variable mWage is used to store the computed total weekly wage.

The program segment for computing wages can be written as follows:

```
mWage=mHours*mWageRate
IF mHours>40
   mWage=(mWageRate*40)+(mHours−40)*mWageRate*1.5
ENDIF
```

Although this program segment produces the correct results, it is not an efficient approach. The program always computes the wage using the first formula (mHours*mWageRate).

The program would be more efficient if the first formula were used only when no overtime is involved. You can modify the program to direct the processing by adding an ELSE clause to the IF..ENDIF statement in the following format:

```
IF <a condition>
    The program segment to be executed if the condition
    is met
    . . . . .
    . . . .
ELSE
    The program segment to be executed if the condition
    is not met
    . . . . .
    . . . .
ENDIF
```

For example, the program shown earlier can be rewritten as follows:

```
IF mHours>40
        mWage=(mWageRate*40)+(mHours–40)*mWageRate*1.5
ELSE
    mWage=mHours*mWageRate
ENDIF
```

This program is a more efficient approach to computing wages because the wage is always computed only once.

Trick:

To speed processing, use the IIF( ) function to handle a two-branch decision operation.

If you're using the IF..ELSE..ENDIF command to process a two-branch decision, you can speed up the processing by replacing the command with an IIF( ) function. The format of the IIF( ) command is

IIF(<condition>, <expression for the cases when the condition is met>, <expression for the cases when the condition is not met>)

When the IIF( ) function is executed, the condition specified in the argument is evaluated. If the condition is met, the first expression defined in the function is executed. Otherwise, the second expression is processed.

As you have seen, the program segment for computing wages by using the IF..ELSE..ENDIF command can be written as:

```
IF mHours>40
    mWage=(mWageRate*40)+(mHours-40)*mWageRate*1.5
ELSE
    mWage=mHours*mWageRate
ENDIF
```

The wage is computed by multiplying the number of hours (mHours) by the wage rate (mWageRate) if the number of hours is 40 or less. Otherwise, overtime pay is calculated by using 150 percent of the normal wage rate for the hours over 40.

To simplify the program segment, use the IIF( ) function:

```
mWage=IIF(mHours<=40,mHours*mWageRate,(mWageRate*40)+
       (mHours-40)*mWageRate*1.5
```

Trick:

Use parentheses to group compound conditions.

The conditions you can specify in IF, CASE, or other statements that involve logical decisions may use one or more logical operators (.OR., .AND.) to define a compound condition.

For example, specifying each of the following conditions in an IF statement is acceptable:

```
IF AREA_CODE="206"
IF AREA_CODE="206".OR.AREA_CODE="503"
IF AREA_CODE="206".OR.AREA_CODE="503".OR.AREA_CODE="212"
IF AREA_CODE="206".AND.LAST_NAME="John".AND.MALE
IF AREA_CODE="206".OR.AREA_CODE="503".AND.FIRST_NAME="John"
IF mVarA=mVarB.AND.mVarC=mVarD.OR.mVarE>mVarF.AND.mVarG
```

Logical operators (.OR. and .AND.) are used to define a compound condition in a decision statement. They are powerful programming tools and should be used with great care.

For example, when you use only one logical operator (the second IF statement) or multiple operators of the same type (the third and fourth IF statements), the meaning of the compound condition is quite clear.

However, when you use more than two logical operators of mixed types, the compound condition may be confusing and difficult to interpret. The compound conditions in the fifth and sixth IF statements, for example, use a series of .OR. and .AND. logical operators. These statements are interpreted based on the priority rules used for evaluating the conditions. To make sure the conditions are interpreted correctly, group the conditions with pairs of parentheses.

For example, the sixth IF statement can be clarified by rewriting it in the following form, using two pairs of parentheses:

IF (mVarA=mVarB.AND.mVarC=mVarD).OR.(mVarE>mVarF.AND.mVarG)

You must place the parentheses carefully and correctly; misplaced parentheses will produce quite a different result.

Tip:

Use DO CASE..ENDCASE commands to handle multidecision branching operations.

An IF..ELSE..ENDIF command is an efficient way to select one of two courses of action depending on a specified condition being met.

If more than two courses of action are to be selected from a set of alternatives, use the DO CASE and ENDCASE commands. Between the DO CASE and ENDCASE commands, you specify a course of action for each of the alternative conditions defined in several CASE statements:

```
DO CASE
    CASE <condition 1>
        Course of action for condition 1
    CASE <condition 2>
        Course of action for condition 2
    CASE <condition 3>
        Course of action for condition 3
    . . . .
    . . . .
ENDCASE
```

For example, your program can compute a quantity discount that is a function of quantity sold. Use the DO

CASE..ENDCASE command to specify a discount rate for each level of quantity sold in CASE statements:

```
DO CASE
   CASE mQtySold<100
       mDiscRate=.05                                    && 5% discount
   CASE mQtySold>=100 .AND. mQtySold<300
       mDiscRate=.10                                    && 10% discount
   CASE mQtySold>=300
       mDiscRate=.15                                    && 15%
ENDCASE
mNetSale=mGrossSale*(1-mDiscRate)
```

Notice that the discount rate (mDiscRate) is set to *0.05*, *0.10*, and *0.15*, respectively, for each case of quantity sold (mQtySold). The net sales figure (mNetSale) is then computed by discounting the gross sales (mGrossSale) by the appropriate discount rate.

The DO CASE..ENDCASE command can be used also for designing a menu-driven program. Different program modules are executed for each case specified, depending on the menu option selected. (A discussion of such a menu design is given in a separate program tip in Chapter 9.)

Tip:

Use an OTHERWISE statement to handle open-ended cases in decision branching operations.

When you use the DO CASE..ENDCASE command to direct execution in a multiple branching operation, add an OTHERWISE statement to handle the open-ended cases. Here is an example:

```
DO CASE
CASE mChoice="A"
. . . . .

      . . . . .
   CASE mChoice="B"
   . . . . .
   . . . . .
   OTHERWISE
   . . . . .
   . . . . .
ENDCASE
```

In this case, the program segment specified following the OTHERWISE statement is executed only when the conditions defined in all the other CASE statements are not met.

Program Loops

Understand the basic structure of a program loop.

Use a *program loop* to instruct the computer to perform a repetitive set of tasks. The set of tasks can be specified as a program segment that is carried out over and over, as long as a specified condition is met.

To define a program loop, you can use the DO WHILE..ENDDO statements, specifying between these commands the set of instructions to be carried out repeatedly:

```
DO WHILE <a condition>
    The program segment to be repeated
    . . . .
    . . . .
ENDDO
```

The condition defined in the DO WHILE statement instructs the computer to execute the program segment specified in the loop as long as the condition is met. Otherwise, the computer skips the program segment and exits the program loop.

To set up an infinite program loop, use .T. as a condition.

If you need to process a program segment repeatedly in an infinite loop, specify the logical value of .T. as the condition:

```
DO WHILE .T.
    The program segment to be repeatedly processed
    . . . .
    . . . .
ENDDO
```

Because the condition is always *True* (.T.), the program segment within the loop is executed over and over.

Infinite loops play an important role in data processing. They will be discussed in other sections of this chapter.

Tip:

Use the LOOP command to skip a program loop.

The LOOP command directs the program to go to the beginning of the loop. When the command is encountered within a program segment in the loop, control is transferred to the beginning of the loop, and the rest of the commands in the segment are ignored:

```
DO WHILE . . . .
    . . . . .
    . . . . .
    LOOP
    . . . . .
    . . . . .
ENDDO
```

To skip a segment of instructions in the program loop, use the LOOP command with a conditional transfer statement.

```
DO WHILE . . .
    . . . . .
    . . . . .
    DO CASE
        CASE . . . . .
            . . . .
            LOOP
        CASE . . . . .
            . . . .
            . . . .
        OTHERWISE
            . . . .
            . . . .
    ENDCASE
    . . . . .
    . . . . .
ENDDO
```

The program segment instructs the program to go back to the beginning of the loop after executing the instructions when the first case condition is met.

Tip:

Use the EXIT command to interrupt a program loop.	In the normal course of processing, a program loop is terminated when the condition specified in the DO WHILE statement is no longer true. But you can interrupt processing and terminate the program loop at any time by using the EXIT command in the program segment within the loop:

DO WHILE . . .

    . . . . .

    . . . . .

EXIT

   . . . .

ENDDO

Whenever the EXIT statement is encountered in the loop, the normal processing sequence is interrupted and program control is transferred to the command immediately following the ENDDO command.

Trick:

Use the Esc key to exit from an infinite loop.	To set up an infinite program loop to process a set of instructions repeatedly, specify *.T.* as the condition in the DO WHILE statement:

DO WHILE .T.

    The program segment to be repeatedly processed

    . . . .

    . . . .

ENDDO

The program segment defined within the program loop executes in a continuous cycle. If you want to terminate processing, press the Esc key while the program loop is being executed. If SET ESCAPE OFF is not in effect, the program will halt, and you'll see the following message:

```
*** INTERRUPTED ***
Called from - <name of the program>
Cancel, Ignore, or Suspend? (C, I, or S)
```

Press *C* to terminate program execution. Press *I* to continue. Press *S* to halt processing temporarily. End resume processing by issuing the RESUME command at the dot prompt.

Applications for Program Loops

Tip:

Use a program loop to access records sequentially in a database file.

To access each record in a database file, use a DO WHILE..ENDDO program loop. Use the EOF( ) function to terminate the loop when it reaches the end-of-file mark.

The following program segment allows you to display sequentially the contents of each record in EMPLOYEE.DBF:

```
*** LISTNAME.PRG
* List FIRST_NAME and LAST_NAME in EMPLOYEE.DBF
SET TALK OFF
SET ECHO OFF
CLEAR
USE EMPLOYEE
?"Name of Employee"
?
* Set up program loop to scan record
DO WHILE .NOT. EOF( )
    ?TRIM(FIRST_NAME)+" "+LAST_NAME
   SKIP                        && go to next record
ENDDO
RETURN
```

Remember to use the SKIP command to move the record pointer to the next record to be accessed. Otherwise, the end-of-file mark will never be reached—and you'll display the same record and remain in an infinite loop.

The LISTNAME.PRG program scans each data record in EMPLOYEE.DBF and displays the values of the LAST_NAME and FIRST_NAME data fields.

Tip:

Use a program to sum values in a numeric field.

Using the DO WHILE..ENDDO command, you can set up a program loop to sum the values in a database file numeric field. Such a loop examines sequentially the data field value in each database record and then adds it to an accumulator variable.

You can sum the values in INVENTRY.DBF's ON_HAND data field, for example. To do so, you can set up a program loop to access each data record in the file and add the value of the data field to the accumulator variable mTotal:

```
*** SUMVALUE.PRG
* Sum ON_HAND field values in INVENTRY.DBF
SET TALK OFF
SET ECHO OFF
CLEAR
USE ACCOUNTS
USE INVENTRY
* Clear the accumulator
STORE 0 to mTotal
* List values in ON_HAND
?"ON_HAND Quantity"
?
* Set up program loop to scan data records
DO WHILE .NOT. EOF()
    ?ON_HAND                    && display field value
    mTotal=mTotal+ON_HAND       && add value to total
    SKIP                        && go to next record
ENDDO
* Show total
@10,10 SAY "Total ON_HAND quantity . . . . ";
    GET mTotal PICTURE "###"
RETURN
```

Don't forget to include the SKIP command, which moves the record pointer to the next record to be accessed. Otherwise, you will access the same record over and over.

Figure 10.1 shows the output of SUMVALUE.PRG. As you can see, the program provides not only a computed total but also a listing of the values in the ON_HAND data field.

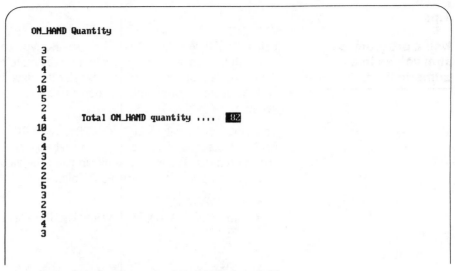

Fig. 10.1. The total value in the ON_HAND data field.

Tip:

Use a program loop to count data records in a database file.

You can set up a program to count data records that meet certain conditions.

If you want to count the phone numbers in different area codes in ACCOUNTS.DBF, for example, set up a program loop to scan the AREA_CODE data field and count the phone numbers selectively:

```
*** AREACODE.PRG
* Count phone numbers in area codes 206 and 503
SET TALK OFF
SET ECHO OFF
CLEAR
USE ACCOUNTS
* Clear counter variables
STORE 0 TO mCount206
STORE 0 TO mCount503
?"Area Code Scanned"
?
* Set up program loop to scan area codes
```

```
DO WHILE .NOT. EOF( )
    * Display the area code scanned
    ?AREA_CODE
    * Count area codes
    DO CASE
        CASE AREA_CODE="206"
            mCount206=mCount206+1       && count one "206"
        CASE AREA_CODE="503"
            mCount503=mCount503+1       && count one "503"
    ENDCASE
    SKIP
ENDDO
* Display counts
@5,10 SAY "Number of 206 area codes . . . .";
    GET mCount206 PICTURE "###"
@7,10 SAY "Number of 503 area codes . . . .";
    GET mCount503 PICTURE "###"
RETURN
```

The output produced by AREACODE.PRG is shown in figure 10.2. A list of area codes that have been scanned by the program loop is displayed with the computed totals.

```
Area Code Scanned

503
503
503         Number of 206 area codes ....  ██
503
503         Number of 503 area codes ....  ██
206
206
206
415
503
```

Fig. 10.2. Counting area codes in ACCOUNTS.DBF.

Tip:

Use a program loop to find the maximum or minimum field value in a database file.

If you want to find a data field's maximum or minimum value, use the DO CASE..ENDCASE command to set up a program loop to scan the field values.

To find a maximum field value, choose as the initial maximum either a very small value or the value of the first record. As you scan the field value of each record, replace the maximum value with any field value that is greater than the current maximum value; otherwise, scan the next record. The maximum value is always the largest value in the records scanned. When the end of the file is reached, the maximum value is the largest field value in the database file.

The following sample program segment will find the hardware item with the highest value in HARDWARE.DBF's COST field:

```
*** FINDMAX.PRG
* Find the maximum value in the COST field
SET TALK OFF
SET ECHO OFF
CLEAR
USE HARDWARE
* Use a very small value as an arbitrary maximum value
STORE 0 TO mMaxCost
?"Values of COST scanned"
?
* Set up the program loop to scan records in HARDWARE.DBF
DO WHILE .NOT. EOF( )
    ?COST
    IF COST>mMaxCost         && a new maximum is found
        mMaxCost=COST        && update the maximum
    ENDIF
    SKIP                     && scan the next record
ENDDO
* Display the maximum value
@7,10 SAY "The maximum value in COST field .... ";
    GET mMaxCost PICTURE "#,###.##"
RETURN
```

As you can see from figure 10.3, the loop finds and displays the highest value in the COST field. A list of the data field's values is shown also.

To find the *minimum* cost in the HARDWARE.DBF file, you can begin the search process by arbitrarily choosing the value of the first record (or a very large value) as the minimum value. As you scan a record, replace the minimum value with a field value only if that field value is less than the current minimum:

```
Values of COST scanned

1359.00
1695.00
3790.00
  89.00
 560.00    The maximum value in COST field ....  3,790.00
 269.00
 390.00
2190.00
 279.00
 199.00
```

Fig. 10.3. Finding the maximum value in the COST data field.

```
*** FINDMIN.PRG
* Find the minimum value in the COST field
SET TALK OFF
SET ECHO OFF
CLEAR
USE HARDWARE
* Use COST in the first record as an arbitrary minimum value
STORE COST TO mMinCost
?"Values of COST scanned"
?
* Set up the program loop to scan records in HARDWARE.DBF
DO WHILE .NOT. EOF( )
    ?COST
    IF COST<mMinCost          && a new minimum is found
        mMinCost=COST         && update the minimum
    ENDIF
    SKIP                      && scan the next record
ENDDO
* Display the minimum value
@7,10 SAY "The minimum value in COST field . . . . ";
    GET mMinCost PICTURE "#,###.##"
RETURN
```

The program's output shows the smallest value in the COST field as well as a list of the COST values scanned by the loop (see fig. 10.4).

```
Values of COST scanned

1359.00
1695.00
3790.00
  89.00
 560.00    The minimum value in COST field ....    89.00
 269.00
 398.00
2190.00
 279.00
 199.00
```

Fig. 10.4. Finding the minimum value in the COST data field.

Tip:

Use a program loop to compute statistics based on the values in a specific data field.

A program loop allows you to scan the values in a specific data field and compute such descriptive statistics as the *mean* (average) and *standard deviation*.

To compute the mean value of a set of field values, divide the sum of these values (denoted as *x*s) by the number of values (*N*):

$$\bar{x} = \Sigma \ x_i \ /N \qquad \text{for } i=1,2,3,\ldots, N$$

The symbol x_i is used to denote the field value of the *i*th data record where *i* is an index that takes on a value from *1* to *N* (number of records in the file). The Σ symbol is used to represent the sum of all the field values.

Several formulas can be used to compute the standard deviation of a set of values (*x*s). A definitional formula for computing a sample standard deviation is

$$s = \sqrt{\Sigma \ (x_i - \bar{x})^2 \ /(N-1)} \qquad \text{for } i=1,2,3,\ldots, N$$

The numerator in the formula is the sum of the squared differences between the field values and the mean value.

The following sample program segment computes the mean and standard deviation of the values in HARDWARE.DBF's COST data field. The variables mSum and mSSD are used to store the sum of the field values and the sum of the squared

differences. The variable mNOBS (number of observations) is
used to keep track of the number of records in the file. And a
program loop is set up to scan the value of the COST data field
in each record:

```
*** STATISTS.PRG
* Compute descriptive statistics of COST in HARDWARE.DBF
   SET TALK OFF
   SET ECHO OFF
   CLEAR
   USE HARDWARE
* Clear accumulator variables
   STORE 0 TO mSum
   STORE 0 TO mSSD
   STORE 0 TO mNOBS
* Display the list of raw data
   ?"      >> Raw Data <<"
   ?
   ?SPACE(3)+"Obs.#   Cost"
   ?SPACE(3)+"-----   -------"
* Sum values in the COST field
   DO WHILE .NOT. EOF( )        && set up loop to scan records
     mNOBS=mNOBS+1              && count a record
     * Display COST as raw data
     ?SPACE(3)+STR(mNOBS,2,0)+STR(COST,12,2)
     mSum=mSum+COST             && add COST to sum
     SKIP
   ENDDO
* Compute mean COST value
  mMean=mSum/mNOBS
* Compute the sum of squared differences
   GO TOP
   DO WHILE .NOT. EOF( )
     mSSD=mSSD+(COST-mMean)*(COST-mMean)
     SKIP
   ENDDO
* Compute the standard deviation
  mStdDev=SQRT(mSSD/(mNOBS-1))
* Display computed results
  @7,30 SAY ">> Descriptive Statistics <<"
  @9,27  SAY "Mean . . . . . . . . . . . . . . . . . ";
   GET mMean PICTURE "#,###.##"
  @11,27 SAY "Standard Deviation . . . . ";
   GET mStdDev PICTURE "#,###.##"
RETURN
```

Figure 10.5 shows the results of executing STATISTS.PRG. Notice that the descriptive statistics and the values in the COST field are displayed.

```
   >> Raw Data <<

   Obs.#  Cost
   ───────────
     1    1359.00
     2    1695.00
     3    3790.00          >> Descriptive Statistics <<
     4      89.00
     5     560.00     Mean .................. [1,002.00]
     6     269.00
     7     390.00     Standard Deviation .... [1,193.74]
     8    2190.00
     9     279.00
    10     199.00
```

Fig. 10.5. Computing descriptive statistics for the COST data field.

Tip:

Use a program loop to compute regression coefficients.

Although the dBASE III Plus command language was developed to be used as a general-purpose programming language, it can be used to compute many complex, sophisticated statistics.

For example, you can save the values of two economic variables as two data fields, and then write a program using these two variables to compute a regression equation.

The general form of a simple linear regression can be defined as follows:

$$Y_i = a + b\ X_i \qquad \text{for } i=1,2,3, \ldots, N$$

Y and *X* are the dependent and independent variables. *N* denotes the number of observations to be used in the regression. The *a* and *b* are the regression coefficients that can be computed with the following formulas:

$$b = (N \Sigma\ X_i \bullet Y_i - \Sigma\ X_i\ \Sigma\ Y_i)/(N \Sigma\ X_i^2 - (\Sigma\ X_i)^2)$$
$$a = (\Sigma\ Y_i/N) - b\bullet(\Sigma\ X_i/N)$$

For example, you can regress the values in HARDWARE.DBF's
COST data field (the dependent variable) on the value of the
PRICE data field (the independent variable) by using the
following program:

```
*** REGRESS.PRG
* Regressing COST (the dependent variable, Y) on PRICE
* (the independent variable, X) in HARDWARE.DBF
SET TALK OFF
SET ECHO OFF
CLEAR
* Initialize accumulator variables
STORE 0 TO mSumX
STORE 0 TO mSumY
STORE 0 TO mSumXY
STORE 0 TO mSumXSq
STORE 0 TO mNOBS
* Select the database containing the COST and PRICE fields
USE HARDWARE
?SPACE(10)+">> Raw Data << "
?
?"The dependent variable . . . . . COST"
?"The independent variable . . . PRICE"
?
?SPACE(3)+"Obs.#    Cost         Price"
?SPACE(3)+"-----    ------       -------"
* Summing up X's, Y's, products of X by Y, X-squares
DO WHILE .NOT. EOF( )
    mNOBS=mNOBS+1                        && count a record
    ?SPACE(3)+STR(mNOBS,2,0)+STR(COST,12,2)+STR(PRICE,12,2)
    mSumX=mSumX+PRICE
    mSumY=mSumY+COST
    mSumXY=mSumXY+PRICE*COST
    mSumXSq=mSumXSq+PRICE*PRICE
    SKIP                                && scan the next record
ENDDO
* Compute regression coefficients, a and b
mB=(mNOBS*mSumXY-mSumX*mSumY)/(mNOBS*mSumXSq-mSumX*mSumX)
mA=(mSumY/mNOBS) - mB*(mSumX/mNOBS)
* Display results
```

```
?
?"  >> Estimated Regression Coefficients << "
?
?"        The intercept, a . . . . " + STR(mA,12,4)
?"        The slope, b . . . . . . . " + STR(mB,12,4)
RETURN
```

Figure 10.6 shows the results of REGRESS.PRG's regression analysis.

```
              >> Raw Data <<

The dependent variable ..... COST
The independent variable ... PRICE

   Obs.#  Cost          Price
   -----  -----         -----
     1    1359.00       1095.00
     2    1695.00       2399.00
     3    3790.00       4490.00
     4      89.00        159.00
     5     560.00        820.00
     6     269.00        389.00
     7     398.00        495.00
     8    2190.00       2790.00
     9     279.00        389.00
    10     199.00        239.00

  >> Estimated Regression Coefficients <<

     The intercept, a ....    -73.9497
     The slope, b ........       0.8224
```

Fig. 10.6. Displaying the estimated regression results.

Figure 10.6 shows the estimated regression coefficients and the listing of raw data that represents the values of HARDWARE.DBF's COST and PRICE data fields.

Subprograms and Procedures

Tip:

Design your database system around small program modules.

When you design and develop a database management system, consider organizing the system in several small program modules. A small program module is easy to create and maintain.

Keeping program modules small is especially important if you're using the dBASE III Plus text editor. The maximum size of a text file created and edited by the text editor must be no more than 5,000 characters (5K) long.

During the system's development stage, individual program modules can be tested separately to eliminate all syntax and logic errors before the modules are linked as a complete system. These program modules can be reorganized as the function of the database management system changes.

Tip:

Use a program module to perform a specific data-management function.

A program module consists of a set of instructions for performing a specific task. One program module can call another whenever it is needed.

As you design your database management system, you may want to design a number of program modules, each of which will be used to carry out a specific data-maintenance function.

For example, you can write a program module that appends a new record to a specific database file:

```
*** ADDRECRD.PRG
* A program module for adding a new record to EMPLOYEE.DBF
SET STATUS ON
USE EMPLOYEE
STORE "Y" TO mContinue
DO WHILE UPPER(mContinue)="Y"
    CLEAR
    APPEND BLANK
    @4,27 SAY "EMPLOYEE DATA ENTRY FORM"
    @8,8   SAY "Employee's Social Security # : ";
        GET ID_NO   PICTURE "999-99-9999"
    @8,56 SAY "Sex* : " GET MALE
    @10,22 SAY "Employee's Name: " GET FIRST_NAME
    @10,56 GET LAST_NAME   PICTURE "!AAAAAAAAAAAAA"
    @12,29 SAY "Position: " GET POSITION
    @14,24 SAY "Date Employed: " GET EMPLY_DATE
    @17,18 SAY "<< * Note: Enter T for male, F for female >>"
    @1,0 TO 19,79 DOUBLE       && draw a double-line frame
    @3,24 TO 5,53              && draw a single-line box
```

```
        READ
        @20,20 SAY "Do you want to add another record [Y/N] ?";
           GET mContinue
        READ
     ENDDO
     RETURN
```

Whenever this ADDRECRD.PRG program module is executed, it appends a data record to EMPLOYEE.DBF. Although the module may be executed as an independent program, you probably will prefer to invoke it from another program whenever you need to add a record to the database file.

The program module that calls ADDRECRD.PRG may be written as follows:

```
    *** ADDDATA.PRG
    * Adding data to a database file
    SET TALK OFF
    SET ECHO OFF
    STORE " " TO mChoice
    DO WHILE .T.
       CLEAR
       SET STATUS OFF
       @10,10 SAY "Enter [A] to Add a new record, [E] to Exit ";
          GET mChoice
       READ
       DO CASE
         CASE  UPPER(mChoice)="A"
             DO ADDRECRD              && call the program module
             LOOP
         CASE UPPER (mChoice)="E"
             EXIT
       ENDCASE
    ENDDO
    * End of ADDDATA.PRG
```

When the ADDDATA.PRG module is executed, a prompt is displayed requesting that you press either *A* to add a record or *E* to exit the program.

Press *A* to call the ADDRECRD.PRG program module (DO ADDRECRD) and transfer control to that module. Then use the custom data-entry screen defined in the ADDRECRD.PRG module to append a record to EMPLOYEE.DBF.

After you enter values in the data fields of the custom data-entry form, you are asked whether you want to add another record to the file. If you press *Y*, a blank data-entry form is displayed. Press *N* to exit the program module (see fig. 10.7).

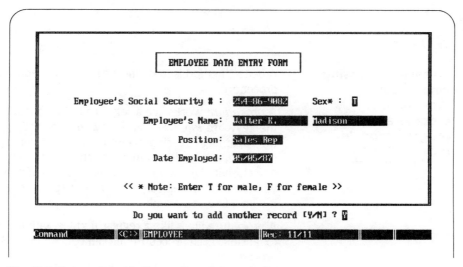

EMPLOYEE DATA ENTRY FORM

Employee's Social Security # : 254-86-9082   Sex* : T

Employee's Name: Walter K.   Madison

Position: Sales Rep

Date Employed: 05/05/87

<< * Note: Enter T for male, F for female >>

Do you want to add another record [Y/N] ? Y

Command   <C:> EMPLOYEE   Rec: 11/11

Fig. 10.7. Data entered in the custom data-entry form.

When you press *N* at the prompt, the character string is assigned to the memory variable mContinue. As a result, the DO WHILE UPPER (mContinue)="Y"..ENDDO program loop terminates and the RETURN command immediately after the loop is executed. At this point, control is transferred back to the ADDDATA.PRG calling program.

As you can see, program modules are powerful. They allow you to process instructions repeatedly by simply calling a module whenever you need it.

Using Procedures

When you are developing a database management system, you probably will use certain key modules repeatedly. There are two ways to use these program modules.

In the first method, discussed in the preceding section, you call one program module from another program. When a program module is used in this manner, the disk file containing the module is opened and loaded in memory whenever the module is called. When you exit the called module, the module is erased from memory. Because the file is opened and loaded in memory each time you call the module, processing time can be very slow if the module is large.

Trick:

To save processing time, use a procedure to process a key program module repeatedly.

A better method is to define a frequently used module as a procedure.

A *procedure* works like a regular module but is identified with the keyword *PROCEDURE* followed by an assigned name at the beginning of each procedure section. When a procedure is called up, it is loaded in memory and remains in memory until you close it. After a procedure has been loaded in memory, you can use it repeatedly to perform a specified task by calling it with a DO command.

A procedure file is like a regular text file with a .PRG file extension. Each procedure file can contain up to 32 procedures.

You can define a program module (ADDRECRD.PRG, from the preceding section, for example) as a procedure in the DATAPROC.PRG procedure file as follows:

```
*** DATAPROC.PRG
* A procedure file
PROCEDURE ADDRECRD          && define the procedure name
    SET STATUS ON
    USE EMPLOYEE
    STORE "Y" TO mContinue
    DO WHILE UPPER(mContinue)="Y"
        CLEAR
        APPEND BLANK
        @4,27 SAY "EMPLOYEE DATA ENTRY FORM"
        @8,8  SAY "Employee's Social Security # : ";
          GET ID_NO   PICTURE "999-99-9999"
        @8,56 SAY "Sex* : " GET MALE
        @10,22 SAY "Employee's Name: " GET FIRST_NAME
        @10,56 GET LAST_NAME   PICTURE "!AAAAAAAAAAAAA"
        @12,29 SAY "Position: " GET POSITION
        @14,24 SAY "Date Employed: " GET EMPLY_DATE
```

```
   @17,18 SAY "<< * Note: Enter T for male, F for female >>"
   @1,0 TO 19,79 DOUBLE          && draw a double-line frame
   @3,24 TO 5,53                 && draw a single-line box
   READ
   @20,20 SAY "Do you want to add another record [Y/N] ?";
       GET mContinue
   READ
ENDDO
RETURN
* End of the ADDRECRD procedure
```

In this example, only one procedure is defined in the DATAPROC.PRG procedure file. To add other procedures to the file, specify each of them in a section that begins with the keyword *PROCEDURE* and an assigned name.

Tip:

Call the procedure file with the DO command.

After a procedure has been defined and saved in a procedure file, you can call it (as you would a program module) by using a DO command. By issuing the DO ADDRECRD command, for example, you can call the ADDRECD procedure from the ADDDATA.PRG program module.

Before calling the procedure, however, you must select the procedure file by using the SET PROCEDURE TO command at the beginning of the calling program:

```
*** ADDDATA.PRG
* Data maintenance menu
SET PROCEDURE TO DATAPROC      && select the procedure file
SET TALK OFF
SET ECHO OFF
STORE " " TO mChoice
DO WHILE .T.
   CLEAR
   SET STATUS OFF
   @10,10 SAY "Enter [A] to Add a new record, [E] to Exit ";
       GET mChoice
```

```
READ
DO CASE
    CASE  UPPER(mChoice)="A"
        DO ADDRECRD            && call the program module
        LOOP
    CASE UPPER (mChoice)="E"
        EXIT
ENDCASE
ENDDO
```

The results of executing the procedure are the same as they would be if the procedure were in the form of an independent program module. But, in most cases, using a procedure greatly reduces the amount of disk accessing time. This is especially true if the procedure contains a large set of instructions.

Whenever feasible, use a procedure rather than a program module.

Tip:

Release memory space by closing a procedure file when you no longer need it.

Because loaded procedure files compete with other operations for memory space, you should release memory space whenever a procedure file is no longer needed.

To remove the contents of a procedure from memory, use the CLOSE PROCEDURE command (see the following Trap).

Trap:

To avoid losing data, close a procedure file only in the calling program.

You can remove the contents of an active procedure file from memory by issuing the CLOSE PROCEDURE command.

However, be sure to close a procedure file only in the calling program. The system hangs if you close a procedure when you are in that procedure, and you have to reboot the computer. As a result, you risk losing valuable data.

Trap:

Be sure to allocate sufficient memory to dBASE III Plus if you use a large procedure file.

The contents of a procedure file are loaded in memory whenever the file is selected with the SET PROCEDURE TO command and remain in memory until you close the file. Memory space allocated to dBASE III Plus is thereby diminished.

If you anticipate using a large procedure file, be sure to allocate sufficient memory to the program by setting a higher MAXMEM value in CONFIG.DB. Otherwise, you won't be able to continue processing and may run the risk of losing some of the immediate results. (Refer to Chapter 2 for a discussion of memory allocation.)

Tip:

Design a general-purpose program module or procedure to perform a key operation.

A program module or procedure is an efficient way to process a frequently needed operation in database management.

You may want to include in your database management system, for example, a program module or procedure for finding data records in a database file. You can design the module to find a record in a database file by searching a specific data field for a prespecified key value.

For example, if EMPLOYEE.DBF has been indexed on the LAST_NAME field, you can use the following FINDLAST.PRG program module to find the record for a given key value in the indexed field:

```
*** FINDLAST.PRG
* Find a given last name in the LAST_NAME of EMPLOYEE.DBF
CLEAR
USE EMPLOYEE INDEX BYLAST
SEEK mKeyValue
IF FOUND( )
   @15,10 SAY "The record found:"
   ?
   DISPLAY
ELSE
   @15,30 SAY "No such record!"
```

```
ENDIF
@22,1
WAIT
RETURN
```

This program can be called from another program module. The FINDLAST.PRG module selects and indexes EMPLOYEE.DBF with the information saved in BYLAST.NDX (which was created by using the INDEX ON LAST_NAME TO BYLAST command). Then the SEEK command finds a specific record in the database file. The key value for the index field is stored in the memory variable mKeyValue. If the SEEK operation finds a record, the contents of that record will be displayed. Otherwise, a **No such record!** message is returned.

Before invoking the module, the calling program must supply the information contained in the memory variable mKeyValue because the FINDLAST.PRG module needs the information for the SEEK operation.

In the calling program LOCATE.PRG, for example, the character string "Taylor" is assigned to the memory variable before the DO FINDLAST command is issued:

```
***  LOCATE.PRG
SET  TALK  OFF
SET  ECHO  OFF
CLEAR
*  Find  record  for  "Taylor"  in  LAST_NAME  field  of  EMPLOYEE.DBF
STORE  "Taylor"  TO  mKeyValue
*  Call  the  program  module
   DO  FINDLAST
RETURN
```

When you execute LOCATE.PRG, the key value for the index field ("Taylor") is passed to the FINDLAST.PRG module and the record found by the SEEK operation (SEEK "Taylor") is displayed (see fig. 10.8).

FINDLAST.PRG is useful for finding a specific record based on the value in the LAST_NAME field of EMPLOYEE.DBF, but it lacks the flexibility to be used as a general-purpose module. Because the names of the predefined database and index files (EMPLOYEE.DBF and BYLAST.NDX) are prespecified in the program module, FINDLAST.PRG cannot be used to find a

```
     The record found:

Record#  ID_NO       FIRST_NAME      LAST_NAME      POSITION    EMPLY_DATE MALE
    4    732-88-4589 Doris Y.        Taylor         Sales Rep   08/14/83   .F.



Press any key to continue...
```

Fig. 10.8. The record found by LOCATE.PRG.

record in other database files with key values in other data fields.

However, you can use the names of the database and index files in the modules as parameters. Then different values can be passed to the module from the calling program, and you can use the program module to find a record in any database file.

The following FINDRECD.PRG module, for example, results from modifying FINDLAST.PRG:

```
*** FINDRECD.PRG
* Find and display a data record in a given database file
PARAMETERS mDBF,mNDX,mKeyValue
* Display parameters passed from the calling program
CLEAR
@5,20 SAY ">> Search parameters specified <<"
@7,10 SAY "Name of the database file (.dbf)    : " GET mDBF
@9,10 SAY "    Name of the index file (.ndx) : " GET mNDX
@11,10 SAY "        Value for the key field       : " GET mKeyValue
USE &mDBF INDEX &mNDX
SEEK mKeyValue
IF FOUND( )
   @15,10 SAY "The record found:"
   ?
   DISPLAY
ELSE
   @15,30 SAY "No such record!"
ENDIF
@22,1
WAIT
RETURN
```

In FINDRECD.PRG, you can see the names of the database and index files to be passed as parameters (mDBF and mNDX). And the value of the key field is supplied (as mKeyValue) by the calling program. The variables mDBF and mNDX are used with the macro functions to select and index the database file:

USE &mDBF INDEX &mNDX

The character string in mKeyValue is used in the SEEK operation:

SEEK mKeyValue

If they are to be passed from the calling program, these parameters must be defined with the PARAMETERS command at the beginning of the program modules. The order of the parameters determines the order in which they are passed from the calling program. They must be passed in the following order: database file name, index file name, and key value for the index field.

The following program calls the FINDRECD.PRG module:

```
*** FINDDATA.PRG
SET TALK OFF
SET ECHO OFF
CLEAR
* Find record for Taylor in LAST_NAME field of EMPLOYEE.DBF
* Call the program module
  DO FINDRECD WITH "EMPLOYEE","BYLAST","Taylor"
* Find record for ASH-DB300 in STOCK_NO field of SOFTWARE.DBF
  DO FINDRECD WITH "SOFTWARE","SWSTCKNO","ASH-DB300"
RETURN
```

As you can see, when the FINDRECD program module is called, the WITH operator passes the values of the parameters in the DO command.

For example, to find the record with "Taylor" in the LAST_NAME data field in EMPLOYEE.DBF (which has been indexed with BYLAST.NDX), call FINDRECD.PRG by issuing the following command:

DO FINDRECD WITH "EMPLOYEE","BYLAST","Taylor"

In this command, the three items defined following the WITH operator are values for the three parameters (mDBF, mNDX, and mKeyValue) specified in the FINDRECD.PRG module.

These values are used for the values of the memory variables in the macro functions. As a result, the following commands will be executed:

USE EMPLOYEE INDEX BYLAST
SEEK "Taylor"

Figure 10.9 shows the output for the record search.

```
              >> Search parameters specified <<
      Name of the database file (.dbf) :  EMPLOYEE
      Name of the index file (.ndx) :  BYLAST
      Value for the key field Key :  Taylor


      The record found:

Record#  ID_NO      FIRST_NAME    LAST_NAME      POSITION    EMPLY_DATE MALE
      4  732-88-4589 Doris Y.     Taylor         Sales Rep   08/14/83    .F.



Press any key to continue...
```

Fig. 10.9. The record found by the FINDRECD.PRG program module.

Similarly, you can use the FINDRECD.PRG program module to find a record in another database file based on another key field.

For example, when you issue the following command from FINDDATA.PRG, a record in SOFTWARE.DBF (which has been indexed on the STOCK_NO field in SWSTCKNO.NDX) will be found by using "ASH–DB300" as the key value:

DO FINDRECD WITH "SOFTWARE","SWSTCKNO","ASH–DB300"

Trick:

Share common variables by declaring them PUBLIC.

There are two types of memory variables: *public* and *private*. A *public* variable is used to store values that are accessible by any program module at any level. Public variables can be declared in any program module.

For example, you can let all program modules gain access to the values of the mAcct_No and mAcct_Name memory variables. Declare them as public variables in the program module in which they are initialized:

PUBLIC mAcct_No, mAcct_name

Trick:

Hide a public variable by declaring it PRIVATE.

After a variable has been declared public, it is considered a *global* variable. Its values can be shared by all program modules.

However, you can use the same variable name as a local variable in a given module, storing a value relevant only to that module. To do so, declare the variable in the program module as *PRIVATE*. For example, the variable mSubTotal (which has been declared PUBLIC) may be declared in a program module as PRIVATE:

PRIVATE mSubTotal

As a result, while you are in that program module, the value of mSubTotal is meaningful to that module only. When you are outside that module, the value stored in the public variable is used when mSubTotal is referenced.

Trick:

Declare all common variables in the main program.

If you need to share a set of common variables among all program modules, initialize them in the main program instead of declaring them as PUBLIC variables. The values of variables created in a program can be accessed by any lower-level program module that is called from that program.

As an example, the variables mAcctName, mInvDate, and mInvAmount are initialized in MAIN.PRG:

```
*** MAIN.PRG
* The main program that calls PROGA.PRG
SET TALK OFF
SET ECHO OFF
* Initialize common variables
STORE "The Evergreen Lumber Store" TO mAcctName
STORE CTOD("5/14/87") TO mInvDate
```

```
STORE 799.97 TO mInvAmount
CLEAR
@2,15 SAY ">> Values of memory variables in MAIN.prg <<"
@4,15 SAY " mAcctName : " GET mAcctName
@5,15 SAY " mInvDate : " GET mInvDate
@6,15 SAY "mInvAmount : " GET mInvAmount PICTURE "$###.##"
* Calling PROGA.PRG program module
DO PROGA
RETURN
```

Notice that the values of these variables are assigned in MAIN.PRG by using the STORE commands. To show that these variables can be shared by the subprograms, MAIN.PRG calls subprogram PROGA.PRG. PROGA.PRG, in turn, calls another subprogram—PROGB.PRG:

```
*** PROGA.PRG
* Program module sharing common variables with MAIN.PRG
@9,15 SAY ">> Values of memory variables in PROGA.PRG <<"
@11,15 SAY " mAcctName : " GET mAcctName
@12,15 SAY " mInvDate : " GET mInvDate
@13,15 SAY "mInvAmount : " GET mInvAmount PICTURE "$###.##"
* Calling PROGB.PRG
DO PROGB
* Return to MAIN.PRG
RETURN
```

```
*** PROGB.PRG
* Program module sharing common variables with MAIN.PRG
@16,15 SAY ">> Values of memory variables in PROGB.PRG <<"
@18,15 SAY " mAcctName : " GET mAcctName
@19,15 SAY " mInvDate : " GET mInvDate
@20,15 SAY "mInvAmount : " GET mInvAmount PICTURE "$###.##"
* Return to PROGA.PRG
RETURN
```

The output produced by executing MAIN.PRG (DO MAIN) is shown in figure 10.10. You can see that the values of the common variables assigned in the main program are passed correctly among the program modules.

```
>> Values of memory variables in MAIN.prg <<

mAcctName :  The Evergreen Lumber Store
  mInvDate :  05/14/87
mInvAmount :  $799.97

>> Values of memory variables in PROGA.prg <<

mAcctName :  The Evergreen Lumber Store
  mInvDate :  05/14/87
mInvAmount :  $799.97

>> Values of memory variables in PROGB.prg <<

mAcctName :  The Evergreen Lumber Store
  mInvDate :  05/14/87
mInvAmount :  $799.97
```

Fig. 10.10. Values of the variables in all the program modules.

Graphics Programs

Trick:

Use a text character to produce a bar graph.

Although dBASE III Plus's programming language offers a limited capability for producing a wide range of business graphs, you can use it (and a few tricks) to design basic graphs. For example, you can use a series of text graphic characters to form a histogram or bar graph (see figure 10.11).

The data used to generate the bar graph in figure 10.11 includes the values in the two BARDATA.DBF data fields. This database file structure and records are

```
. USE BARDATA
. DISPLAY STRUCTURE
Structure for database     : C:BARDATA.DBF
Number of data records     : 5
Date of last update        : 04/15/87
Field   Field Name    Type        Width   Dec
  1     CLASSCOUNT    Numeric       2
  2     CLASSLABEL    Character    20
** Total **                        23
```

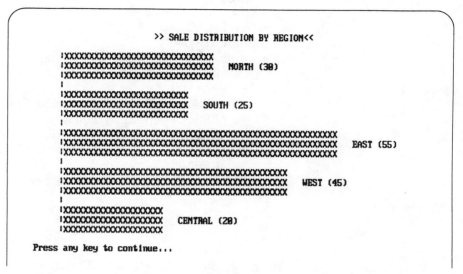

Fig. 10.11. Using text characters to display a bar graph.

```
. LIST
Record#   CLASSCOUNT    CLASSLABEL
    1            30     NORTH
    2            25     SOUTH
    3            55     EAST
    4            45     WEST
    5            20     CENTRAL
```

CLASSCOUNT represents the sales in a given region (identified by a label in the CLASSLABEL field).

From figure 10.11, you can see that each bar is displayed as three lines. The length of each bar represents the value in the CLASSCOUNT data field. The following program was used to produce the bar graph:

```
*** BARGRAF.PRG
* A bar chart by using records in BARDATA.DBF
SET TALK OFF
SET ECHO OFF
CLEAR
* Display chart title
@2,24 SAY ">> SALE DISTRIBUTION BY REGION<<"
?
* Define the graphic symbol
```

```
                    STORE "X" TO mSymbol
                    * Select database file
                    USE BARDATA
                    * Process one record at a time
                    DO WHILE .NOT. EOF( )
                        * Display the bar
                        ?SPACE(5)+"|"+REPLICATE(mSymbol,CLASSCOUNT)
                        ?SPACE(5)+"|"+REPLICATE(mSymbol,CLASSCOUNT)+SPACE(3);
                            +TRIM(CLASSLABEL)+"  ("+STR(CLASSCOUNT,2,0)+")"
                        ?SPACE(5)+"|"+REPLICATE(mSymbol,CLASSCOUNT)
                        ?SPACE(5)+"|"
                        SKIP                    && go to next data record
                    ENDDO
                    @23,1
                    WAIT
                    RETURN
```

You can see that the text symbol "X" is stored in the memory variable mSymbol. The horizontal bar is formed by using the REPLICATE( ) function to display the symbol in mSymbol the number of times stored in CLASSCOUNT.

Trick:

Use a series of ASCII graphics characters to produce a bar graph.

You can use a series of ASCII graphics characters as well as text characters to form a bar in a bar graph. In the preceding section, the program BARGRAF.PRG uses a series of text characters ("X") to produce the bar graph shown in figure 10.11. The text character is stored in the memory variable named mSymbol.

If you replace the character in the memory variable with an ASCII graphics character, you can produce a bar graph with solid bars (see fig. 10.12).

To form a solid bar, use ASCII character 219—a solid square symbol (see the ASCII table in Appendix A at the end of this book).

The bar graph shown in figure 10.12 was produced by using BARGRAF.PRG (as described in the preceding section) after modifying one of the commands in the program as follows:

```
    STORE CHR(219) TO mSymbol
```

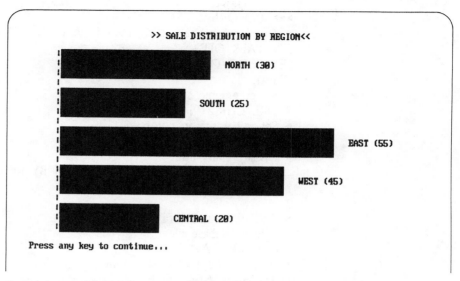

Fig. 10.12. Using ASCII graphic characters to display a bar graph.

Experiment with other ASCII characters to determine which you prefer to use for your graphs.

Trick:

Add colors to a bar graph.

If you have a color monitor connected to the appropriate adapter card, you can display a bar graph in color.

To produce a color bar graph, you use a program with the same logic as that in BARGRAF.PRG (refer to the preceding section) and the data in BARDATA.DBF.

The additional instructions that produce the color bars include a series of SET COLOR TO commands. A different set of colors is defined for each record's text and background. A memory variable (mColorCode) is set up to keep track of which data record is being processed, which in turn determines which set of color combinations should be used to display its value. The memory variable mColor is used to store the color letter codes ("R/B", "W/B", and so on) for the text and its background colors:

```
*** COLORBAR.PRG
* A color bar chart using records in BARDATA.DBF
SET TALK OFF
SET ECHO OFF
CLEAR
* Select graphic symbol
STORE CHR(219) TO mSymbol
* Set initial screen colors
SET COLOR TO W/B,R/W,B
* Display chart title
@3,24 SAY ">> SALE DISTRIBUTION BY REGION<<"
?
?
STORE 0 to mColorCode
* Select database file
USE BARDATA
* Process one record at a time
DO WHILE .NOT. EOF( )
   mColorCode=mColorCode+1
   DO CASE        && determine the color combinations
      CASE mColorCode=1
         mColor="R/B"
      CASE mColorCode=2
         mColor="G/B"
      CASE mColorCode=3
         mColor="R+/B"
      CASE mColorCode=4
         mColor="W/B"
      CASE mColorCode=5
         mColor="RB/B"
   ENDCASE
   SET COLOR TO &mColor
   * Display the bar
   ?SPACE(5)+"|"+REPLICATE(mSymbol,CLASSCOUNT)
   ?SPACE(5)+"|"+REPLICATE(mSymbol,CLASSCOUNT)+SPACE(3);
      +TRIM(CLASSLABEL)+" ("+STR(CLASSCOUNT,2,0)+")"
   ?SPACE(5)+"|"+REPLICATE(mSymbol,CLASSCOUNT)
   SKIP                  && go to next data record
ENDDO
SET COLOR TO W/B          && set frame color
@1,1 TO 22,79 DOUBLE      && frame the bar chart
@23,1
WAIT
RETURN
```

This program can accommodate up to five classes, each displayed in a separate color. Each bar is formed by three lines of graphics symbols (ASCII character 219). If you need to display additional horizontal bars, modify the program by using additional CASE statements to select the color combinations and use a shorter bar length to fit the graph on the screen.

Debugging Your Program

Test each program module and remove errors in syntax and logic (or bugs) before linking the modules as a complete system. If there are errors in a program module, you need to find and correct them. The processing of finding and correcting problems is called *debugging*.

A number of debugging tools are available for tracing program errors. You may need to monitor program execution by using a number of commands provided by dBASE III Plus.

Trick:

Use HISTORY to display an executed program segment.

During debugging, you may want to review the program segment that has just been executed. You can do this by saving to the HISTORY buffer all instructions as they are executed. Then you can display and analyze the contents of the HISTORY buffer.

The use of the HISTORY buffer is discussed in detail in Chapter 3. It basically involves setting the size of the HISTORY buffer by using the SET HISTORY TO command:

SET HISTORY TO <number of commands>

Unless specified differently, the HISTORY buffer can accommodate up to 20 command lines. However, you can store a large section of text temporarily by changing the size of the buffer to hold up to 16,000 commands. Setting the HISTORY buffer to 0 records will empty the buffer.

After setting the necessary buffer size, issue the SET DOHISTORY ON command to activate the HISTORY buffer. The buffer will save the executed instructions in a program. To stop the HISTORY operation, issue the SET DOHISTORY OFF command.

For example, to save all the instructions carried out when you execute the FINDMAX.PRG program (for finding the maximum value in the COST fields in HARDWARE.DBF), issue the following commands at the dot prompt:

. SET HISTORY TO 0
. SET HISTORY TO 100
. SET DOHISTORY ON
. DO FINDMAX

. . . . .

. . . . .
. SET DOHISTORY OFF

As each instruction in FINDMAX.PRG is executed, it is saved in the HISTORY buffer. Then you can use the LIST HISTORY command to display the contents of the HISTORY buffer so that you can analyze the commands which have been executed. A partial list of the contents of the HISTORY buffer after executing FINDMAX.PRG is shown in figure 10.13.

```
. LIST HISTORY
SET DOHISTORY ON
DO FINDMAX
SET TALK OFF
SET ECHO OFF
CLEAR
USE HARDWARE
STORE 0 TO mMaxCost
?"Values of COST scanned"
?
DO WHILE .NOT. EOF()
    ?COST
    IF COST>mMaxCost          && a new maximum is found
        mMaxCost=COST         && update the maximum
    ENDIF
    SKIP                      && scan the next record
ENDDO
    ?COST
    IF COST>mMaxCost          && a new maximum is found
        mMaxCost=COST         && update the maximum

*** INTERRUPTED ***
.
```

Fig. 10.13. A list of commands captured by the HISTORY buffer.

Notice that the HISTORY buffer has captured all the instructions that have been executed.

The SET DOHISTORY ON and SET DOHISTORY OFF commands can be incorporated in the program to selectively capture a certain segment of the program and save it to the HISTORY buffer.

To monitor program execution, use SET ECHO ON during the program development stage.

When you're debugging your program, it is often necessary to monitor the program execution as each command in the program is being processed.

To monitor execution, issue the SET ECHO ON command at the beginning of the program so that the command being processed and its intermediate results will be displayed.

For example, if you add the SET ECHO ON command at the beginning of FINDMAX.PRG, the instructions will be echoed on the screen when you execute the program. Figure 10.14 shows a partial list of the commands.

```
USE HARDWARE
STORE 0 TO mMaxCost
?"Values of COST scanned"
Values of COST scanned
?

DO WHILE .NOT. EOF()
   ?COST
1359.00
   IF COST>mMaxCost          && a new maximum is found
      mMaxCost=COST          && update the maximum
   ENDIF
   SKIP                      && scan the next record
ENDDO
   ?COST
1695.00
   IF COST>mMaxCost          && a new maximum is found
      mMaxCost=COST          && update the maximum
*** INTERRUPTED ***
Called from - C:FINDMAX.prg
Cancel, Ignore, or Suspend? (C, I, or S)
```

Fig. 10.14. Executed commands displayed by the ECHO operation.

Use SET DEBUG ON to send echoed commands to the printer.

You can use the SET ECHO ON command to display instructions on your screen as they are being executed. But the instructions and the results of the program are displayed on the same screen, which can be quite confusing.

Use the SET DEBUG ON command in the program to separate the echoed commands from the output. The echoed commands will be directed to the printer while the results of the program are shown on the screen. You can monitor program execution by looking at the screen and the printer.

Tip:

Use the Suspend option to check intermediate results.

As you debug a program, you often need to know (during program execution) what values are currently in the memory variables.

You can interrupt program execution at any point (if you're using SET ECHO ON to monitor the instructions being executed) by pressing the Esc key. Pressing Esc interrupts program execution. A Cancel, Ignore, or Suspend? (C, I, or S) prompt asks you how you want to proceed.

If you want to examine the values of the memory variables, choose *S* to *suspend* execution. Pressing *S* returns you to the dot prompt. Then you can display the current values in the active memory variables by issuing the DISPLAY MEMORY command (see fig. 10.15).

```
?
DO WHILE .NOT. EOF()
   ?COST
1359.00
   IF COST>mMaxCost        && a new maximum is found
      mMaxCost=COST        && update the maximum
   ENDIF
*** INTERRUPTED ***
Called from - C:FINDMAX.prg
Cancel, Ignore, or Suspend? (C, I, or S) Suspend
Do suspended




. DISPLAY MEMORY
MMAXCOST     priv  N        1359.00  (      1359.00000000)      C:FINDMAX.prg
    1 variables defined,        9 bytes used
  255 variables available,   5991 bytes available

.
```

Fig. 10.15. Continue program execution by using the RESUME command.

As you can see, the current status of the memory variables is displayed.

If you want to continue program execution from the point of interruption, issue the RESUME command.

Tip:

Use SET STEP ON to step through a section of the program during execution.

A powerful command you can use to trace program execution is the SET STEP ON command. When you issue the SET STEP ON command, you can execute the program line-by-line (in steps).

For example, if you want to trace the execution process while you are executing FINDMAX.PRG, issue the following commands:

```
. SET STEP ON
. DO FINDMAX
```

Before each command line in FINDMAX.PRG is executed you are prompted for directions:

Press SPACE to step, S to suspend, or Esc to cancel...

By pressing the space bar in sequence, you can execute the program in steps and observe the intermediate results between steps. To suspend or terminate the execution process, press *S* or the Esc key.

To return to normal processing mode after the SET STEP ON operation, issue the SET STEP OFF command.

Utility Programs

Tip:

Use a documentation utility to help organize your programs.

When you are designing a large database system, you may need a utility program. A utility program can help you document all the program modules and provide detailed references about the components of the system. One such utility program is dPROBE™, developed and marketed by Analytical Software, Inc., Seattle, Washington.

dPROBE, a dBASE Source Code Analysis Utility, is a comprehensive program-development, documentation, and debugging utility designed to evaluate and report on dBASE III Plus application programs. The utility can be used to list all the program modules and file structures of all databases used in the application.

One of dPROBE's powerful features is that it can be used to scan all the program modules and produce a tree diagram (see figure 10.16).

You can see that the tree diagram describes all the linkages between the program modules at various levels. (These program modules are taken from the last chapter of Que Corporation's *dBASE III Plus Handbook*, 2nd Edition, which I wrote.)

In addition to the tree diagram, dPROBE produces a comprehensive set of cross-reference tables that reveal where programs, memory variables, and data fields are referenced and where index files and databases are opened.

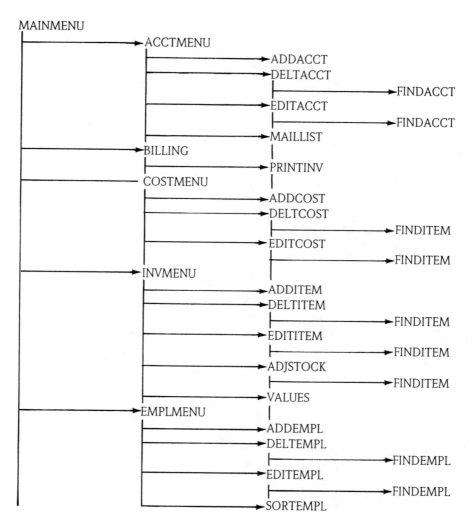

Fig. 10.16. A sample tree diagram describing the program modules.

11

Advanced Topics

This chapter covers topics for advanced users. Here you find (1) how to exchange data between dBASE III Plus and other computer programs (including spreadsheet programs such as Lotus 1-2-3, VisiCalc, and Microsoft Multiplan), (2) how to use a non-dBASE program to access data in a dBASE III Plus database file, and (3) how to import data created in other programs (written in such programming languages as BASIC, Pascal, and FORTRAN).

Another powerful feature—using a compiler to speed execution of a program written in the dBASE III Plus command language—is also discussed.

Tip:

You may have to alter file formats to exchange data with other programs.

When you create a database file within dBASE III Plus, the contents of each record in that file are saved sequentially to a disk file in a unique format. This format may be quite different from that of a file created by other database programs. Similarly, the format of data in disk files created by a word processor or by a spreadsheet program (such as 1-2-3) will be different.

Before you attempt to import a data file created by another computer program, you must determine its data format so that you can retrieve the information from the file. And if you need to use another program to process data files created by dBASE III Plus, you must convert those files into a format which the other program can understand.

To illustrate different formats for text files that can be created from a dBASE III Plus database file, the EMPLOYEE.DBF file is used for the following tips, tricks, and traps. The file structure and its contents are

```
. USE EMPLOYEE
. DISPLAY STRUCTURE
Structure for database    : C:EMPLOYEE.DBF
Number of data records : 10
Date of last update      : 04/20/87
Field    Field Name      Type          Width    Dec
  1      ID_NO           Character        11
  2      FIRST_NAME      Character        15
  3      LAST_NAME       Character        15
  4      POSITION        Character        10
  5      EMPLY_DATE      Date              8
  6      MALE            Logical           1
** Total **                               61
```

```
. LIST
Record#   ID_NO          FIRST_NAME   LAST_NAME POSITION    EMPLY_DATE MALE
      1   123-45-6789    Thomas T.    Smith     President   03/01/81   .T.
      2   254-63-5691    Tina Y.      Thompson  VP          09/22/82   .F.
      3   467-34-6789    Peter F.     Watson    Manager     10/12/82   .T.
      4   732-08-4589    Doris Y.     Taylor    Sales Rep   08/14/83   .F.
      5   563-55-8900    Tyrone T.    Thorsen   Engineer    06/20/82   .T.
      6   823-46-6213    Cathy J.     Faust     Secretary   04/15/83   .F.
      7   554-34-7893    Vincent M.   Corso     Sales Rep   07/20/84   .T.
      8   321-65-9087    Jane W.      Kaiser    Accountant  11/22/82   .F.
      9   560-56-9321    Tina K.      Davidson  Trainee     05/16/86   .F.
     10   435-54-9876    James J.     Smith     Trainee     01/23/86   .T.
```

Tip:

To exchange data with other programs, use the SDF format.

When you convert a database file to *System Data Format* (SDF), all data is coded in ASCII format. SDF is considered a universal data format because most computer programs can retrieve data from an ASCII file.

If you convert the contents of a database file created in dBASE III Plus to a text file in SDF format, for example, that file can be read by a word processor or by an application program written in BASIC.

Tip:

Use the COPY TO command to convert a database file to a text file in SDF format.

To convert an active database file to a text file in SDF format, use the COPY TO command and specify *SDF* as the file format at the end of the command:

    . COPY TO <name of text file> SDF

Each record in the file you have converted is now written as a text line in ASCII format. A carriage return and line feed are added at the end of each record.

(The carriage return positions the data pointer at the beginning of the text line. The line feed moves the data pointer to the next text line to be processed. The combination of a line feed and a carriage return is equivalent to pressing the Enter key.)

Each text line ends with *Enter* (or *RETURN*). This information is important if you need to use other application programs to access data in an SDF format file.

Tip:

Export the contents of a database file to a text file in SDF format with the COPY TO command.

For example, to export the contents of EMPLOYEE.DBF to a text file (in SDF format) named EMPLOYEE.TXT, use the following commands:

    . USE EMPLOYEE
    . COPY TO EMPLOYEE.TXT SDF

After the COPY operation, the EMPLOYEE.TXT will contain the data records of the EMPLOYEE.DBT in SDF format.

You can display the text file created by the COPY TO command by using the TYPE command:

. TYPE <name of text file>

Use the *TYPE EMPLOYEE.TXT* command, for example, to display the contents of the EMPLOYEE.TXT file.

You can stop the screen display temporarily by pressing *Ctrl-S*. Press any key to resume the screen listing after you have viewed a segment of text.

As you can see from figure 11.1, the contents of each EMPLOYEE.DBF data record have been converted into a text line. Information in the data fields is saved as continuous character strings (no separators divide the strings).

```
. TYPE EMPLOYEE.TXT
123-45-6789Thomas T.        Smith      President 19810301T
254-63-5691Tina Y.          Thompson   VP        19820922F
467-34-6789Peter F.         Watson     Manager   19821012T
732-00-4589Doris Y.         Taylor     Sales Rep 19830814F
563-55-8900Tyrone T.        Thorsen    Engineer  19820620T
823-46-6213Cathy J.         Faust      Secretary 19830415F
554-34-7893Vincent M.       Corso      Sales Rep 19840720T
321-65-9087Jane W.          Kaiser     Accountant19821122F
560-56-9321Tina K.          Davidson   Trainee   19860516F
435-54-9876James J.         Smith      Trainee   19860123T

.
```

Fig. 11.1. Contents of the EMPLOYEE.TXT text file.

Characters in a character field are saved as a fixed-length string (the length of the string is determined by the field length specified in the database file's structure). Dates are converted to a different format, and the value of the logical field is represented as *T* or *F* (without the familiar enclosing periods).

Tip:

To list contents of a file to the printer, add the phrase TO PRINT at the end of the TYPE command.

The format for this command is

. TYPE <name of text file> TO PRINT

For example, the following command will list the contents of the EMPLOYEE.TXT file to the printer:

. TYPE EMPLOYEE.TXT TO PRINT

Tip:

Use delimiters to separate character strings in the text file.

In SDF format, the contents of each record in the database file are saved as a continuous text line and the contents of the record's data fields are saved as consecutive character strings, without separators.

Data items saved in this continuous format may not be suitable for access by other application programs.

For example, if you want to write a BASIC program to read the contents of data fields in a text line, these data field values must be separated by a specific character (such as a comma).

To insert separators between the character strings in a text line, use the DELIMITED operator in the COPY TO command when you create a text file:

. COPY TO <name of text file> DELIMITED

The DELIMITED operator encloses the contents of a character field in a pair of double quotation marks and uses commas to separate the contents of data fields.

For example, if you want to separate the character strings in a text file named EMPLOYEE.DAT (which is to be converted from EMPLOYEE.DBF), use the DELIMITED operator in the COPY TO command:

. USE EMPLOYEE
. COPY TO EMPLOYEE.DAT DELIMITED

Figure 11.2 shows the results of using delimiters for separating the character strings in the EMPLOYEE.DAT text file.

```
. TYPE EMPLOYEE.DAT
"123-45-6789","Thomas T.","Smith","President",19810301,T
"254-63-5691","Tina Y.","Thompson","VP",19820922,F
"467-34-6789","Peter F.","Watson","Manager",19821012,T
"732-88-4589","Doris Y.","Taylor","Sales Rep",19830814,F
"563-55-8900","Tyrone T.","Thorsen","Engineer",19820620,T
"823-46-6213","Cathy J.","Faust","Secretary",19830415,F
"554-34-7893","Vincent M.","Corso","Sales Rep",19840720,T
"321-65-9087","Jane W.","Kaiser","Accountant",19821122,F
"560-56-9321","Tina K.","Davidson","Trainee",19860516,F
"435-54-9876","James J.","Smith","Trainee",19860123,T

.
```

Fig. 11.2. Contents of the text file delimited with quotation marks.

In figure 11.2, each line of the EMPLOYEE.DAT text file represents the contents of a data record in the EMPLOYEE.DBF database file. Values in the data fields are separated by commas. The character string in a character field is "trimmed" to exclude trailing spaces and enclosed in a pair of double quotation marks. Dates are saved as a string of digits representing the year, month, and day (as in *19810301* for *March 1, 1981*). The logical values *.T.* and *.F.* are stored as a single letter, *T* or *F*, without periods. Values in numeric fields are saved in their original form.

Tip:

Use the DELIMITED WITH operator to define your own delimiters.

You can use the DELIMITED operator in a COPY TO command to convert the contents of a dBASE III Plus database file to a text file. In this file, the character strings in the text file's character fields are delimited by default with a pair of double quotation marks. If you want to use another symbol as the delimiter, specify it by using the DELIMITED WITH operator in the COPY TO command:

. COPY TO <name of text file> DELIMITED WITH <delimiter symbol>

For example, you can use a backslash in the text file as a delimiter for enclosing the contents of a character field in the database file. Figure 11.3 shows the text file created with the following commands:

. USE EMPLOYEE
. COPY TO STAFF.DAT DELIMITED WITH \

```
. USE EMPLOYEE
. COPY TO STAFF.DAT DELIMITED WITH \
      10 records copied
. TYPE STAFF.DAT
\123-45-6789\,\Thomas T.\,\Smith\,\President\,19810301,T
\254-63-5691\,\Tina Y.\,\Thompson\,\VP\,19820922,F
\467-34-6789\,\Peter F.\,\Watson\,\Manager\,19821012,T
\732-88-4589\,\Doris Y.\,\Taylor\,\Sales Rep\,19830814,F
\563-55-8900\,\Tyrone T.\,\Thorsen\,\Engineer\,19820620,T
\823-46-6213\,\Cathy J.\,\Faust\,\Secretary\,19830415,F
\554-34-7893\,\Vincent M.\,\Corso\,\Sales Rep\,19840720,T
\321-65-9087\,\Jane W.\,\Kaiser\,\Accountant\,19821122,F
\560-56-9321\,\Tina K.\,\Davidson\,\Trainee\,19860516,F
\435-54-9876\,\James J.\,\Smith\,\Trainee\,19860123,T
.
```

Fig. 11.3. Contents of the text file delimited with backslashes.

It is important to note that, as shown in figure 11.3, the character strings in the character fields are "trimmed" when the DELIMITED WITH operator is used in the COPY TO command.

Tip:

Use DELIMITED WITH BLANK to insert a blank space between two character strings in the text file.

A common way to separate field values in the text file created from a database file with the COPY TO command is to use a blank space as a delimiter. To do this, use the DELIMITED WITH BLANK clause in the COPY TO command while you are converting the database file.

The field values in each EMPLOYEE.DBF record are separated with a single space when the record is converted to a text line in the STAFF1.DAT text file (see fig. 11.4).

```
. USE EMPLOYEE
. COPY TO STAFF1.DAT DELIMITED WITH BLANK
      10 records copied
. TYPE STAFF1.DAT
123-45-6789 Thomas T. Smith President 19810301 T
254-63-5691 Tina Y. Thompson VP 19820922 F
467-34-6789 Peter F. Watson Manager 19821012 T
732-88-4589 Doris Y. Taylor Sales Rep 19830814 F
563-55-8900 Tyrone T. Thorsen Engineer 19820620 T
823-46-6213 Cathy J. Faust Secretary 19830415 F
554-34-7893 Vincent M. Corso Sales Rep 19840720 T
321-65-9007 Jane W. Kaiser Accountant 19821122 F
560-56-9321 Tina K. Davidson Trainee 19860516 F
435-54-9876 James J. Smith Trainee 19860123 T

.
```

Fig. 11.4. Contents of the text file delimited with blank spaces.

You can see in figure 11.4 that all the field values, regardless of their types, are separated by single spaces. The character strings in the original character fields are "trimmed."

Trick:

Use the FIELDS operator to copy the contents of selected data fields to a text file.

When you create a text file in SDF format from an existing database file, you can select a specific data field or fields from the database file by using the FIELDS operator in the COPY TO command:

. COPY FIELDS <field list> TO <name of text file> SDF

For example, to create the ROSTER.TXT file shown in figure 11.5, which contains only the first and last names from EMPLOYEE.DBF, issue the following commands:

. USE EMPLOYEE
. COPY FIELDS FIRST_NAME, LAST_NAME TO ROSTER.TXT SDF

```
. USE EMPLOYEE
. COPY FIELDS FIRST_NAME, LAST_NAME TO ROSTER.TXT SDF
      10 records copied
. TYPE ROSTER.TXT
Thomas T.     Smith
Tina Y.       Thompson
Peter F.      Watson
Doris Y.      Taylor
Tyrone T.     Thorsen
Cathy J.      Faust
Vincent M.    Corso
Jane W.       Kaiser
Tina K.       Davidson
James J.      Smith

.
```

Fig. 11.5. ROSTER.TXT created with the COPY TO operation.

You may notice in figure 11.5 that the character strings in the character fields (FIRST_NAME and LAST_NAME) are not "trimmed" when you use the COPY FIELDS TO command to save text in SDF format.

If you want to "trim" the character strings and delimit them with the default delimiter symbols (double quotation marks) or a custom delimiter symbol, use the DELIMITED WITH operator in the COPY FIELDS commands. Examples follow:

. USE EMPLOYEE
. COPY FIELDS FIRST_NAME, LAST_NAME TO ROSTER.TXT DELIMITED
. COPY FIELDS FIRST_NAME, LAST_NAME TO ROSTER.TXT DELIMITED WITH \
. COPY FIELDS FIRST_NAME, LAST_NAME TO ROSTER.TXT DELIMITED WITH BLANK

Trick:

Use SET FILTER TO to copy selected records from a database file to a text file.

If you use the SET FILTER TO command to filter the data records in a database file before issuing the COPY TO command, you can copy selected records from the database file to a text file. The SET FILTER TO command allows you to set a filter condition so that only those data records that meet the condition are subjected to the COPY TO operation.

If you want to copy the EMPLOYEE.DBF records that belong to female employees, for example, specify the filter condition before copying the records to a text file named FEMALES.DAT. Use the following commands:

. USE EMPLOYEE
. SET FILTER TO .NOT. MALE
. COPY TO FEMALES.DAT SDF

The SET FILTER command specifies that only those records whose values in the logical field *MALE* are *.F.* are to be selected for the COPY TO operation that follows. The text file (FEMALES.DAT) created by the COPY TO operation contains only records belonging to female employees in EMPLOYEE.DBF (see fig. 11.6).

```
. USE EMPLOYEE
. SET FILTER TO .NOT. MALE
. LIST
Record#   ID_NO        FIRST_NAME    LAST_NAME     POSITION    EMPLY_DATE MALE
      2   254-63-5691  Tina Y.       Thompson      VP          09/22/82    .F.
      4   732-88-4589  Doris Y.      Taylor        Sales Rep   08/14/83    .F.
      6   823-46-6213  Cathy J.      Faust         Secretary   04/15/83    .F.
      8   321-65-9887  Jane W.       Kaiser        Accountant  11/22/82    .F.
      9   560-56-9321  Tina K.       Davidson      Trainee     05/16/86    .F.

. COPY TO FEMALES.TXT SDF
      5 records copied
. TYPE FEMALES.TXT
254-63-5691Tina Y.       Thompson      VP         19820922F
732-88-4589Doris Y.      Taylor        Sales Rep  19830814F
823-46-6213Cathy J.      Faust         Secretary  19830415F
321-65-9887Jane W.       Kaiser        Accountant19821122F
560-56-9321Tina K.       Davidson      Trainee    19860516F

.
```

Fig. 11.6. Setting filter conditions for the COPY TO operation.

Other examples of filter conditions are

. SET FILTER TO POSITION="Trainee"
. SET FILTER TO POSITION="Trainee".OR.MALE
. SET FILTER TO POSITION="Trainee".AND.
EMPLY_DATE>CTOD("1/1/85")

Trick:

To copy a block of records from a database file to a text file, set the record range in a scope condition.

If you want to copy a block of data records from a dBASE III Plus database file to a text file, specify the record range as a scope condition in the COPY TO command. To select the set of records to be copied, use the RECNO( ) function to define the record range.

For example, if you want to copy the first five records of EMPLOYEE.DBF to a text file named PARTONE.TXT, specify the record range as follows:

. COPY TO PARTONE.TXT SDF FOR RECNO( )<=5

You can copy one or more sections of the records in EMPLOYEE.DBF to a text file with the commands:

. COPY TO TEXTFILE SDF FOR RECNO( )>=5 .AND. RECNO( )<=8
. COPY TO TEXTFILE DELIMITED FOR (RECNO( )>=2 .AND. RECNO( )<=4) .OR. (RECNO( )>=6 .AND. RECNO( )<=8)

The first of these COPY TO operations copies records 5 through 8 from EMPLOYEE.DBF to a text file; the second COPY TO command copies records 2 through 4 and 6 through 8 to another text file.

Tip:

Use DIF format to share dBASE III Plus database files with VisiCalc.

You can use the VisiCalc® spreadsheet program to process data you've saved in a dBASE III Plus database file. First, use the COPY TO command to convert the contents of the file to a disk file in DIF (data interchange format) format. To do this, specify DIF as the file type to be converted with the COPY TO command:

. COPY TO <name of DIF file> DIF

When you convert a database file to a DIF file, each record in the database file is converted as a row in the VisiCalc spreadsheet. Each data field of the database file is saved as a spreadsheet column in DIF format.

For example, you can convert the data in EMPLOYEE.DBF to a disk file in DIF format by using the following commands:

```
. USE EMPLOYEE
. COPY TO EMPLOYEE DIF
```

The COPY TO operation creates a disk file in DIF format and automatically attaches a *.DIF* file extension if you don't specify a file extension.

If you want to view the DIF file in spreadsheet format, you must use the VisiCalc program to display the file. (You can't use the TYPE command to display the contents of the disk file in a meaningful format.)

Tip:

Use WKS format to share dBASE III Plus database files with 1-2-3.

To use the 1-2-3 spreadsheet program to access data you've saved in a dBASE III Plus database file, use the COPY TO command. COPY TO converts the contents of the database file to a disk file in WKS format. Specify *WKS* as the file type to be converted with the COPY TO command:

```
. COPY TO <name of WKS file> WKS
```

When you convert a database file to a WKS file, each record in the database file is converted to a row in the 1-2-3 spreadsheet. Each data field is saved as a spreadsheet column in WKS format.

To convert the data in EMPLOYEE.DBF to a disk file in WKS format, for example, use the following commands:

```
. USE EMPLOYEE
. COPY TO EMPLOYEE WKS
```

The COPY TO operation creates a disk file in WKS format and automatically attaches the file extension *.WKS* if you don't specify a file extension.

If you want to view the WKS file in spreadsheet format, you must use 1-2-3 to display it. (You cannot use the TYPE command to display the contents of the disk file in a meaningful format.) A WKS file created with the COPY TO command is shown in figure 11.7. Notice that the field names are saved as the first row of the spreadsheet table.

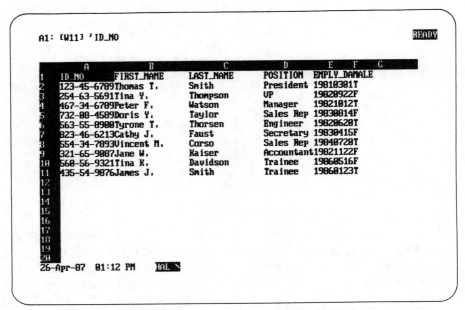

```
A1: [W11] 'ID_NO                                                    READY

         A              B            C            D          E      F      G
 1  ID_NO       FIRST_NAME    LAST_NAME    POSITION   EMPLY_DAMALE
 2  123-45-6789Thomas T.      Smith        President  19010301T
 3  254-63-5691Tina Y.        Thompson     VP         19020922F
 4  467-34-6789Peter F.       Watson       Manager    19021012T
 5  732-00-4509Doris Y.       Taylor       Sales Rep  19030814F
 6  563-55-8900Tyrone T.      Thorsen      Engineer   19020620T
 7  823-46-6213Cathy J.       Faust        Secretary  19030415F
 8  554-34-7093Vincent M.     Corso        Sales Rep  19040720T
 9  921-65-9087Jane W.        Kaiser       Accountant19021122F
10  560-56-9321Tina K.        Davidson     Trainee    19060516F
11  435-54-9876James J.       Smith        Trainee    19060123T
12
13
14
15
16
17
18
19
20
26-Apr-87  01:12 PM    HAL
```

Fig. 11.7. The spreadsheet file converted from EMPLOYEE.DBF.

Trick:

Use WKS format to exchange data between dBASE III Plus and Release 2 of 1-2-3.

When you are using Release 1A of 1-2-3, spreadsheet files are saved in WKS format.

Although Release 2.01 of the program stores its spreadsheet files in *WK1* format, spreadsheets saved in WKS format can be read by Release 2.01.

If you need to use Release 2.01 of 1-2-3 to access the data in a dBASE III Plus database file, convert the database file to a disk file in WKS format by using the COPY TO command:

. COPY TO <name of WKS file> WKS

Trap:

When you use the COPY TO operation to convert a database file to a spreadsheet for Release 2.01 of 1-2-3, do not specify WK1 as the file type.

If you specify *WK1* as the file type when you use the COPY TO operation to convert a database file to a spreadsheet for Release 2.01 of 1-2-3, the error message `Unrecognized phrase/ keyword in command` is displayed and the COPY operation will be ignored.

Tip:

Use SYLK format to share dBASE III Plus database files with the Microsoft Multiplan spreadsheet program.

You can use the Microsoft Multiplan® spreadsheet program to access data you've saved in a dBASE III Plus database file. Use the COPY TO command to convert the contents of the database file to a disk file in SYLK (symbolic link) format. To do this, specify SYLK as the file type to be converted with the COPY command:

   . COPY TO <name of SYLK file> SYLK

When you convert a database file to a SYLK file, each record in the database file is converted to a row in the spreadsheet used by Multiplan. Each data field of the database file is saved as a spreadsheet column in SYLK format.

For example, you can convert the data in EMPLOYEE.DBF to a disk file in SYLK format with the following commands:

   . USE EMPLOYEE
   . COPY TO PERSONEL SYLK

The disk file created by the COPY TO command is in SYLK format. Note that no file extension is added to the disk file unless you specify one in the COPY TO command.

To view the SYLK file in spreadsheet format, you must use the Multiplan spreadsheet program to display it. (You cannot use the TYPE command to display the contents of the disk file in a meaningful format.)

Trap:

The contents of a memo field in a database file cannot be copied to a text file with the COPY TO command.

If you store textual information in a memo field in a database file, the text is saved in a separate disk file with a .DBT file extension. Although memo fields can be useful for storing a large block of text in a database file, they are excluded from many data manipulation operations.

For example, you can't search a memo field for a specific record, and you can't use a memo field as a key for sorting or indexing records. And when you use the COPY TO command to convert a database file that includes one or more memo fields to a text file, the contents of the memo fields will be ignored.

However, if you need to make a backup copy of a database file that includes one or more memo fields, you can use the COPY FILE command to copy the .DBF and .DBT files.

For example, if you want to make a backup copy of the contents of the BULLETIN.DBF file (which has a memo field), copy both the BULLETIN.DBF and BULLETIN.DBT files by using the following commands:

    . COPY FILE BULLETIN.DBF TO BULLEBAK.DBF
    . COPY FILE BULLETIN.DBT TO BULLEBAK.DBT

Using the same file name for both the .DBF and .DBT files is important.

Tip:

Use the EXPORT TO command to convert a database file to a PFS file.

To convert a database file created by dBASE III Plus to a disk file in PFS format, use the EXPORT TO command:

    . EXPORT TO <name of the PFS file> PFS

The EXPORT TO command creates a disk file in PFS format. Because a PFS file normally has no file extension, the command will not add a file extension to this PFS file unless you specify an extension. However, you must include a period at the end of the file name if you do not want a file extension for the PFS file:

    . EXPORT TO APFSFILE. PFS

The EXPORT TO command performs a function similar to that of a COPY TO command when it is used to convert a database file to a disk file in a particular data format. But the EXPORT TO command does more than the COPY TO command—it allows you to format the data fields in the database file with a format (.FMT) file before exporting the data to the PFS file.

For example, you can export to a PFS file the contents of EMPLOYEE.DBF, whose data fields are defined with a format file EMPLOYEE.FMT, by using the following commands:

```
. USE EMPLOYEE
. SET FORMAT TO EMPLOYEE
. EXPORT TO EMPLOYEE. PFS
```

Trap:

Do not use an existing file name for the converted disk file unless SET SAFETY ON is in effect.

When you use the COPY TO or EXPORT TO command to convert a database file created by dBASE III Plus to a disk file of another format, *do not* use an existing file name. If you do, the converted disk file may replace the original database file.

For example, the following command is *not* recommended:

```
. USE EMPLOYEE
. COPY TO EMPLOYEE.DBF SYLK
```

If the default setting SET SAFETY ON is in effect when the COPY TO command is executed, you are informed that the file already exists and prompted whether to overwrite it. However, if you have set SET SAFETY to OFF in previous operations, the original database file will be overwritten automatically and without warning.

To protect your data during the file conversion operation, issue the SET SAFETY ON command so that you will be warned if you try to overwrite an existing file.

Trick:

Use an external program to process data created by dBASE III Plus.

Although the dBASE III Plus command language is one of the most powerful programming languages offered as part of a database program, it lacks many of the mathematical capabilities provided by such programming languages as FORTRAN, Pascal, or BASIC. These mathematical tools are necessary for developing programs that involve complex computations.

The dBASE III Plus command language, for example, does not allow dimensioned arrays in a program. But you can compensate by using an external program within dBASE III Plus.

In other words, you can process data created within dBASE III Plus by executing a program written in another language (such as BASIC) at the dot prompt. To do so, convert the contents of a database file to a text file in the format the external program can read. Then execute the external program at the dot prompt.

Trick:

Use a BASIC program to process dBASE III Plus data in a dimensioned array.

When you are in dBASE III Plus, data is stored in a database file in the form of a data table. Each row of the table corresponds to a record, and each data field is considered as a table column.

To process the data in the database file, you need to scan each data record and process it sequentially. You can't store these data values in a dimensioned array that gives you access at random to one or more of these values. This sequential mode of processing imposes a significant restriction on data manipulation if complex mathematical operations are needed.

To solve this problem, first export the data values from the database file to a text file. Then use a program written in a conventional programming language to store the data in a dimensioned array.

For example, you can process the data values in the COST and PRICE data fields in PRODUCTS.DBF in two single-dimensioned arrays. To do so, save these values in a text file by using the COPY TO command. The file structure and contents of PRODUCTS.DBF are

```
. USE PRODUCTS
. DISPLAY STRUCTURE
Structure for database   : C:PRODUCTS.DBF
Number of data records : 20
Date of last update      : 02/07/87
```

Field	Field Name	Type	Width	Dec
1	STOCK_NO	Character	9	
2	DIVISION	Character	2	
3	TYPE	Character	20	
4	COST	Numeric	7	2
5	PRICE	Numeric	7	2
** Total **			46	

```
. LIST
```

Record#	STOCK_NO	DIVISION	TYPE	COST	PRICE
1	CPQ-SP256	HW	system	1359.00	1895.00
2	ZEN-SL181	HW	system	1695.00	2399.00
3	IBM-AT640	HW	system	3790.00	4490.00
4	ZEN-MM012	HW	monitor	89.00	159.00
5	NEC-PC660	HW	printer	560.00	820.00
6	HAY-M1200	HW	modem	269.00	389.00
7	HAY-M1200	HW	modem	398.00	495.00
8	IOM-HD040	HW	hard disk	2190.00	2790.00
9	PAR-GC100	HW	graphics card	279.00	389.00
10	HER-GC100	HW	graphics card	199.00	239.00
11	ASH-DB300	SW	database	395.00	595.00
12	ANS-DB110	SW	database	525.00	695.00
13	CLP-DB100	SW	database compiler	450.00	595.00
14	WOR-DB100	SW	database compiler	469.00	595.00
15	LOT-LO123	SW	spreadsheet	289.00	359.00
16	MIC-WS330	SW	word processing	229.00	269.00
17	MIS-WD300	SW	word processing	229.00	289.00
18	AST-FW200	SW	integrated	345.00	395.00
19	MIC-QB100	SW	language	79.00	109.00
20	BOL-PA300	SW	language	39.50	69.50

You need to create a text file (VALUES.DAT) to hold the values of the COST and PRICE data fields of the PRODUCTS.DBF database file. To do so, use the following commands:

```
. USE PRODUCTS
. COPY FIELDS COST, PRICE TO VALUES.DAT DELIMITED
```

The contents of the text file VALUES.DAT are shown in figure 11.8.

```
. TYPE VALUES.DAT
1359.00,1895.00
1695.00,2399.00
3790.00,4490.00
89.00,159.00
560.00,820.00
269.00,389.00
390.00,495.00
2190.00,2790.00
279.00,389.00
199.00,239.00
395.00,595.00
525.00,695.00
450.00,595.00
469.00,595.00
289.00,359.00
229.00,269.00
229.00,289.00
345.00,395.00
79.00,109.00
39.50,69.50

.
```

Fig. 11.8. Contents of the text file VALUES.DAT.

Note that the values in each record's COST and PRICE data fields are saved as a text line and separated by a comma. These values can be read into two single-dimensioned arrays (such as X and Y) by the BASIC program ARRAYS.BAS as follows:

```
10 REM ARRAYS.BAS
20 REM Read values in VALUES.DAT and assign them to
30 REM arrays X( ) and Y( )
40 DIM X(20),Y(20)           ' declare array dimensions
50 OPEN "VALUES.DAT" FOR INPUT AS #1      'select the input file
60 N=0                'count number of values
70 IF EOF(1) THEN 120
80 N=N+1
90 INPUT #1,X(N),Y(N)
100 GOTO 70
110 REM Display values in the arrays
120 KEY OFF:CLS
130 PRINT "  >> Values in the arrays <<"
140 PRINT " i ", "X(i)", "Y(i)"
150 PRINT "---", "----", "----"
160 FOR I=1 TO N
170 PRINT I,X(I),Y(I)
```

180 NEXT I
190 LOCATE 12,38:PRINT "Press any key to return to dBASE III Plus!"
200 A$=INKEY$:IF A$="" THEN 200
210 SYSTEM   'return to dBASE III Plus

To execute the ARRAYS.BAS program, issue the RUN command at the dot prompt. If the program is written in an interpretive BASIC (such as BASICA or GWBASIC), execute it by using the interpretive language:

. RUN BASICA ARRAYS

or

. RUN GWBASIC ARRAYS

When the RUN command is processed, the program is executed and control is transferred to the BASIC program. The results of executing ARRAYS.BAS at the dot prompt (. RUN BASICA ARRAYS) are shown in figure 11.9.

```
>> Values in the arrays <<
 i          X(i)            Y(i)
---         ----            ----
 1          1359            1895
 2          1695            2399
 3          3790            4490
 4          89              159
 5          560             820
 6          269             389
 7          398             495
 8          2190            2790
 9          279             389        Press any key to return to dBASE III Plus!
10          199             239
11          395             595
12          525             695
13          450             595
14          469             595
15          289             359
16          229             269
17          229             289
18          345             395
19          79              189
20          39.5            69.5
```

Fig. 11.9. Output of the ARRAYS.BAS BASIC program.

After the BASIC program has been processed and a key is pressed, you pass control back to dBASE III Plus by issuing the SYSTEM command from within the BASIC program.

If the BASIC program has been compiled and saved as an executable (.EXE) or command (.COM) file, you may execute the program directly by issuing the RUN command for processing a DOS file:

. RUN ARRAYS

When you use the RUN command to execute an external program at the dot prompt, all the system programs needed for processing the external program must be present in the current directory. Or they must have been defined in the DOS PATH command. (Refer to Chapter 1 for a discussion of how to execute an external program by using the RUN command in dBASE III Plus.)

Trick:

Use a BASIC program to produce a pie graph based on the data in a database file.

dBASE III Plus does not provide commands for drawing lines and circles needed for many business graphs (such as line and pie graphs).

A solution to this problem is to write an external program in a conventional language (such as BASIC). In this way, you can produce the graphs you need, based on the data stored in your dBASE III Plus database file. To do this, convert the contents of the database file to a text file format that the external program can recognize.

For example, you can write a program in BASIC to create a pie graph based on the values in SWSALES.DBF. The file structure and contents of SWSALES.DBF are

```
. USE SWSALES
. DISPLAY STRUCTURE
Structure for database   : C:SWSALES.DBF
Number of data records : 6
Date of last update      : 04/22/87
Field    Field Name        Type        Width    Dec
  1      PROD_TYPE         Character     20
  2      SALE              Numeric       10       2
** Total **                             31
```

```
. LIST
Record#    PROD_TYPE              SALE
      1    Database            2200.00
      2    Accounting          1200.00
      3    Word Processor      1700.00
      4    Spreadsheet         2400.00
      5    Language            1200.00
      6    Graphics             800.00
```

Before processing the data in the SWSALES.DBF database file, convert its contents to a text file (named PIEDATA.DAT) in the format BASIC can read. To do this, issue the following commands:

```
. USE SWSALES
. COPY TO PIEDATA.DAT DELIMITED
```

The text file (PIEDATA.DAT) created by the COPY TO command contains the labels and values needed to display a pie graph (see fig. 11.10).

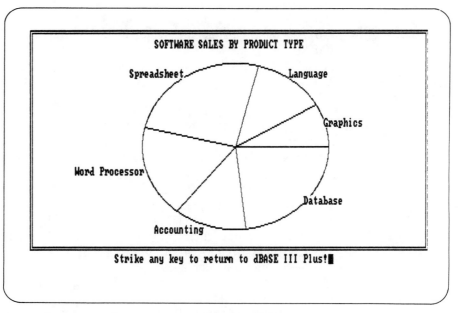

Fig. 11.10. The pie graph produced by PIECHART.BAS.

After the converted data has been stored in the format BASIC can read, execute the program. The following BASIC program (PIECHART.BAS) displays the data in the PIEDATA.DAT file as a pie graph:

```
10 '*** PIEGRAPH.BAS
20 'L$(I), V(I) are arrays for storing the labels and values
30 'for the Ith record of PIEDATA.DBF
40 'N=number of data records
50 KEY OFF:SCREEN 1:WIDTH 80:CLS
60 DIM L$(10),V(10)
80 PI=3.14159                    ' Value of pi
90 XC=330: YC=95                 ' Set center of the pie graph
100 RADIUS=150                    ' Set radius of the circle
110 '*** Reading data from the data file PIEDATA.DAT
120 OPEN "PIEDATA.DAT" FOR INPUT AS #1
130 K=0
140 IF EOF(1) THEN 180
150 K=K+1
160 INPUT #1,L$(K),V(K)
170 GOTO 140
180 N=K            ' number of records or divisions
190 '*** Summing up the values in the V-array
200 SUM=0
210 FOR I=1 TO N
220 SUM=SUM+V(I)
230 NEXT
240 '*** Assign the graph title
250 TITLE$="SOFTWARE SALES BY PRODUCT TYPE"
260 CLS
270 '*** Draw a double-line box
280 LINE(0,0) - (639,180),,B
290 LINE(3,2) - (636,178),,B
300 '*** Display the graph title
310 LOCATE 2,(80-LEN(TITLE$))/2:PRINT TITLE$
320 '*** Draw the circle center at (XC,YC)
330 CIRCLE(XC,YC),RADIUS,,,,5/11
340 '*** Draw division lines
350 A0=0                          'The beginning angle
360 FOR I=1 TO N
370 A=A0+2*3.14156*(V(I)/SUM)                    'The angle of the arc
380 X=XC+RADIUS*COS(A)
390 Y=YC+RADIUS*SIN(A)*5/11
```

```
400 LINE (XC,YC) – (X,Y)
410 '*** Position a label at (R,C)
420 MIDPOINT= A0+(A–A0)/2
430 YL=YC+(RADIUS+4)*SIN(MIDPOINT)*5/11
440 XL=XC+(RADIUS+4)*COS(MIDPOINT)
450 IF XL>(XC+10) THEN 500
460 IF XL<(XC–10) THEN 490
470 XL=XL–LEN(L$(I))/16
480 GOTO 500
490 XL=XL–LEN(L$(I))*8
500 R=INT(YL/8)+1
510 C=INT(XL/8)+1
520 LOCATE R,C:PRINT L$(I)
530 A0=A
540 NEXT I
550 LOCATE 24,18:INPUT "Strike any key to return to dBASE III
Plus!", AKEY
560 SYSTEM
570 END
```

The pie graph shown in figure 11.10 was produced by executing the BASIC program at the dot prompt:

. RUN BASICA PIECHART

When the RUN command is processed, the program is executed and control is transferred to the BASIC program. After the BASIC program has been processed, issue the SYSTEM command within the BASIC program to pass control back to dBASE III Plus.

System programs needed to process an external program with the RUN command must be present in the current directory or have been defined in the DOS PATH command. (See Chapter 1 for a discussion of how to execute an external program by using the RUN command in dBASE III Plus.)

Tip:

Save a report to a text file for possible editing.

Once you've designed a report based on the contents of a database file, you can print the report or display it on the screen.

If you need to make any changes, modify the report form by using the MODIFY REPORT operation and then regenerating the report. This approach may be necessary if you need to make major modifications.

To correct minor errors, such as misspelled report headings, or to rearrange some of the column figures, you can use a word processor or text editor to modify the report. To do this, save the report to a text file by adding the name of the text file to the REPORT FORM command:

. REPORT FORM <name of .FRM file> TO <name of text file>

For example, you can use a word processor or text editor to modify the report produced by using the data records in PRODSOLD.DBF with the SALERPT3.FRM report form. Invoke the following commands to save the report to SALERPT3.TXT:

. USE PRODSOLD
. REPORT FORM SALERPT3 TO SALERPT3.TXT

After the report has been saved in a text file, use a word processor or text editor to make the changes you need. In figure 11.11, for instance, the text file (SALERPT3.TXT) created with the REPORT FORM command is displayed for editing with WordStar.

Importing Data from a Non-dBASE Disk File

Tip:

Use the APPEND command to import data from a text file.

Data created by other application programs and saved in an ASCII text file can be read into a dBASE III Plus file.

Depending on the way in which data elements in the file are delimited, you can append the contents of the text file to a database file with a defined file structure. The format of the APPEND command is

. APPEND FROM <name of the text file> DELIMITED WITH <the delimiter>

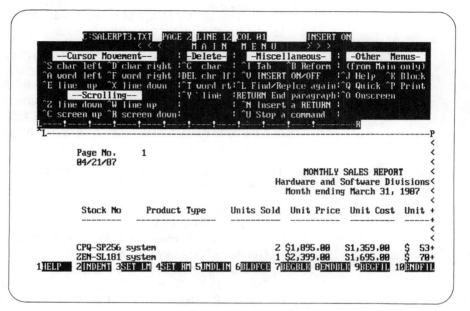

Fig. 11.11. Editing the sales report with a word processor.

For example, to read the data in the STAFF.DAT text file into the database file named PERSONAL.DBF, issue the following commands:

```
. USE PERSONAL
. APPEND FROM STAFF.DAT DELIMITED WITH \
```

The backslash is defined as the delimiter in the APPEND command. To see what the contents of the text file look like, refer to figure 11.12. All the character strings are delimited with a backslash and all the data elements are separated by commas.

```
. TYPE STAFF.DAT
\123-45-6789\,\Thomas T.\,\Smith\,\President\,19010301,T
\254-63-5691\,\Tina Y.\,\Thompson\,\VP\,19020922,F
\467-34-6789\,\Peter F.\,\Watson\,\Manager\,19021012,T
\732-88-4589\,\Doris Y.\,\Taylor\,\Sales Rep\,19030814,F
\563-55-8900\,\Tyrone T.\,\Thorsen\,\Engineer\,19020620,T
\823-46-6213\,\Cathy J.\,\Faust\,\Secretary\,19030415,F
\554-34-7893\,\Vincent M.\,\Corso\,\Sales Rep\,19040720,T
\321-65-9087\,\Jane W.\,\Kaiser\,\Accountant\,19021122,F
\560-56-9321\,\Tina K.\,\Davidson\,\Trainee\,19060516,F
\435-54-9876\,\James J.\,\Smith\,\Trainee\,19060123,T
```

Fig. 11.12. The database file created by using the APPEND operation.

The data elements of the text file's fields are determined by the file structure of the active database file.

For example, the letter *T* or *F* at the end of each line in the STAFF.DAT text file can be interpreted as the value of either a character field or a logical field, depending on the file structure of PERSONAL.DBF. Similarly, the string of numeric digits in a text line (such as *19810301*) can be treated as a date (*3/1/81*) or a numeric value, based on the type of data field to which it is to be appended.

The file structure of PERSONAL.DBF, which is used to store the data imported from STAFF.DAT, is

```
. USE PERSONAL
. DISPLAY STRUCTURE
Structure for database   :  C:PERSONAL.DBF
Number of data records :  0
Date of last update      :  04/23/87
Field    Field Name       Type         Width    Dec
  1      ID_NO            Character      11
  2      FIRST_NAME       Character      15
  3      LAST_NAME        Character      15
  4      POSITION         Character      10
  5      EMPLY_DATE       Date            8
  6      MALE             Logical         1
** Total **                              61
```

When you convert the contents of a text file to a database file with the APPEND command, each line of the text file is saved as a data record. Data elements in a text line are saved in the data fields, whose types and lengths are defined by the file structure of the database file.

For example, the contents of PERSONAL.DBF, whose records are appended by importing the contents of the STAFF.DAT text file, are shown in figure 11.13.

Tip:

Use a delimiter to identify a character string in an imported text file.

Although you can import an ASCII text file in SDF format (System Data Format) without using a delimiter to identify the character strings, doing so is not recommended. If you don't delimit character strings with a delimiter symbol (quotation marks or backslashes, for example), all the character strings

```
. USE PERSONAL
. APPEND FROM STAFF.DAT DELIMITED WITH \
     10 records added
. LIST
Record#   ID_NO         FIRST_NAME    LAST_NAME    POSITION    EMPLY_DATE MALE
     1    123-45-6789   Thomas T.     Smith        President   03/01/81   .T.
     2    254-63-5691   Tina Y.       Thompson     VP          09/22/82   .F.
     3    467-34-6789   Peter F.      Watson       Manager     10/12/82   .T.
     4    732-08-4509   Doris Y.      Taylor       Sales Rep   08/14/83   .F.
     5    563-55-8900   Tyrone T.     Thorsen      Engineer    06/20/82   .T.
     6    823-46-6213   Cathy J.      Faust        Secretary   04/15/83   .F.
     7    554-34-7893   Vincent M.    Corso        Sales Rep   07/20/84   .T.
     8    321-65-9087   Jane W.       Kaiser       Accountant  11/22/82   .F.
     9    560-56-9321   Tina K.       Davidson     Trainee     05/16/86   .F.
    10    435-54-9876   James J.      Smith        Trainee     01/23/86   .T.
```

Fig. 11.13. The database file converted from the STAFF.DAT text file.

must be defined in fixed length. And each string occupies the same number of characters regardless of the actual length of the string.

For example, you can read the first data element in a line of a file in SDF format into the character field LAST_NAME, whose field length is defined as 10 characters. The first 10 characters of the text line will be used for the field contents. As a result, every character string in the beginning of the text line must be ten characters long. If the actual string is shorter than 10 characters, you must fill the string with blank spaces:

```
JOHN       SMITH
JONATHAN   DAVIDSON
JO         LEE
```

These blank spaces waste disk space.

A better approach is to enclose the character strings with delimiters (such as quotation marks) so that only the actual string of characters is saved in the text file:

```
"JOHN","SMITH"
"JONATHAN","DAVIDSON"
"JO","LEE"
```

Tip:

Use the TYPE operator to import data from disk files created by a spreadsheet program.

You can convert data files created by a spreadsheet program (such as 1-2-3, VisiCalc, or Multiplan) to database files by using the TYPE operator in the APPEND command:

    . APPEND FROM <name of the disk file> TYPE <file type>

The file types for the three most commonly used spreadsheet programs are

Name of Spreadsheet Program	File Type
Lotus 1-2-3	WKS
VisiCalc	DIF
Microsoft Multiplan	SYLK

Here are examples of how they are used:

    . USE SALEDATA
    . APPEND FROM SALES.WKS TYPE WKS

or

    . USE PRODUCTS
    . APPEND FROM SALEITEM.DIF TYPE DIF

or

    . USE PERSONAL
    . APPEND FROM STAFF TYPE SYLK

Trick:

Use TYPE WKS in an APPEND command to import data from a spreadsheet file of WK1 format.

Release 2.01 of 1-2-3 saves all spreadsheet files in WK1 format. However, you can't use the APPEND command to specify *TYPE WK1* as a file type when you attempt to import data from the spreadsheet to a dBASE III Plus database file. *WKS* is the only 1-2-3 file type recognized by the command. If you specify *TYPE WKS*, the APPEND command does not prevent you from reading a spreadsheet in WK1 format.

For example, you can import the data in the EMPLOYEE.WK1 spreadsheet file to the EMPLOYEE.DBF database file with the following commands:

    . USE EMPLOYEE
    . APPEND FROM EMPLOYEE.WK1 TYPE WKS

Tip:

Use the IMPORT command to convert a PFS file to a database file.

If you need to import data from a PFS file and store it in a dBASE III Plus database file, use the IMPORT command:

. IMPORT FROM <name of PFS file> TYPE PFS

Executing the IMPORT command creates a database file (which has the same name as the PFS file, with a .DBF file extension) and associated format (.FMT) and view (.VUE) files. These database, format, and view files are saved in disk files and selected and used automatically. In other words, the following commands are carried out automatically when the IMPORT command is executed:

. USE <name of the database file created>
. SET FORMAT TO <name of the format file created>
. CREATE VIEW <name of view file created> FROM ENVIRONMENT

If you want to convert the data in the PFS file named *STAFF* to a database file, for example, issue the following command:

. IMPORT FROM STAFF TYPE PFS

This IMPORT command creates a database file named STAFF.DBF, a format file named STAFF.FMT, and a view file named STAFF.VUE. As soon as these files are created, they are selected and used automatically, as if you had issued the following commands after executing the IMPORT command:

. USE STAFF
. SET FORMAT TO STAFF
. CREATE VIEW STAFF FROM ENVIRONMENT

Using Compilers

If you are an advanced user of dBASE III Plus and want to perform data manipulation operations with programs written in the dBASE III Plus command language, you can benefit greatly from using a dBASE compiler. The tips and tricks in the following sections cover the principles and benefits of a dBASE III compiler.

Tip:

To improve the execution speed of a program written in dBASE III Plus command language, use a compiler.

The dBASE III Plus command programming language offers a great deal of versatility and flexibility for designing a database management system. It's a high-level programming language with a set of syntax and semantic rules that are relatively close to English. Most programmers find it easy to learn.

However, when you execute a program written in the dBASE III Plus programming language, each command in the program must be translated into machine language before it can be carried out by the computer. And the translation process is repeated whenever you execute the program. The translation operation increases execution time significantly.

You can speed up the execution process by using a compiler to translate the commands into a set of machine-language instructions. The compiler then stores these commands as a disk file. With this operation already performed, the machine language can be processed whenever you need to execute the program. The program has to be translated only once and can be executed repeatedly.

Tip:

Understand the principles of a compiler.

A compiler is a computer program that translates each of the instructions written in a programming language (such as the dBASE III Plus command language) into language that can be understood by the computer.

Because information to be processed by a computer must be represented by binary codes consisting of a series of ones and zeros, any program commands or instructions must be converted to such a machine language before they can be carried out by the computer.

The main function of a compiler is to scan each command in a program and translate it into binary machine language. The process requires two steps. First, commands are translated into machine code, which is called *object code*. Second, a *linker* program produces a program the computer can use. The linker combines your program's object code with other library files (for internal interpretation of the machine codes) to generate an executable (.EXE) program. The process of compilation is summarized in figure 11.14.

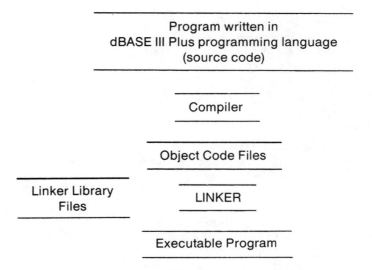

Fig. 11.14. The process of compiling a dBASE III Plus program.

For example, if you want to speed up the program ADDDATA.PRG, which was written in dBASE III Plus, you can use a compiler to produce an executable file named ADDDATA.EXE. Executing the compiled program (ADDDATA.EXE) will take much less time than executing ADDDATA.PRG within dBASE III Plus.

Tip:

Understand the compiler's translation process.

A number of database compilers have been developed for compiling dBASE III Plus programs. Two of the most popular dBASE compilers are Quicksilver, by WordTech Systems, and Clipper, by Nantucket Corporation. Although the procedures and features they offer differ, these compilers achieve a similar objective—converting the program from source code to an executable machine code and thus significantly speeding up program execution.

To give you a better understanding of the compilation process, here is an example. The Quicksilver compiler will be used to compile a dBASE III Plus program, ADDDATA.PRG, which is written in dBASE III Plus command language:

```
*** ADDDATA.PRG
* Data maintenance menu
SET PROCEDURE TO DATAPROC
SET TALK OFF
SET ECHO OFF
STORE " " TO mChoice
DO WHILE .T.
   CLEAR
   SET STATUS OFF
   @10,10 SAY "Enter [A] to Add a new record, [E] to Exit ";
      GET mChoice
   READ
   DO CASE
       CASE   UPPER(mChoice)="A"
       DO ADDRECRD              && call the program module
       LOOP
     CASE UPPER (mChoice)="E"
       EXIT
   ENDCASE
ENDDO
```

ADDDATA.PRG is a data-maintenance menu that calls the
ADDRECRD.PRG program module to append a new data
record to the EMPLOYEE.DBF database file.
ADDRECRD.PRG, a dBASE III Plus procedure, is saved in the
procedure file named DATAPROC.PRG. A listing of
DATAPROC.PRG follows:

```
*** DATAPROC.PRG
* A procedure file
PROCEDURE ADDRECRD        && define the procedure name
     SET STATUS ON
     USE EMPLOYEE
     STORE "Y" TO mContinue
     DO WHILE UPPER(mContinue)="Y"
         CLEAR
         APPEND BLANK
         @4,27 SAY "EMPLOYEE DATA ENTRY FORM"
         @8,8  SAY "Employee's Social Security # : ";
             GET ID_NO   PICTURE "999-99-9999"
         @8,56 SAY "Sex* : " GET MALE
         @10,22 SAY "Employee's Name: " GET FIRST_NAME
```

```
      @10,56 GET LAST_NAME   PICTURE "!AAAAAAAAAAAAAA"
      @12,29 SAY "Position: " GET POSITION
      @14,24 SAY "Date Employed: " GET EMPLY_DATE
      @17,18 SAY "<< * Note: Enter T for male, F for female >>"
      @1,0 TO 19,79 DOUBLE        && draw a double-line frame
      @3,24 TO 5,53               && draw a single-line box
      READ
      @20,20 SAY "Do you want to add another record [Y/N] ?";
        GET mContinue
      READ
   ENDDO
   RETURN
   * End of the ADDRECRD procedure
```

To begin the compilation, invoke the Quicksilver compiler program DB3C.EXE at the DOS prompt:

```
   C>DB3C -A -W ADDDATA.PRG
```

The option –A is used in the command to instruct the compiler to compile automatically all the files associated with ADDDATA.PRG. These files include all the program modules which are called from ADDDATA.PRG.

The –W option is used in the compilation command to suppress warning messages for trivial errors. Because some of the commands in dBASE III Plus, such as SET TALK OFF, are not supported by the compiler, a warning message is displayed when such a command is encountered. To simplify the compilation process, the –W option is chosen so that these trivial error messages will be ignored.

When the DB3C command is carried out, each line in the source file ADDDATA.PRG is scanned and translated into machine code. While scanning the ADDDATA.PRG file, any program module that is called from the program also will be translated into machine language. As you can see from figure 11.15, both ADDDATA.PRG and the procedure file DATAPROC.PRG (containing the program module ADDRECRD.PRG) have been compiled.

To view the object files created by the DB3C program, list the directory by using the DIR @???????.* command (see fig. 11.16).

```
C>DB3C -A -W ADDDATA.PRG

The QuickSilver(TM) Compiler  Version 1.0, September, 1986
Copyright (C) 1985,1986 WordTech Systems, Inc.  All Rights Reserved

Compiling ADDDATA.PRG
   LINE 20
   Constructing object file .... ADDDATA.PRG compilation complete
Compiling DATAPROC.PRG
   LINE 29
   Constructing object file .... DATAPROC.PRG compilation complete

Modules compiled : 2

C>
```

Fig. 11.15. Program files compiled by the DB3C compiler.

```
C>DIR @???????.*

 Volume in drive C is DBASE_DISK1
 Directory of  C:\QKSILVER

@ADDDATA PRG      312   4-24-87  10:22p
@DATAPRO PRG      826   4-24-87  10:22p
        2 File(s)  10723320 bytes free

C>
```

Fig. 11.16. The object files created by the DB3C compiler.

Tip:

Understand the compiler's linking process.

The second step in the compilation process involves the linking operation, in which you execute at the DOS prompt the linker program named DB3L.EXE:

C>DB3L –W ADDDATA

During the linking process, the object files which were created earlier (@ADDDATA.PRG and @DATAPRO.PRG) are combined with the DOS library program to produce an executable program named ADDDATA.EXE (see fig. 11.17).

```
C>DB3L -W ADDDATA

The QuickSilver(TM) dCode Linker Version 1.0, September, 1986
Copyright (C) 1985,1986 WordTech Systems, Inc.  All Rights Reserved

Phase I
Linking @ADDDATA.PRG
Linking @DATAPRO.PRG
Phase II
Linking Library : DB3PCL.LIB

   ADDDATA.EXE      133760
   ADDDATA.OVL       70052
   ADDDATA.DBC        2716

C>
```

Fig. 11.17. The executable and overlay files produced by the DB3L linker.

As you can see from figure 11.17, two other files (ADDDATA.OVL and ADDDATA.DBC) also are created. These are overlay files which are needed by the ADDDATA.EXE file at the time of execution. They hold the program's pseudocode, or *d-code*, which is executed by ADDDATA.EXE.

After the executable file ADDDATA.EXE has been produced, you can execute it at the DOS prompt as an independent program (without using dBASE III Plus):

C>ADDDATA

When ADDDATA.EXE is executed, the instructions in ADDDATA.PRG are processed. ADDDATA.PRG returns the following prompt:

Enter [A] to Add a new record, [E] to Exit

If you press *A* at this prompt, program control is transferred from ADDDATA.PRG to the program module ADDRECRD.PRG. The program module displays a data-entry form for adding a new data record to EMPLOYEE.DBF (see fig. 11.18).

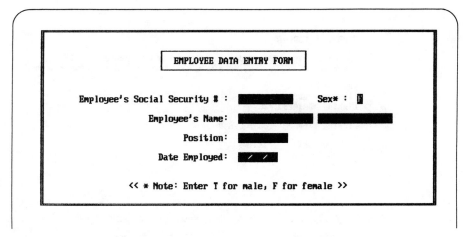

Fig. 11.18. The data-entry form produced by ADDRECRD.PRG.

Tip:

Compile your dBASE III program to protect your program code.

A compiled program is useful not only because it increases the speed of execution but also because most people can't read the compiled program's machine code. If you don't want people to be able to view or modify your program, convert it to machine code by using a compiler.

Trap:

dBASE compilers do not support all dBASE III Plus commands.

Because a compiled program is used in batch processing mode rather than in interactive mode, many commands that are entered interactively (such as BROWSE, APPEND, CREATE, and EDIT) are not supported by most compilers.

The functions performed by some of these interactive commands may be accomplished by other commands provided by the compilers. However, due to their design, many of the commands which are issued at the dot prompt cannot be used in a compiled program.

A

ASCII Character Set

The table lists the ASCII characters and their codes in decimal notation. Characters can be displayed with

? CHR(n)

where *n* is the ASCII value. Characters not appearing on the keyboard can be entered by holding down the Alt key while you enter the ASCII value, using the numeric keypad. The standard interpretations of ASCII codes 0 to 31 are presented in the Control Character column.

ASCII Value	Character	Control Character	ASCII Value	Character	Control Character
000	(null)	NUL	009	(tab)	HT
001	☺	SOH	010	(line feed)	LF
002	●	STX	011	(home)	VT
003	♥	ETX	012	(form feed)	FF
004	♦	EOT	013	(carriage return)	CR
005	♣	ENQ	014	♫	SO
006	♠	ACK	015	☼	SI
007	(beep)	BEL	016	►	DLE
008	◘	BS	017	◄	DC1

ASCII Value	Character	Control Character	ASCII Value	Character
018	↕	DC2	056	8
019	‼	DC3	057	9
020	¶	DC4	058	:
021	§	NAK	059	;
022	▬	SYN	060	<
023	↨	ETB	061	=
024	↑	CAN	062	>
025	↓	EM	063	?
026	→	SUB	064	@
027	←	ESC	065	A
028	(cursor right)	FS	066	B
029	(cursor left)	GS	067	C
030	(cursor up)	RS	068	D
031	(cursor down)	US	069	E
032	(space)		070	F
033	!		071	G
034	"		072	H
035	#		073	I
036	$		074	J
037	%		075	K
038	&		076	L
039	'		077	M
040	(		078	N
041	)		079	O
042	*		080	P
043	+		081	Q
044	,		082	R
045	-		083	S
046	.		084	T
047	/		085	U
048	0		086	V
049	1		087	W
050	2		088	X
051	3		089	Y
052	4		090	Z
053	5		091	[
054	6		092	\
055	7		093	]

ASCII Value	Character	ASCII Value	Character
094	∧	132	ä
095	—	133	à
096	`	134	ä
097	a	135	ç
098	b	136	ê
099	c	137	ë
100	d	138	è
101	e	139	ï
102	f	140	î
103	g	141	ì
104	h	142	Ä
105	i	143	Å
106	j	144	É
107	k	145	æ
108	l	146	Æ
109	m	147	ô
110	n	148	ö
111	o	149	ò
112	p	150	û
113	q	151	ù
114	r	152	ÿ
115	s	153	Ö
116	t	154	Ü
117	u	155	¢
118	v	156	£
119	w	157	¥
120	x	158	Pt
121	y	159	ƒ
122	z	160	á
123	{	161	í
124	|	162	ó
125	}	163	ú
126	~	164	ñ
127	⌂	165	Ñ
128	Ç	166	ª
129	ü	167	º
130	é	168	¿
131	â	169	⌐

ASCII Value	Character	ASCII Value	Character
170	⌐	207	⊥
171	½	208	⊥
172	¼	209	⊤
173	¡	210	⊤
174	«	211	⊔
175	»	212	⊨
176		213	⊨
177	▒	214	⊓
178	▓	215	╫
179	│	216	╪
180	┤	217	┘
181	╡	218	┌
182	╢	219	█
183	╖	220	▬
184	╕	221	▌
185	╣	222	▐
186	║	223	▀
187	╗	224	α
188	╝	225	β
189	╜	226	Γ
190	╛	227	π
191	┐	228	Σ
192	└	229	σ
193	┴	230	μ
194	┬	231	τ
195	├	232	Φ
196	─	233	Θ
197	┼	234	Ω
198	╞	235	δ
199	╟	236	∞
200	╚	237	∅
201	╔	238	∈
202	╩	239	∩
203	╦	240	≡
204	╠	241	±
205	═	242	≥
206	╬	243	≤

ASCII Value	Character
244	$\lceil$
245	J
246	$\div$
247	$\approx$
248	$\circ$
249	•

ASCII Value	Character
250	·
251	$\sqrt{\ }$
252	ⁿ
253	²
254	■
255	(blank 'FF')

B

Summary of Function and Control Keys

I. Default Settings for the Function Keys

Key	Command*
F1	HELP
F2	ASSIST
F3	LIST
F4	DIR
F5	DISPLAY STRUCTURE
F6	DISPLAY STATUS
F7	DISPLAY MEMORY
F8	DISPLAY
F9	APPEND
F10	EDIT

*Different commands can be assigned to these keys with the SET FUNCTION commands.

II. Control Keystrokes for Screen Editing

Keystroke	*Function*
Enter (↵)	Moves the cursor to the next data field or line
	In APPEND: exits and saves the contents of a file when issued from the first character of a blank data record
	In EDIT: exits and saves the file contents when issued from the last field of the last data record
	In text editor: inserts a new line in insert mode
Up arrow (↑)	Moves the cursor up one line or one data field
Down arrow (↓)	Moves the cursor down one line or one data field
Left arrow (←)	Moves the cursor left one space
Right arrow (→)	Moves the cursor right one space
Ctrl-left arrow (^←)	In BROWSE: pans one data field to the left
	In MODIFY STRUCTURE: scrolls down the file structure display
	In MODIFY COMMAND: moves the cursor to the beginning of the line
Ctrl-right arrow (^→)	In BROWSE: pans one data field to the right
	In MODIFY STRUCTURE: scrolls up the file structure display
	In MODIFY COMMAND: moves the cursor to the end of the line
Backspace (←)	Erases the character to the left of the cursor

Delete (Del)	Erases the character above the cursor
End	Moves the cursor right one word
Home	Moves the cursor left one word
Insert (Ins)	Toggles INSERT mode on and off
Page Up (PgUp)	Moves back to previous data record
Page Down (PgDn)	Moves to next data record
Ctrl-End (^End)	Exits and saves modified data items
Escape (Esc)	Exits without saving modified data items
Ctrl-KW (^KW)	In text editor: writes the file to another file
Ctrl-KR (^KR)	In text editor: reads another file into the current text at the cursor position
Ctrl-N (^N)	In MODIFY STRUCTURE: inserts a new line or data field
Ctrl-T (^T)	Erases one word to the right of the cursor
Ctrl-U (^U)	In BROWSE or EDIT: marks a record for deletion
	In MODIFY REPORT or MODIFY STRUCTURE: deletes a data field
Ctrl-Y (^Y)	Erases the entire line at the cursor

III. Keystrokes for Control Processing

Keystroke	Function
Ctrl-P (^P)	Toggles printer on and off
Ctrl-S (^S)	Starts and stops the screen scroll
Ctrl-X (^X)	Erases the command line in interactive processing mode

G

Summary of dBASE III Plus Commands

The commands used in interactive-processing and batch-processing modes are summarized in this appendix. Many of these commands have been discussed in this book, but you will find some commands that have not been used. In many cases, several different commands can be used to perform the same task. Feel free to explore any unfamiliar commands, using the information in this appendix.

I. Definition of Terms

The following special terms are used in this appendix. When entering the commands, enter only the file name or other element; do not enter the angle brackets (<>).

<file name>

A string of up to 10 characters, including the underscore, with a file extension (for example, .DBF, .DBT, .FMT, .FRM, .LBL, .MEM, .NDX, .PRG, and .TXT). A sample file name is EMPLOYEE.DBF.

\<data field name\>

A string of up to 8 characters, including the underscore, such as

LAST_NAME

\<data field list\>

A series of data field names separated by commas, such as

LAST_NAME, FIRST_NAME, AREA_CODE, PHONE_NO

\<variable name\>

A string of up to 10 characters, including underscores, such as

TOTALPRICE

\<variable list\>

A series of variable names separated by commas, such as

HOURS, PAYRATE, GROSSWAGE, TOTALSALE

\<expression\>

An alphanumeric or numeric expression.

\<alphanumeric expression\>

A collection of alphanumeric data joined with plus signs, such as

"Employee's Name: "+TRIM(LAST_NAME)+
FIRST_NAME+MIDDLENAME

\<numeric expression\>

A collection of numeric data joined with arithmetic operators (+, −, *, /, ^), such as

40*PAYRATE+(HOURS−40)*PAYRATE*1.5

\<expression list\>

A series of expressions separated by commas, such as

\<expression 1\>, \<expression 2\>, \<expression 3\>, . . .

<qualifier>

A clause that begins with FOR, followed by one or more conditions.

> FOR AREA_CODE="206"
> FOR ANNUAL_PAY>=25000
> FOR LAST_NAME="Smith" .AND. FIRST_NAME="James C."

II. A Listing of dBASE III Commands by Function

To Create, Modify, and Manipulate Files

APPEND FROM
CLOSE ALTERNATE
CLOSE DATABASES
CLOSE FORMAT
CLOSE INDEX
CLOSE PROCEDURE
COPY FILE
COPY STRUCTURE TO
COPY TO
CREATE
CREATE LABEL
CREATE QUERY
CREATE REPORT
CREATE SCREEN
CREATE VIEW
EXPORT
IMPORT
INDEX ON
JOIN
MODIFY COMMAND
MODIFY LABEL
MODIFY QUERY
MODIFY REPORT
MODIFY SCREEN
MODIFY STRUCTURE
MODIFY VIEW
REINDEX
RENAME
SAVE TO

SELECT
SORT
TOTAL
USE

To Add Data Records to a Database File

APPEND
BROWSE
INSERT

To Edit Data in a Database File

BROWSE
CHANGE
DELETE
EDIT
PACK
READ
RECALL
REPLACE
UPDATE

To Display Data

@ . . . SAY
?
??
AVERAGE
BROWSE
COUNT
DISPLAY
LIST
REPORT
SUM
TEXT

To Control the Record Pointer

CONTINUE
FIND
GO BOTTOM
GOTO
GO TOP
LOCATE
SEEK
SKIP

To Use Memory Variables

ACCEPT
AVERAGE
CLEAR ALL
CLEAR MEMORY
COUNT
DISPLAY MEMORY
INPUT
READ
RELEASE
RESTORE FROM
SAVE TO
STORE
SUM
WAIT

To Program

ACCEPT TO
CANCEL
CASE
DO
DO WHILE . . . ENDDO
DO CASE . . . ENDCASE
EXIT
IF . . . ENDIF
IF . . . ELSE . . . ENDIF
INPUT
LOOP
MODIFY COMMAND
PARAMETERS
PRIVATE

PROCEDURE
PUBLIC
QUIT
RETRY
RETURN
TEXT
WAIT TO

To Control Media Display*

CLEAR
EJECT
SET COLOR TO
SET CONFIRM on/OFF
SET CONSOLE ON/off
SET INTENSITY ON/off
SET PRINT on/OFF
SET DEVICE TO PRINT
SET DEVICE TO SCREEN
SET MARGIN TO

*Uppercase indicates default settings.

To Specify Control Parameters*

SET ALTERNATE TO
SET ALTERNATE on/OFF
SET BELL ON/off
SET CARRY on/OFF
SET CATALOG ON/off
SET CATALOG TO
SET DATE
SET DEBUG
SET DECIMALS TO
SET DEFAULT TO
SET DELETED on/OFF
SET DELIMITERS on/OFF
SET DOHISTORY on/OFF
SET DOHISTORY TO
SET ECHO on/OFF
SET ESCAPE ON/off
SET EXACT on/OFF
SET FIELDS on/OFF
SET FIELDS TO
SET FILTER TO

SET FIXED on/OFF
SET FORMAT TO
SET FUNCTION TO
SET HEADING ON/off
SET HELP ON/off
SET HISTORY ON/off
SET INDEX TO
SET MARGIN TO
SET MENUS ON/off
SET MESSAGE TO
SET ORDER TO
SET PATH TO
SET PROCEDURE TO
SET RELATION TO
SET SAFETY ON/off
SET SCOREBOARD ON/off
SET STATUS ON/off
SET STEP on/OFF
SET TALK ON/off
SET TITLE ON/off
SET TYPEAHEAD TO
SET UNIQUE on/OFF

*Uppercase indicates default settings.

III. Summary of Commands

?

Displays the contents of an alphanumeric or numeric expression on a new display line, such as

? "Employee's name . . . "+FIRST_NAME+LAST_NAME
? HOURS*PAYRATE
? "Gross Pay . . . "+STR(GROSSPAY,7,2)

??

Displays output on the same display line, such as

?? "Invoice number: "+INVNO

@<row,column> GET

Displays user-formatted data at the screen location specified by <row,column>, as in

@5,10 GET LAST_NAME
@8,10 GET SC_NO PICTURE "###-##-####"

@<row,column> SAY

Displays user-formatted data on the screen or printer at the location specified by <row,column>, as in

@5,10 SAY LAST_NAME
@5,10 SAY "Last name . . . " LAST_NAME
@10,5 SAY "Annual salary:" ANNUAL_PAY PICTURE "$##,###.##"

@<row,column> SAY . . . GET

Displays user-formatted data on-screen at the location specified by <row,column>; used for appending or editing a data field.

@5,10 SAY "Last name : " GET LAST_NAME

ACCEPT

Assigns an alphanumeric string to a memory variable, with or without a prompt.

ACCEPT "Enter your last name . . . " TO LASTNAME
ACCEPT TO LASTNAME

APPEND

Adds a data record to the end of the active database file. The data fields are the field labels on the entry form.

USE EMPLOYEE
APPEND

APPEND BLANK

Same as APPEND, but does not display an entry form.

USE EMPLOYEE
APPEND BLANK

APPEND FROM

Adds data records from one database file (FILE1.DBF) to another
database file (FILE2.DBF), with or without a qualifier.

    USE FILE2
    APPEND FROM FILE1

    USE FILE2
    APPEND FROM FILE1 FOR ACCT_NO<="10123"

ASSIST

Activates The Assistant.

AVERAGE

Computes the average of a numeric expression and assigns the value
to a memory variable, with or without a condition.

    AVERAGE ANNUAL_PAY TO AVERAGEPAY
    AVERAGE QTY_SOLD TO AVG_SALE FOR MODEL_NO="XYZ"
    AVERAGE HOURS*PAYRATE TO AVERAGEPAY FOR .NOT. MALE

BROWSE

Displays for review or modification up to 17 records from the active
database file.

    USE EMPLOYEE
    GO TOP
    BROWSE

BROWSE FIELDS

Browses selected data fields in the current database file.

    USE EMPLOYEE
    GO TOP
    BROWSE FIELDS FIRST_NAME, LAST_NAME, PHONE_NO

CANCEL

Terminates the processing of a program file and returns the program
to the dot prompt.

    IF EOF( )
       CANCEL
    ENDIF

CHANGE

Displays the data records in an active database file sequentially, with or without a qualifier.

```
USE EMPLOYEE
CHANGE

USE EMPLOYEE
CHANGE FOR AREA_CODE="206"
```

CHANGE FIELDS

Displays selected data fields sequentially, with or without a qualifier.

```
USE EMPLOYEE
CHANGE FIELDS ANNUAL_PAY

USE EMPLOYEE
CHANGE FIELDS AREA_CODE,PHONE_NO FOR AREA_CODE="206"
```

CLEAR

Clears the screen.

CLEAR ALL

Closes all open database files (including .DBF, .NDX, .FMT, and .DBT files) and releases all memory variables.

CLEAR FIELDS

Releases the data fields that have been created by the SET FIELDS TO command.

CLEAR GETS

Causes the subsequent READ command to be ignored for the @. . . SAY . . . GET commands issued before the command, such as

```
@5,10 SAY "Account number : " GET ACCT_NO
CLEAR GETS
@7,10 SAY "Account name : " GET ACCT_NAME
READ
```

CLEAR MEMORY

Releases or erases all memory variables.

CLEAR TYPEAHEAD

Empties the type-ahead buffer.

CLOSE

Closes various types of files:

CLOSE ALL
CLOSE ALTERNATIVE
CLOSE DATABASES
CLOSE FORMAT
CLOSE INDEX
CLOSE PROCEDURE

CONTINUE

Resumes the search started with the LOCATE command.

USE EMPLOYEE
LOCATE FOR AREA_CODE="206"
DISPLAY
CONTINUE
DISPLAY

COPY FILE

Duplicates an existing dBASE III Plus file of any type.

COPY FILE MAINPROG.PRG TO MAIN.PRG
COPY FILE COST.FMT TO NEWCOST.FMT
COPY FILE ROSTER.FRM TO NAMELIST.FRM

COPY STRUCTURE

Copies the data structure to another database file.

USE COST
COPY STRUCTURE TO NEWCOST.DBF

COPY TO

Copies the contents of a source database file to a destination file, with or without a qualifier.

USE SALE
COPY TO NEWSALE.DBF
COPY TO OLDSALE.DBF FOR ACCT_NO<="100123"

COPY TO

Copies selected fields of a source database file to a new file, with or without a qualifier.

```
USE EMPLOYEE
COPY TO ROSTER.DBF FIELDS FIRST_NAME, LAST_NAME
COPY TO SALARY.DBF FIELDS LAST_NAME, ANNUAL_PAY FOR MALE
```

COUNT

Counts the number of records in the active database file and assigns the number to a memory variable.

```
USE EMPLOYEE
COUNT TO NRECORDS
COUNT FOR ANNUAL_PAY>="50000" .AND. MALE TO RICHMEN
```

CREATE

Sets up a new file structure and adds data records, if desired.

```
CREATE EMPLOYEE
```

CREATE LABEL

Displays a design form to set up a label file (.LBL).

```
CREATE LABEL MAILLIST
```

CREATE QUERY

Creates a new query file (.QRY).

```
USE EMPLOYEE
CREATE QUERY FINDEMPL.QRY
```

CREATE REPORT

Displays a design form to set up a report-form file (.FRM).

```
CREATE REPORT WEEKLY
```

CREATE SCREEN

Creates a new screen file (.SCR).

```
USE EMPLOYEE
CREATE SCREEN SHOWEMPL.SCR
```

CREATE VIEW

Creates a new view file (.VUE).

USE EMPLOYEE
CREATE VIEW SAMPLE.VUE

DELETE

Marks the records in the active database file with a deletion symbol (∗).

USE EMPLOYEE
DELETE
DELETE RECORD 5
DELETE FOR AREA_CODE="503"

DIR

Displays the file directory:

DIR   *(Displays .DBF files)*

DIR ∗.∗   *(Displays all files)*

DIR ∗.PRG   *(Displays program files)*

DIR ∗.NDX   *(Displays index files)*

DIR X∗.DBF   *(Displays .DBF file names beginning with X)*

DIR ??X???.PRG   *(Displays .PRG file names having up to six letters and X as the third character)*

DIR ???.∗   *(Displays all file names that are up to three characters long)*

DISPLAY

Shows the contents of the data records.

USE EMPLOYEE
DISPLAY
DISPLAY RECORD 3
DISPLAY NEXT 2
DISPLAY LAST_NAME,FIRST_NAME
DISPLAY AREA_CODE,PHONE_NO FOR AREA_CODE="206"

DISPLAY MEMORY

Shows the contents of active memory variables.

DISPLAY STATUS

Shows the current processing situation, including the names of active files, the work area number, etc.

DISPLAY STRUCTURE

Shows the data structure of an active database file.

USE EMPLOYEE
DISPLAY STRUCTURE

DO

Executes a program file.

DO MAINPROG

DO CASE . . . ENDCASE

A multiple-avenue branching command, such as

```
DO CASE
    CASE ANSWER="Y"
        . . .
    CASE ANSWER="N"
        . . .
    OTHERWISE
        RETURN
ENDCASE
```

DO WHILE . . . ENDDO

A program loop command, such as

```
DO WHILE .NOT. EOF( )
    . . .
    . . .
ENDDO
```

EDIT

Displays a data record for editing, such as

    USE EMPLOYEE
    GOTO 5
    EDIT

    USE EMPLOYEE
    EDIT RECORD 5

EJECT

Advances the printer paper to the top of the next page.

ERASE

Removes a file from the directory. The file to be erased must be closed.

    ERASE SALE.DBF
    ERASE SAMPLE.PRG

EXIT

Exits from a program loop, such as one created with DO WHILE . . . ENDDO.

    DO WHILE .T.
        . . .
        . . .
    IF EOF( )
        EXIT
    ENDIF
        . . .
    ENDDO

EXPORT TO

Converts a dBASE III Plus file to a PFS file.

    EXPORT TO <name of the PFS file> TYPE PFS

FIND

Searches for the first data record in an indexed file with a specified search key, such as

```
USE EMPLOYEE
INDEX ON AREA_CODE TO AREAS
FIND "206"
DISPLAY
```

GO BOTTOM

Positions the record pointer at the last record in the database file.

```
USE EMPLOYEE
GO BOTTOM
```

GO TOP

Positions the record pointer at the first record in the database file.

```
USE EMPLOYEE
GO TOP
```

GOTO

Positions the record pointer at a specified record.

```
USE EMPLOYEE
GOTO 4
```

HELP

Calls up the help screens. Can be used with a key word to specify the subject, such as

```
HELP
HELP CREATE
HELP STR
```

IF

A conditional branching command, such as

```
WAIT "Enter your choice ([Q] to quit) " TO CHOICE
IF CHOICE="Q"
   RETURN
ELSE
   . . .
   . . .
ENDIF
```

IMPORT FROM

Converts a PFS file to a dBASE III Plus file.

IMPORT FROM <name of the PFS file> TYPE PFS

INDEX

Creates a key file in which all records are ordered according to the contents of the specified key field. The records can be arranged in alphabetical, chronological, or numerical order.

INDEX ON AREA_CODE TO AREACODE
INDEX ON AREA_CODE+PHONE_NO TO PHONES

INPUT

Assigns a data element to a memory variable, using information entered from the keyboard.

INPUT PAYRATE
INPUT "Enter units sold :" TO UNITSSOLD

INSERT

Adds a new record to the database file at the current record location.

USE EMPLOYEE
GOTO 4
INSERT
GOTO 6
INSERT BEFORE
GOTO 5
INSERT BLANK

JOIN

Creates a new database file by merging specified data records from two open database files.

SELECT A
USE NEWSTOCKS
SELECT B
USE STOCKS
JOIN WITH NEWSTOCKS TO ALLSTOCK FOR
STOCK_NO=A->STOCK_NO

JOIN WITH NEWSTOCKS TO ALLSTOCK FOR
STOCK_NO=A–>STOCK_NO;
FIELDS MODEL_NO, ON_HAND, ON_ORDER

LABEL FORM

Displays data records with labels specified in a label file.

USE EMPLOYEE
LABEL FORM ROSTER
LABEL FORM ROSTER TO PRINT
LABEL FORM ROSTER TO AFILE.TXT
LABEL FORM ROSTER FOR AREA_CODE="206" .AND. MALE

LIST

Shows the contents of selected data records in the active database
file.

USE EMPLOYEE
LIST
LIST RECORD 5
LIST LAST_NAME,FIRST_NAME
LIST LAST_NAME,FIRST_NAME FOR AREA_CODE="206" .OR. MALE

LIST MEMORY

Shows name, type, and size of each active memory variable.

LIST STATUS

Lists current processing situation, including the names of active files,
work area number, etc.

LIST STATUS
LIST STATUS TO PRINT

LIST STRUCTURE

Displays the data structure of the active database file, such as

USE EMPLOYEE
LIST STRUCTURE
LIST STRUCTURE TO PRINT

LOCATE

Sequentially searches data records of the active database file for a record that satisfies a specified condition, such as

USE EMPLOYEE
LOCATE FOR LAST_NAME="Smith"
LOCATE FOR UPPER(FIRST_NAME)="JAMES"
LOCATE FOR FIRST_NAME="J" .AND. LAST_NAME="S"

LOOP

Transfers execution from the middle of a program loop to the beginning of the loop:

DO WHILE .T.
 . . .
 . . .
 IF . . .
  LOOP
 ENDIF
 . . .
ENDDO

MODIFY COMMAND

Invokes the text editor to create or edit a program file (.PRG), a format file (.FMT), or a text file (.TXT). The default file extension is .PRG.

MODIFY COMMAND MAINPROG
MODIFY COMMAND BILLING.PRG
MODIFY COMMAND EMPLOYEE.FMT
MODIFY COMMAND TEXTFILE.TXT

MODIFY LABEL

Creates or edits a label file (.LBL) for the active database file.

USE EMPLOYEE
MODIFY LABEL MAILLIST

MODIFY QUERY

Creates or edits a query file (.QRY).

USE EMPLOYEE
MODIFY QUERY FINDEMPL.QRY

MODIFY REPORT

Creates or edits a report file (.FRM) for the active database file.

USE QTYSOLD
MODIFY REPORT WEEKLY

MODIFY SCREEN

Creates or edits a screen file (.SCR).

USE EMPLOYEE
MODIFY SCREEN SHOWEMPL.SCR

MODIFY STRUCTURE

Displays for modification the structure of the active database file.

USE EMPLOYEE
MODIFY STRUCTURE

MODIFY VIEW

Creates or edits a view file (.VUE).

USE EMPLOYEE
MODIFY VIEW SAMPLE.VUE

NOTE

Marks the beginning of a remark line in a program.

SET TALK OFF*
SET ECHO OFF
NOTE Enter hours worked and payrate from the keyboard
INPUT "Enter hours worked . . . " TO HOURS
INPUT "hourly rate . . . " TO PAYRATE

. . .

. . .

*This is a simplified payroll program.

PACK

Removes data records marked for deletion by the DELETE command.

USE EMPLOYEE
DELETE RECORD 5
PACK

PARAMETERS

Assigns local variable names to data items that are to be passed from a calling program module.

```
***** Program: MULTIPLY.PRG *****
* A program to multiply variable A by variable B
PARAMETERS A,B,C
C=A*B
RETURN
```

The preceding program is called from the main program:

```
* The main program
HOURS=38
PAYRATE=8.5
DO MULTIPLY WITH HOURS,PAYRATE,GROSSPAY
?"Gross Wage =",GROSSPAY
RETURN
```

PRIVATE

Declares private variables in a program module, for example

```
PRIVATE VARIABLEA, VARIABLEB, VARIABLEC
```

PROCEDURE

Identifies the beginning of each procedure in a procedure file.

PUBLIC

Declares public variables to be shared by all program modules.

```
PUBLIC VARIABLEA, VARIABLEB, VARIABLEC
```

QUIT

Closes all open files, terminates dBASE III Plus processing, and exits to DOS.

READ

Activates all the @ . . . SAY . . . GET commands issued since the last CLEAR GET was issued.

```
USE EMPLOYEE
@5,10 SAY "Last name : " GET LAST_NAME
@6,10 SAY "First name : " GET FIRST_NAME
READ
```

RECALL

Recovers data records marked for deletion.

    RECALL
    RECALL ALL
    RECALL RECORD 5

REINDEX

Rebuilds all active index (.NDX) files.

    USE EMPLOYEE
    SET INDEX TO AREACODE
    REINDEX

RELEASE

Deletes all or selected memory variables, such as

    RELEASE ALL
    RELEASE ALL LIKE NET*
    RELEASE ALL EXCEPT ???COST

RENAME

Changes the name of a disk file, such as

    RENAME FILE XYZ.DBF TO ABC.DBF
    RENAME MAINPROG.PRG TO MAIN.PRG
    RENAME MAILIST.LBL TO MAILLIST.LBL

REPLACE

Changes the contents of specified data fields in an active database file.

    USE EMPLOYEE
    REPLACE ALL ANNUAL_PAY WITH ANNUAL_PAY*1.05
    REPLACE FIRST_NAME WITH "James K." FOR FIRST_NAME="James C."
    REPLACE ALL AREA_CODE WITH "206" FOR AREA_CODE="216"

REPORT FORM

Displays information from the active database file with the custom form specified in the report form (.FRM) file.

    USE QTYSOLD
    REPORT FORM WEEKLY   (Sends output to screen)
    REPORT FORM WEEKLY TO PRINT   (Sends output to printer)
    REPORT FORM WEEKLY TO TEXTFILE.TXT   (Sends output to text file)

RESTORE FROM

Retrieves memory variables from a memory (.MEM) file.

RESTORE FROM MEMLIST.MEM
RESTORE FROM MEMLIST ADDITIVE

RESUME

Resumes execution of a program or procedure after it has been stopped by the SUSPEND command.

RETURN

Terminates a program and either returns to the dot prompt or transfers execution to the calling program module.

RUN

Executes an .EXE, . COM, or . BAT DOS disk file from within dBASE III Plus.

RUN B:XYZ   *(Where XYZ.EXE, XYZ.COM, or XYZ.BAT is an executable disk file in a DOS directory)*

SAVE TO

Stores all or selected memory variables to a memory (.MEM) file.

SAVE TO ALLVARS
SAVE TO VARLIST ALL EXCEPT NET*
SAVE TO VARLIST ALL LIKE COST????

SEEK

Searches an indexed database file for the first data record containing the specified key expression.

USE EMPLOYEE
INDEX ON AREA_CODE TO AREACODE
SEEK "206"

SELECT

Places a database file in a specified work area.

SELECT 1
USE EMPLOYEE
SELECT A
USE COSTS

SET

Sets control parameters for processing. The default settings (indicated by uppercase letters) are appropriate for most purposes.

SET ALTERNATE on/OFF

Creates a text file, as designated by the SET ALTERNATE TO command, to record the processing activities.

SET BELL ON/off

Turns on/off the warning bell.

SET CARRY on/OFF

Carries the contents of the previous record into an APPENDED record.

SET CATALOG ON/off

Adds files to open catalog.

SET CATALOG TO

Creates, opens, and closes a catalog file.

SET CENTURY on/OFF

Shows the century in date displays.

SET COLOR ON/OFF

Sets output display to color/monochrome monitor. The default is the mode from which dBASE III Plus is started.

SET COLOR TO

Sets color screen attributes. Available colors and their letter codes are

Color	Letter
black	N
blue	B
green	G
cyan	BG
blank	X
red	R
magenta	RB
brown	GR
white	W

An asterisk indicates blinking characters, and a plus sign (+) indicates high intensity. Format of the command is

SET COLOR TO <standard>,<enhanced>,<border>,<background>

For example,

SET COLOR TO GR+/R,W/R,GR

sets standard video to yellow characters on a red background and enhanced video to white letters on a red background, with a yellow screen border.

SET CONFIRM on/OFF

Controls the cursor movement from one variable to the next when the first variable is filled.

SET CONSOLE ON/off

Turns the video display on/off.

SET DATE

Specifies the format for date expressions.

SET DATE AMERICAN	(mm/dd/yy)
SET DATE ANSI	(yy.mm.dd)
SET DATE BRITISH	(dd/mm/yy)
SET DATE ITALIAN	(dd-mm-yy)
SET DATE FRENCH	(dd/mm/yy)
SET DATE GERMAN	(dd.mm.yy)

SET DEBUG on/OFF

Traces the command errors during processing. When DEBUG is ON, messages from SET ECHO ON are routed to the printer.

SET DECIMALS TO

Sets the number of decimal places for values, such as

SET DECIMALS TO 4

SET DEFAULT TO

Designates the default disk drive, such as

SET DEFAULT TO B:

SET DELETED on/OFF

Determines whether data records marked for deletion are to be ignored.

SET DELIMITERS on/OFF

Marks field widths with the delimiter defined by means of the SET DELIMITERS TO command.

SET DELIMITERS TO

Specifies the characters for marking a field.

```
SET DELIMITERS TO '[ ]'
SET DELIMITERS ON
```

SET DEVICE TO SCREEN/print

Selects a display medium.

SET ECHO on/OFF

Displays instructions during execution.

SET ESCAPE ON/off

Controls the capability of aborting execution with the Esc key. When ESCAPE is ON, pressing Esc aborts execution of a program.

SET EXACT on/OFF

Determines how two alphanumeric strings are compared.

SET FIELDS on/OFF

Activates the selection of data fields named with the SET FIELDS TO command.

SET FIELDS TO

Selects a set of data fields to be used in one or more files.

```
USE EMPLOYEE
SET FIELDS TO LAST_NAME, FIRST_NAME
SET FIELDS ON
```

SET FILTER TO

Defines the filter conditions.

```
USE EMPLOYEE
SET FILTER TO AREA_CODE="216"
```

SET FIXED on/OFF

Sets all numeric output to the fixed number of decimal places defined by SET DECIMALS TO.

SET FORMAT

Selects custom format defined in a format (.FMT) file.

SET FUNCTION

Redefines a function key for a specific command, such as

SET FUNCTION 10 TO "QUIT"

SET HEADING ON/off

Uses field names as column titles for display of data records with the DISPLAY, LIST, SUM, and AVERAGE commands.

SET HELP ON/off

Determines whether Help screen is displayed.

SET HISTORY ON/off

Turns on the history feature.

SET HISTORY TO

Specifies the number of executed commands to be saved in the HISTORY buffer.

SET HISTORY TO 10

SET INDEX

Opens the specified index files.

SET INTENSITY ON/off

Displays data fields in reverse video with EDIT and APPEND commands.

SET MARGIN

Adjusts the left margin for all printed output, such as

SET MARGIN TO 10

SET MEMOWIDTH TO

Defines the width of memo field output (default width is 50).

SET MEMOWIDTH TO 30

SET MENUS ON/off

Displays a cursor-movement key menu.

SET MESSAGE TO

Displays an alphanumeric string in the message window.

SET MESSAGE TO "Hello!"

SET ORDER TO

Sets up an open index file as the controlling index file. The
format is

SET ORDER TO <n>

where <n> is the number of the file within the series of index files
named with the INDEX command. The following commands cause
AREACODE.NDX to be used:

USE EMPLOYEE INDEX LASTNAME.NDX, PAYRANK.NDX,
AREACODE.NDX
SET ORDER TO 3

SET PATH TO

Defines the search directory path.

SET PATH TO C:\DBDATE\SALES

SET PRINT on/OFF

Directs output generated with @ . . . SAY commands to the printer
and the screen.

SET PROCEDURE

Opens a specified procedure file.

SET RELATION TO

Links two open database files according to a common key
expression.

SET SAFETY ON/off

Displays a warning message when overwriting an existing file.

SET SCOREBOARD ON/off

Displays or hides dBASE messages on the status line.

SET STATUS ON/off

Displays or hides the status bar at the bottom of the screen.

SET STEP on/OFF

Causes execution to pause after each command.

SET TALK ON/off

Displays interactive messages during processing.

SET TITLE ON/off

Displays the catalog file title prompt.

SET TYPEAHEAD TO

Specifies the size of the type-ahead buffer (possible values are 0 to 32,000 characters; default is 20 characters).

SET TYPEAHEAD TO 30

SET UNIQUE on/OFF

Prepares an ordered list with the INDEX command, allowing only the first record of records with identical keys to be displayed (if set to ON).

SET VIEW TO

Selects the view file.

SET VIEW TO EMPLOYEE.VUE

SKIP

Moves the record pointer forward or backward through the records in the database file, such as

USE EMPLOYEE
GOTO 3
DISPLAY
SKIP 3
DISPLAY
SKIP −1
DISPLAY

SORT

Rearranges data records on one or more key fields in ascending or descending order. The default setting is ascending order.

```
USE EMPLOYEE
SORT ON AREA_CODE TO AREACODE
SORT ON ANNUAL_PAY/D TO RANKED
SORT ON AREA_CODE, LAST_NAME TO PHONLIST FOR
AREA_CODE="206"
```

STORE

Assigns a data element to a memory variable.

```
STORE 1 TO COUNTER
STORE "James" TO FIRSTNAME
```

SUM

Totals the value of a numeric expression and stores the total in a memory variable, such as

```
USE EMPLOYEE
SUM ANNUAL_PAY TO TOTALPAY
SUM ANNUAL_PAY*0.1 TO DEDUCTIONS
```

SUSPEND

Suspends the execution of a program or procedure.

TEXT

Displays a block of text on the screen or printer; used in a program.

```
***** Program: BULLETIN.PRG *****
SET PRINT ON
TEXT
This is a sample message to be displayed on the printer when
this program is executed.
ENDTEXT
```

TOTAL

Sums the numeric values of the active database file on a key field and stores the results to another file.

```
USE STOCKS
TOTAL ON MODEL_NO TO BYMODEL
TOTAL ON STOCK_NO TO BYSTOCNO FOR ON_HAND>=2
```

TYPE

Displays the contents of a disk file to the screen or printer.

TYPE MAINPROG.PRG
TYPE EMPLOYEE.FMT TO PRINT

UPDATE

Uses records in one database file to update records in another file, such as

SELECT A

USE RECEIVED

SELECT B

USE STOCKS

UPDATE ON STOCK_NO FROM RECEIVED REPLACE
ON_HAND WITH ON_HAND+A–>ON_HAND

USE

Opens an existing database file.

USE EMPLOYEE

WAIT

Causes execution to pause until a key is pressed, as in

WAIT
WAIT TO CHOICE
WAIT "Enter your answer (Y/N)? " TO ANSWER

ZAP

Removes all data records from the database file without deleting the data structure, such as

USE EMPLOYEE
ZAP

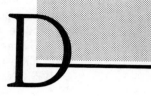

File Structures of
the Database Files

```
Structure for database        : ACCOUNTS.DBF
Number of data records        : 10
Date of last update           : 4/12/87
Field   Field Name      Type        Width   Dec
  1     ACCOUNT_NO      Character       5
  2     NAME            Character      25
  3     ADDRESS         Character      25
  4     CITY            Character      13
  5     STATE           Character       2
  6     ZIP             Character       5
  7     AREA_CODE       Character       3
  8     PHONE_NO        Character       8
  9     MAX_CREDIT      Numeric         7     2
** Total **                            94
```

```
Structure for database       : ALLSTOCK.DBF
Number of data records       : 20
Date of last update          : 3/03/87
Field   Field Name      Type          Width    Dec
   1    STOCK_NO        Character         9
   2    DIVISION        Character         2
   3    TYPE            Character        20
   4    COST            Numeric          7      2
   5    PRICE           Numeric          7      2
   6    ON_HAND         Numeric          2      0
   7    ON_ORDER        Numeric          2      0
** Total **                             50
```

```
Structure for database       : BARDATA.DBF
Number of data records       : 5
Date of last update          : 4/15/87
Field   Field Name      Type          Width    Dec
   1    CLASSCOUNT      Numeric          2      0
   2    CLASSLABEL      Character        20
** Total **                             23
```

```
Structure for database       : BULLETIN.DBF
Number of data records       : 6
Date of last update          : 4/03/87
Field   Field Name      Type          Width    Dec
   1    REF_NO          Character         5
   2    NOTE            Memo             10
   3    NAME            Character        10
** Total **                             26
```

```
Structure for database       : CUSTOMER.DBF
Number of data records       : 6
Date of last update          : 3/02/87
Field   Field Name      Type          Width    Dec
   1    FIRST_NAME      Character        15
   2    LAST_NAME       Character        15
** Total **                             31
```

Route: FJ   SWL   FCG
       KGW   HUM   ~~HPD~~
       RRL   DLS   SLS
       DRA   RDB

...e feel free to take home

& watch w/your family.
Very informational.

Return When Done To:
— John Driggs

Structure for database   : EMPLOYEE.DBF
Number of data records   : 10
Date of last update   : 4/20/87

Field	Field Name	Type	Width	Dec
1	ID_NO	Character	11	
2	FIRST_NAME	Character	15	
3	LAST_NAME	Character	15	
4	POSITION	Character	10	
5	EMPLY_DATE	Date	8	
6	MALE	Logical	1	
** Total **			61	

Structure for database   : HARDWARE.DBF
Number of data records   : 10
Date of last update   : 4/10/87

Field	Field Name	Type	Width	Dec
1	STOCKNO	Character	9	
2	DIVISION	Character	2	
3	TYPE	Character	20	
4	COST	Numeric	7	2
5	PRICE	Numeric	7	2
** Total **			46	

Structure for database   : HWCOST.DBF
Number of data records   : 10
Date of last update   : 3/05/87

Field	Field Name	Type	Width	Dec
1	STOCK_NO	Character	9	
2	COST	Numeric	7	2
3	PRICE	Numeric	7	2
** Total **			24	

Structure for database   : HWLIST.DBF
Number of data records   : 20
Date of last update   : 3/05/87

Field	Field Name	Type	Width	Dec
1	STOCK_NO	Character	9	
2	TYPE	Character	15	
3	DSCRIPTION	Character	30	
** Total **			55	

```
Structure for database        : HWSTOCK.DBF
Number of data records        : 10
Date of last update           : 2/07/87
Field    Field Name     Type            Width    Dec
  1      STOCK_NO       Character          9
  2      ON_HAND        Numeric            3      0
  3      ON_ORDER       Numeric            3      0
** Total **                               16


Structure for database        : HWSTRUC.DBF
Number of data records        : 6
Date of last update           : 4/04/87
Field    Field Name     Type            Width    Dec
  1      FIELD_NAME     Character         10
  2      FIELD_TYPE     Character          1
  3      FIELD_LEN      Numeric            3      0
  4      FIELD_DEC      Numeric            3      0
** Total **                               18


Structure for database        : INVENTRY.DBF
Number of data records        : 20
Date of last update           : 2/14/87
Field    Field Name     Type            Width    Dec
  1      STOCK_NO       Character          9
  2      ON_HAND        Numeric            3      0
  3      ON_ORDER       Numeric            3      0
** Total **                               16


Structure for database        : ITEMSOLD.DBF
Number of data records        : 5
Date of last update           : 3/01/87
Field    Field Name     Type            Width    Dec
  1      INV_NO         Numeric            4      0
  2      ACCOUNT_NO     Character          5
  3      STOCK_NO       Character          9
  4      UNITS_SOLD     Numeric            3      0
** Total **                               22
```

```
Structure for database        : JOINFILE.DBF
Number of data records        : 10
Date of last update           : 3/30/87
Field     Field Name    Type          Width    Dec
  1       STOCK_NO      Character        9
  2       COST          Numeric          7      2
  3       PRICE         Numeric          7      2
  4       ON_HAND       Numeric          3      0
  5       ON_ORDER      Numeric          3      0
** Total **                             30


Structure for database        : LAST.DBF
Number of data records        : 5
Date of last update           : 2/16/87
Field     Field Name    Type          Width    Dec
  1       ID_NO         Character       11
  2       FIRST_NAME    Character       15
  3       LAST_NAME     Character       15
  4       POSITION      Character       10
  5       EMPLY_DATE    Date             8
  6       MALE          Logical          1
** Total **                             61


Structure for database        : LOWSTOCK.DBF
Number of data records        : 5
Date of last update           : 2/14/87
Field     Field Name    Type          Width    Dec
  1       STOCK_NO      Character        9
** Total **                             10


Structure for database        : MAILLIST.DBF
Number of data records        : 5
Date of last update           : 2/25/87
Field     Field Name    Type          Width    Dec
  1       NAME          Character       15
  2       ADDRESS       Character       20
  3       CITY_ST       Character       20
** Total **                             56
```

Structure for database   : NEWHW.DBF
Number of data records   : 6
Date of last update   : 4/20/87

Field	Field Name	Type	Width	Dec
1	REF_NO	Character	5	
2	NOTE	Memo	10	
3	NAME	Character	10	
** Total **			26	

Structure for database   : NEWLAST.DBF
Number of data records   : 5
Date of last update   : 2/16/87

Field	Field Name	Type	Width	Dec
1	ID_NO	Character	11	
2	FIRST_NAME	Character	15	
3	LAST_NAME	Character	15	
4	POSITION	Character	10	
5	EMPLY_DATE	Date	8	
6	MALE	Logical	1	
** Total **			61	

Structure for database   : OFFICERS.DBF
Number of data records   : 2
Date of last update   : 2/16/87

Field	Field Name	Type	Width	Dec
1	FIRST_NAME	Character	15	
2	LAST_NAME	Character	15	
3	POSITION	Character	10	
** Total **			41	

Structure for database   : PAYROLL.DBF
Number of data records   : 10
Date of last update   : 11/17/86

Field	Field Name	Type	Width	Dec
1	ID_NO	Character	11	
2	POSITION	Character	10	
3	SALARY	Logical	1	
4	COMMISSION	Logical	1	
5	BASE_PAY	Numeric	8	2
6	EXEMPTIONS	Numeric	2	0
** Total **			34	

```
Structure for database        : PERSONAL.DBF
Number of data records        : 21
Date of last update           : 4/23/87
Field    Field Name       Type         Width    Dec
  1      ID_NO            Character      11
  2      FIRST_NAME       Character      15
  3      LAST_NAME        Character      15
  4      POSITION         Character      10
  5      EMPLY_DATE       Date            8
  6      MALE             Logical         1
** Total **                              61


Structure for database        : PRODCOST.DBF
Number of data records        : 20
Date of last update           : 3/05/87
Field    Field Name       Type         Width    Dec
  1      STOCK_NO         Character       9
  2      COST             Numeric         7       2
  3      PRICE            Numeric         7       2
** Total **                              24


Structure for database        : PRODLIST.DBF
Number of data records        : 20
Date of last update           : 3/05/87
Field    Field Name       Type         Width    Dec
  1      STOCK_NO         Character       9
  2      TYPE             Character      15
  3      DSCRIPTION       Character      30
** Total **                              55


Structure for database        : PRODSOLD.DBF
Number of data records        : 20
Date of last update           : 3/05/87
Field    Field Name       Type         Width    Dec
  1      STOCK_NO         Character       9
  2      DIVISION         Character       2
  3      TYPE             Character      20
  4      COST             Numeric         7       2
  5      PRICE            Numeric         7       2
  6      UNITS_SOLD       Numeric         3       0
** Total **                              49
```

Structure for database   : PRODSTCK.DBF
Number of data records   : 20
Date of last update   : 3/05/87

Field	Field Name	Type	Width	Dec
1	STOCK_NO	Character	9	
2	ON_HAND	Numeric	3	0
3	ON_ORDER	Numeric	3	0
** Total **			16	

Structure for database   : PRODUCTS.DBF
Number of data records   : 20
Date of last update   : 2/07/87

Field	Field Name	Type	Width	Dec
1	STOCK_NO	Character	9	
2	DIVISION	Character	2	
3	TYPE	Character	20	
4	COST	Numeric	7	2
5	PRICE	Numeric	7	2
** Total **			46	

Structure for database   : ROSTER.DBF
Number of data records   : 5
Date of last update   : 2/16/87

Field	Field Name	Type	Width	Dec
1	FIRST_NAME	Character	15	
2	LAST_NAME	Character	15	
3	POSITION	Character	10	
** Total **			41	

Structure for database   : SALARY.DBF
Number of data records   : 10
Date of last update   : 4/02/87

Field	Field Name	Type	Width	Dec
1	ID_NO	Character	11	
2	LAST_NAME	Character	10	
3	FIRST_NAME	Character	10	
4	POSITION	Character	10	
5	SALARY	Logical	1	
6	BASE_PAY	Numeric	8	2
7	EXEMPTIONS	Numeric	2	0
** Total **			53	

Structure for database   : SALEITEM.DBF
Number of data records   : 6
Date of last update   : 2/28/87

Field	Field Name	Type	Width	Dec
1	STOCK_NO	Character	9	
2	DSCRIPTION	Character	20	
3	TYPE	Character	20	
4	COST	Numeric	7	2
5	PRICE	Numeric	7	2
** Total **			64	

Structure for database   : SOFTWARE.DBF
Number of data records   : 10
Date of last update   : 2/16/87

Field	Field Name	Type	Width	Dec
1	STOCK_NO	Character	9	
2	DSCRIPTION	Character	20	
3	TYPE	Character	20	
4	COST	Numeric	7	2
5	PRICE	Numeric	7	2
** Total **			64	

Structure for database   : STAFF.DBF
Number of data records   : 10
Date of last update   : 3/14/87

Field	Field Name	Type	Width	Dec
1	ID_NO	Character	11	
2	FIRST_NAME	Character	15	
3	LAST_NAME	Character	15	
4	POSITION	Character	10	
5	EMPLY_DATE	Date	8	
6	MALE	Logical	1	
** Total **			61	

Structure for database   : SWINVTRY.DBF
Number of data records   : 10
Date of last update   : 2/17/87

Field	Field Name	Type	Width	Dec
1	STOCK_NO	Character	9	
2	DSCRIPTION	Character	20	
3	ON_HAND	Numeric	3	0
4	COST	Numeric	7	2
** Total **			40	

```
Structure for database      : SWLIST.DBF
Number of data records      : 10
Date of last update         : 2/16/87
Field    Field Name     Type          Width   Dec
  1      STOCK_NO       Character         9
  2      ON_HAND        Numeric          3      0
  3      DSCRIPTION     Character        20
  4      COST           Numeric          7      2
** Total **                              40
```

```
Structure for database      : SWSALES.DBF
Number of data records      : 6
Date of last update         : 4/22/87
Field    Field Name     Type          Width   Dec
  1      PROD_TYPE      Character        20
  2      SALE           Numeric         10      2
** Total **                              31
```

```
Structure for database      : SWSTOCK.DBF
Number of data records      : 10
Date of last update         : 2/25/87
Field    Field Name     Type          Width   Dec
  1      STOCK_NO       Character         9
  2      ON_HAND        Numeric          3      0
  3      ON_ORDER       Numeric          3      0
** Total **                              16
```

Index

D

Q

More Computer Knowledge from Que

MORE COMPUTER KNOWLEDGE FROM QUE

dBASE III Plus Handbook, 2nd Edition
by George T. Chou, Ph.D.

If you need a complete, easy-to-understand guide to dBASE III Plus, you need *dBASE III Plus Handbook*, 2nd Edition. The Handbook takes you from basic database concepts to advanced command-file programming, using a series of step-by-step practice examples. Error messages are explained in detail, and tips on how to avoid and recover from errors are presented. Que's *dBASE III Plus Handbook*, 2nd Edition, is the ideal tutorial and lasting reference for both newcomers to dBASE III Plus and former dBASE users. Get your copy today!

dBASE III Plus Advanced Programming, 2nd Edition
by Joseph-David Carrabis

This book is for experienced programmers who thrive on challenge. Stretch your skills as you tackle sophisticated and proven techniques for writing tighter, faster, more efficient dBASE programs. You will learn proper programming skills as you study underlying theories and inspect examples of code. A special section on utilities examines such programs as dB run, Run Time, and Clipper. Featuring a handy Command Reference, *dBASE III Plus Advanced Programming*, 2nd Edition, will show you the secrets of expert programming.

dBASE III Plus Applications Library
by Thomas W. Carlton

Que's *dBASE III Plus Applications Library* contains complete code listings and step-by-step directions for five business applications: Personnel System, Sales Tracking System, Fixed Asset Manager, Accounts Receivable Manager, and General Ledger and Financial Reporting System. These applications can be used "as is" or adapted to individual needs.

Managing Your Hard Disk, 2nd Edition
by Don Berliner

Proper hard disk management is the key to efficient personal computer use, and Que's *Managing Your Hard Disk* provides you with effective methods to best manage your computer's hard disk. This valuable text shows you how to organize programs and data on your hard disk according to their special applications, and helps you extend your understanding of DOS. This new edition features detailed information on DOS 3.3, IBM's PS/2 hardware, and new application and utility software. If you own a personal computer with a hard disk, you need Que's *Managing Your Hard Disk*, 2nd Edition!

FOLD HERE

_____

_____

_____

_____

Que Corporation
P.O. Box 90
Carmel, IN 46032

REGISTER YOUR COPY OF
dBASE III PLUS TIPS, TRICKS, AND TRAPS

Register your copy of *dBASE III Plus Tips, Tricks, and Traps* and receive information about Que's newest products relating to database applications. Complete this registration card and return it to Que Corporation, P.O. Box 90, Carmel, IN 46032.

Name _____

Company _____ Title _____

Address _____

City _____ State _____ ZIP _____

Phone _____

Where did you buy your copy of *dBASE III Plus Tips, Tricks, and Traps*?

_____

How do you plan to use this book?

_____

_____

_____

What other kinds of publications about microcomputers would you be interested in?

_____

_____

_____

Which operating system and hardware do you use? _____

Do you have any other comments or suggestions?

_____

_____

_____

THANK YOU!

Que Corporation
P.O. Box 90
Carmel, IN 46032